Why Beliefs Matter

Why Beliefs Matter

Reflections on the Nature of Science

E. Brian Davies

Department of Mathematics
King's College London

OXFORD

UNIVERSITY PRESS

2010

OXFORD

UNIVERSITY PRESS

Great Clarendon Street, Oxford OX2 6DP

Oxford University Press is a department of the University of Oxford.
It furthers the University's objective of excellence in research, scholarship,
and education by publishing worldwide in

Oxford New York

Auckland Cape Town Dar es Salaam Hong Kong Karachi
Kuala Lumpur Madrid Melbourne Mexico City Nairobi
New Delhi Shanghai Taipei Toronto

With offices in

Argentina Austria Brazil Chile Czech Republic France Greece
Guatemala Hungary Italy Japan Poland Portugal Singapore
South Korea Switzerland Thailand Turkey Ukraine Vietnam

Oxford is a registered trade mark of Oxford University Press
in the UK and in certain other countries

Published in the United States
by Oxford University Press Inc., New York

British Library Cataloguing in Publication Data

Data available

Library of Congress Cataloging in Publication Data

Data available

Typeset by SPI Publisher Services, Pondicherry, India
Printed in Great Britain
on acid-free paper by
the MPG Books Group, Bodmin and King's Lynn

ISBN 978-0-19-958620-2

1 3 5 7 9 10 8 6 4 2

Preface

This book is about beliefs. It was born from my dissatisfaction with the attempts of many physicists to sell a vision of the world whose 'objective' character disregards most of what makes life interesting. The attempt to separate science from human values and judgements has been of immense value, but it has led in some strange directions. If the brain is no more than a collection of neurons functioning according to physical laws, then it is difficult to understand what everyday conversations could actually mean. If the notion of purpose has no function in a wholly material world, how is one to make sense of kidney transplants? It seems apparent that we cannot make any sense of our lives without reference to notions such as purpose, cause, meaning, and ethics, even if fundamental physics makes no reference to them. Something surely needs to be explained.

At the highest level beliefs become world-views, fundamental beliefs that we use to evaluate other beliefs about the world. They range from the belief that every aspect of reality can ultimately be explained scientifically to young Earth creationism. Needless to say these are not the only options! Some people believe that matter is composed of atoms which move according to definite laws but that this fact does not undermine the validity of religious ideas; a number of different justifications of this position have been given. I will be advocating the following, pluralist world-view: we have limited mental capacities and will always need a multiplicity of ways of looking at the world in order to understand it as well as we are able. Even if the reductionist programme never encounters a final road block, we will continue to need concepts such as purpose and meaning.

My partial support for the notion of final causes should not be interpreted as support for the so-called 'intelligent design' movement – it is a declaration that we may use any form of explanation that has some value within a particular context. It will not perturb most biologists, even though some physicists might regard it as unacceptable. Multiple explanations of a phenomenon may complement each other provided we realize that they are aids that we construct to compensate for our limited intelligence.

My task was helped by reading some of the enormous literature on the philosophy of science, but this book is more a series of snapshots than a systematic treatment of that subject. It is directed more at the educated public than at philosophers. In general philosophers seem to think in linguistic categories, whereas many scientists and mathematicians, including myself, rely on intuitive visualization – without being able to explain quite what that means. Philosophers' descriptions of our subject may therefore seem remote from our own experience. You might think that anyone approaching mathematics visually and intuitively is inevitably going to be a Platonist, but Chapter 3 contains an extended criticism of Platonism, which I am not alone in regarding as a seductive but ultimately unproductive way of looking at mathematics. I argue instead for an approach to mathematical knowledge that adapts ideas of Aristotle, Kant, Poincaré, Popper, and Dummett. Put briefly, mathematical knowledge is objective but mathematical entities are created by us using our innate mental capacities in a particular social context.

Chapters 4 and 5 discuss the two other fields in which Platonism often plays a major role, fundamental physics and theology. It is possible to discuss both subjects in depth without making any reference to Platonism, but some physicists do not realize the extent to which their way of thinking is influenced by the thoughts of Plato and his later interpreter Plotinus. The result is that they take for granted a simplistic approach to facts or problems that have quite different explanations if one goes to the effort of formulating them. Whether or not these alternatives are better must be left to the reader, but they deserve to be brought out into the open.

Discussion by physicists about the ultimate nature of the world are frequently not very convincing. They often ignore those who disagree with them, and present their own point of view as though it were the only sensible option. John Polkinghorne and Stephen Weinberg are notable exceptions; they disagree with each other about religious issues, but both have thought their positions through carefully. Some make clear their contempt for philosophy, and then adopt philosophical positions masquerading as common sense, without being aware that they have been criticized in detail in the philosophical literature. Although I am putting forward my own view of the nature of science, I quote extensively from what others have written, to avoid the charge of setting up straw men in order to indulge myself by knocking them down again.

The perspectives of scientists and philosophers of science are quite different. Philosophers discuss the logical coherence and relative merits of different world-views, with no expectation of altering the course of discovery. A few have had real influence, not always for the better. All scientists believe that they are studying a world that is real and external to themselves, but they are often driven by the simplicity and beauty of their theories as much as they are by external evidence. Some of their theories were not accepted for decades in spite of substantial evidence, while others were incorporated into the scientific consensus long before a substantial body of supporting evidence was forthcoming. In each case there were reasons, but these need to be considered case by case.

Writing for the general public is a challenging task. The success of books by Penrose, Paul Davies (no relation), Gould, Dawkins, and many others demonstrate that there is a real thirst for discussions of our place in the cosmos. As formal religious belief wanes, people hope that science will fill the gap. However, one gradually realizes that people defending science and religion have little to say to each other. At best they co-exist peacefully, and at worst they are engaged in a gladiatorial conflict. Scientists with widely differing religious beliefs, or none, do not bring their religious beliefs into their research papers, whatever they may put in their popular books. They cannot, however, dispense so easily with philosophical beliefs, even if they believe that they have none.

The ideas in this book have been incubating for a long time. I would like to thank Alex Bellamy, Richard Davies, Petros Gelepithis, Donald Gillies, Neil Lambert, Chris Linton, Terry Lyons, John Norton, Peter Palmer, Geoffrey Pugh, Peter Saunders, Ray Streater, and John Taylor for conversations and criticisms that only bore fruit much later. Some of these might not wish to be associated with the ideas here, but I thank them anyway. I am grateful to King's College for providing an environment in which I could develop my thoughts. Finally I thank my wife, Jane, for her constant companionship and good sense, which have meant more to me than anything else.

Contents

1
The Scientific Revolution

The growth of science has depended more on
opportunity and vision than on method.

1.1 Early Memories

One of my clearest memories from my time at Cardiff High School for
Boys is of my history master, Mr Riddell. At the start of every lesson he
would come into the classroom and start dictating at high speed, with the
expectation that everything that he said would be copied down faithfully. In
the 1950s in that school there was no possibility of rebellion, but many of
us could not keep up, and were forced to copy from the boy next to us.
I soon learned that good marks in the examination depended on memorizing as long a list of dates as possible. I was therefore not sorry to give up
history at the age of fourteen – I took it for granted that I would specialize
in the sciences, because my father was the senior mathematics master in the
same school. The result was that, like countless other children of that era,
I left the school knowing nothing about British history after the death of
Queen Elizabeth I in 1603, and nothing at all about the history of other
countries.

My later appreciation of history and philosophy was at least partly the
result of watching a 1950s television programme called *The Brains Trust*.
This was a series of live discussions by a small group of intellectuals, who
answered questions submitted by viewers on any topic, with the exception
of politics and religion. The older of the two scientists in the group was
Julian Huxley, a grandson of Thomas Huxley, also known as 'Darwin's
bulldog'. The other was Jacob Bronowski, who later produced an ambitious television series called *The Ascent of Man*, covering the whole of

human civilization and science in thirteen episodes. Whenever he spoke in *The Brains Trust* he would pause for several seconds and place the tips of his fingers together very precisely as though to emphasize the depth and precision of his thoughts. In retrospect, it is not clear whether this was a deliberate device to persuade his audience of his profundity, but it certainly succeeded.

The effect of these early influences, and of Bertrand Russell's *History of Western Philosophy*, was to persuade me that science must be understood in an historical context. Once one fully accepts that our ancestors four hundred years ago were just as intelligent as we are, one is forced to ask why their attitudes and beliefs were so different. One reason is our possession of scientific instruments that enable us to investigate in detail aspects of the world that they had no inkling of, ranging from ultraviolet light and radioactivity to the structure of DNA. We should try to keep in mind that much that is obscure to us will seem self-evident to our descendants in a few hundred years' time. We cannot begin to imagine their world-views, but they will be very different from ours.

The notion of a world-view is of fundamental importance in any discussion of people's beliefs, however rational they may appear on the surface. A world-view is a set of fundamental beliefs about reality used to evaluate a wide range of other, more particular, beliefs. World-views are often called metaphysical frameworks in academic circles.[1] Examples include religious belief, Platonism, scientific realism and the belief that other people have rights; we will discuss several of these below.

In 1962, the historian of science Thomas Kuhn published *The Structure of Scientific Revolutions*, which made him a household name in philosophy circles. In this book he introduced the term 'paradigm shift', referring to a fairly sudden change in an attitude or world-view, particularly one arising from a new scientific theory. He argued that paradigm shifts were not fully justifiable in rational terms, and defended this claim by detailed historical examples. Unfortunately his concept of incommensurability was used by others to argue that all world-views are equally valid, a development that Kuhn did not dissociate himself from for many years.

Describing alternative scientific theories as embodying different world-views sounds rather pompous. However, the conceptual revolutions involved in quantum theory and general relativity are so fundamental that the use of the term is perhaps justifiable in those cases. In most situations it is more appropriate to refer simply to the framework in which a discussion is taking place, because one may change from one framework to another with little difficulty.

Another term used in this context is the more literary 'narrative'. The idea is that people create narratives that bind their lives, or some aspect of their lives, into coherent wholes and provide the bases on which they make their decisions. The consistency of one narrative does not imply the inconsistency of another. All narratives deal with some aspects of reality better than others, and some people manage to switch between them effortlessly depending on the context. Others regard this as dishonest.

There are people who react with extreme hostility to any mention of world-views. They appear to believe that even accepting the *existence of the notion* leads inevitably to cultural relativism. Indeed, a person's world-view can be prejudiced and unreasonable. If the rational analysis of a world-view (or theory), taking as many considerations as possible into account, leads to bizarre consequences, this forcefully suggests that it should be abandoned, even though it does not *logically* compel one to do so.

World-views can be evaluated, compared and changed, but you cannot avoid having one.

A world-view that depends on rejecting large amounts of evidence about natural processes may be rationally indefensible. For example, young Earth creationism (not exclusively a Christian phenomenon) implies that vast numbers of apparently ancient fossils were built into the strata only a few thousand years ago to deceive us (or test our faith). The logician, philosopher, aristocrat, and statesman Bertrand Russell once pointed out that, if this is accepted, it removes the basis for believing *anything* about the past, because any physical evidence might be a deception. Each of us might have been created five minutes ago, complete with all of our memories. Young Earth creationists may logically, but not reasonably, believe that events after God's act of creation (often said to have been in 4004 BC) happened at the time they appear to have, while everything that appears to have happened before simply did not do so. Why they believe this is another question, whose answer has more to do with group cohesion than with rational argument.

The Catholic and Anglican churches accept that one should take seriously evidence about the natural world revealed by painstaking scientific investigations. If one rejects the possibility of deliberate deception by an effectively omnipotent superbeing, then it is hard to find reasons for rejecting Darwin's account of the origin of species. The status of evolution is not diminished by the existence of controversies within the subject, for example about gradualism versus punctuationism. Nor is the acceptance of evolution dependent on explaining the origin of life itself, hidden in the mists of time almost four billion years ago. It is also possible to argue that evolution occurred over this enormous timescale but that its course was guided by God. Many biologists, including Darwin, find this argument unconvincing because of the extreme cruelty of the struggle for survival, but it could be argued that either argument is too anthropocentric.

In this chapter we will discuss two world-views that led to one of the most famous conflicts in the history of science; the traditional view that planets were points in the sky whose movements should be described mathematically by reference to celestial spheres and epicycles, and the new claim by Copernicus that they were physical objects orbiting around the Sun, as was the Earth. At the start of the seventeenth century both positions were reasonable, but today it would require extraordinary contortions to argue in favour of the former. When men have walked on the Moon and space probes have photographed most of the planets and their satellites in great detail, the only way of rejecting all the evidence is to claim a massive long-term fraud by all relevant scientific bodies and governments. Who can believe that the latter are capable of this when they are incompetent in so many other respects?

We will see in Chapter 5 that comparing the world-views of different religions and those of atheists is much harder than the above examples. However, trying to understand the point of view of others is surely a prerequisite for fruitful discussions between the various groups, and many of those involved are visibly not interested in doing so.

1.2 The Scientific Method

Over the last two hundred years science has transformed our everyday lives. We, or at least our children, take air travel, motor cars, mobile phones, refrigerators, computers, and anaesthetics for granted. I still remember my promise in the 1970s to buy a pocket calculator if the price ever fell below £100 – a possibility that I was sure would never materialize. About fifteen years later I was the owner of a calculator that had been given away free in a packet of breakfast cereal! It may have been puny by comparison with today's desktop computers, but it heralded a revolution in personal computing whose end is still nowhere in sight. Within twenty years people's watches may contain a terabyte of memory that will interface seamlessly with any computer that they sit in front of; more likely the future will bring something wholly unexpected – perhaps the replacement of desktop computers by an entirely different technology.

The positive results of the explosion of science and technology are supposedly the result of applying the 'scientific method' to the study of the world. The negative ones are 'of course' unfortunate consequences of human greed, to be resolved by ever more ingenious applications of science. But what exactly is the scientific method and how did it arise? Clearly science is not just another story – its impact is undeniable and huge – but we must avoid telling tales about it that are too simple. On the one hand science is a human creation, whose historical development has depended on the imagination of many brilliant individuals as well as the patient labour of countless others. On the other it has provided knowledge about the world that has survived the theories and even the philosophical outlooks of many of its creators. In spite of the fact that science has far more to offer than we have seen so far, it has little to say about large areas of human experience.

The scientific method is often said to have been the invention of Francis Bacon. He was born in 1561 to a privileged family and rose rapidly in political and legal circles. He gained the favour of King James I and was knighted in 1603. After becoming Lord Chancellor and Baron of Verulam in 1618, his public career suddenly ended in 1621 as the result of a (possibly politically motivated) conviction for accepting bribes. Bacon also wrote several works on science and philosophy, and these had a substantial influence, particularly on the Royal Society, founded in 1660. In these works he emphasized the importance of experiment and observation, as opposed to the scholastic philosophy, in which the truth about the world was supposed to be deducible by detailed argument based upon a few evident facts about the world. Bacon advocated the patient accumulation of quantities of information that could later be used as the foundation on which to build the next layer of knowledge. His idea that the acquisition of knowledge could be incremental and progressive was of great importance for the future of science. William Harvey's investigation into the circulation of blood provides a good example of this, although he owed nothing to Bacon – he announced his theory in 1616, before the publication of Bacons's *Novum Organum* in 1620. Harvey's conclusions were based on extensive dissections, vivisections and other experiments at a time when the existence of invisibly small capillary vessels was no more than a theory.

Bacon argued that science was the process of deriving the laws of nature from a body of observations by induction, the process of inferring a general law from a sufficiently large number of particular instances. While it has merits in some areas of science, in the eighteenth century David Hume pointed out that it was logically flawed. There is no *purely logical* way one can infer from a finite sequence of events in the past that similar events will occur in the future. Even an appeal to the uniformity of the laws of nature is logically flawed; their validity and uniformity in the past does not guarantee that they will remain valid in the future. We all assume this, but not for logical reasons.

Much more recently the philosopher Karl Popper claimed that basing science on induction misrepresents the scientific process and tried to lay down principles governing the way that scientists did or should behave. He argued that intuitive breakthroughs were beyond explanation, but, once obtained, the process of assessment could be carried out rationally, not by the discredited method of induction, but by attempts at refutation. He considered that a scientific theory can never be proved true and that science advances by carrying out critical tests which may prove its falsity, and hence the need for a better theory. Many people still hail Popper as the true prophet of the scientific method, not knowing that serious flaws in his analysis were eventually revealed. The problem was not his insistence that all theories should be regarded as provisional, but the fact that his system gave no basis for using scientific theories with confidence, as in fact we do. If one does not rely on induction what basis can there be for believing that the sun will rise tomorrow or that opening your eyes is necessary to see things? Both beliefs can be justified by scientific theories, but why do we believe that those theories will continue to hold in the future, if not by induction? Another problem is that Popper was unduly concerned with logic – truth and falsity. All current theories are known to be inadequate in certain situations. In real life a failed prediction is often regarded as reducing or clarifying the domain of applicability of a theoretical model, rather than refuting it in an absolute sense.

The weakness of Popper's ideas about refutation may be illustrated by small anomalies in the orbits of Mercury and Uranus that occupied some astronomers in the nineteenth century. According to Popper both should have led to the abandonment of Newton's theory of gravitation. In fact the problem relating to Uranus motivated astronomers to seek a further planet, leading to the discovery of Neptune in 1846 and then Pluto in 1930. In 1859, the French astronomer Le Verrier proposed that the anomalies in the orbit of Mercury could also be explained by the gravitational influence of a small planet, which he named Vulcan, orbiting even closer to the Sun than Mercury did. Sporadic observations of this hypothetical planet over half a century failed to determine consistent orbital parameters – unsurprisingly, since it did not exist. Eventually the anomalies were only resolved by the introduction of general relativity. This example is typical: the failure of a mature theory is usually *but not always* explicable within the framework of the theory itself by the introduction of new considerations that had not previously been thought necessary. Whether or not a new theory is needed can only be decided by the passage of time, possibly after many decades.

The most extreme example of different reactions to radically new theories might be Einstein's theory of general relativity and Wegener's theory of continental drift, both published in 1915. The first was accepted within a very few years even though the evidence supporting it was very slight. Wegener's theory was more or less universally dismissed in spite of the wealth of detailed evidence that he produced in support of it. There seemed to be no mechanism that allowed continents to move and, without this, his theory was rejected as a mere list of coincidences. If Popper's views about the correct way of assessing science had been in vogue at the time, Wegener's theory might have been accepted and Einstein's regarded as very weak. However, the key issue in both cases was not the quantity of relevant evidence but whether the theory could be fitted into a credible general framework. When the framework was forthcoming, as a result of surveys of the ocean floors in the 1960s, attitudes towards Wegener's theory changed very rapidly.

We turn to Paul Feyerabend, a philosopher of science whose views lay far from the main stream of the subject. He was born in Vienna in 1924, but moved from one country to another frequently during his life. He studied under Popper in the 1950s, but later renounced Popper's views as mere propaganda. Feyerabend's first book *Against Method* was published in 1975, and contained two major arguments, which we discuss below in turn. Both arguments were anarchistic in character, but they were not equally good.

A large part of *Against Method* was a sustained argument against the existence of something called 'the scientific method'. Feyerabend concluded from his analysis of a variety of particular cases that 'the only principle that does not inhibit progress is: *anything goes*'. In other words scientific progress is measured by its eventual success, not by the nature or quality of the reasoning used *en route*. This was totally out of line with the views of Popper, Lakatos, and most other philosophers at the time that Feyerabend was writing. In true anarchistic style, he later denied that it was a valid principle. Since I agree to a substantial extent with this aspect of *Against Method*, I should emphasize that I strongly disagree with his other major thesis.

This was to be further developed in *Science in a Free Society*, which Feyerabend published in 1978 as a reply to the critics of 'Against Method'. Here he endorsed the notion of cultural relativism, that conventional science was just one way of looking at the world, and that it was being imposed on Western society for no good reason. (He later denied being a relativist.) The following is typical of many statements of a similar type in *Against Method*.

> *The theoretical authority of science is much smaller than it is supposed to be. Its social authority, on the other hand, has by now become so over-powering* that political interference is necessary to restore a balanced development....*Such a balanced presentation of the evidence may even convince us that the time is overdue for adding the separation of state and science to the separation of state and church.*[2]

He went on to applaud the actions of the Chinese communists in acting against this scientific chauvinism and in the process (supposedly) improving the practice of medicine. This statement must be taken as support for the so-called 'Cultural Revolution' of Mao Zedong in China between 1966 and 1976, generally regarded as a major disaster. Later he wrote that, objectively speaking, i.e. independently of participation in a tradition, there is not much to choose between humanitarianism and anti-Semitism. It is easy to dismiss such views as ridiculous, or worse, but Feyerabend later said that he was trying to provoke debate and to free up people's minds; he even accused his critics of not having a sense of humour. While there might be an element of truth in this claim, the only response left when someone feels free to disown his own arguments is, ultimately, to ignore him.

Cultural relativism depends on the belief that our interpretations of the world are almost entirely dependent on the cultural context in which we view it. This idea provides some insights, but it is based on the 'blank slate' theory of the mind, in which our responses to situations have no inborn components. In Chapter 2 we will provide evidence that the blank slate theory is simply false. The same criticism applies to what is called post-modernism in literary circles, in which 'deconstruction' of the written word tells one a lot about the intentions of the person writing it but much less about the ostensible topic.

The theoretical physicist Sheldon Glashow has also endorsed the view that scientific progress does not fit neatly into a single pattern, but he has little else in common with Feyerabend. In 2003 he went on a lecture tour of Japan, during which he described a series of important discoveries that arose from chance observations, rather than by the more systematic approach favoured by methodologists. One of these involved Sir William Herschel, best known for his discovery of Uranus in 1781. In 1800 he carried out several experiments to try to understand the heating effect of different colours of light, by using a prism to separate the sun's light into its spectrum. He found that the rays of sunlight at the red end of the spectrum produced a greater heating effect on carefully placed thermometers than did the violet rays at the other end. By chance he noticed that a thermometer placed outside the visible spectrum, beyond the red end, was heated up even more, even though no light was apparently falling on it. This led him to the discovery of infrared light, apparent by its heating effect even though our eyes are not sensitive to it. Herschel's discovery only happened in the context of his enquiry into the heating effect of different colours of light. In the process he revealed a completely unexpected phenomenon that transformed our understanding of light and emphasized the inadequacy of our senses.

The importance of their world-view to scientists is not an accident. Science is a human activity. Scientists, like everyone else, have beliefs, and then try to find evidence to support them. They often persuade others that their discoveries are valid by recasting the process of discovery in the Baconian mold, because scientific journals prefer this. But in fact the beliefs often come first. The obvious example is that of Copernicus, who provided no new observational evidence to support his heliocentric theory; its merit was an economy of description, but this was not initially enough to persuade many to abandon the well entrenched Ptolemaic system. The battles between science and religion have often been about competing world-views, rather than facts. Some now maintain that different world-views can be complementary, but others disagree even about this. Their world-view excludes the possibility that complementary world-views could exist!

1.3   The New Astronomy

When people talk about the 'scientific revolution' they are not referring to the deliberate actions of a group of revolutionaries. They hardly could be when the changes happened over a period of a hundred and fifty years that is traditionally said to start in 1543. Many of the main participants in the events that unfolded, including Newton, had attitudes that were a strange mixture of the old and the new. Nevertheless, whatever they intended, it is now considered that the developments in physics and astronomy during this period were of fundamental importance. The separate revolution that replaced the spiritually loaded alchemy by quantitative chemistry was equally fundamental, but it was not to happen until the end of the eighteenth century.

The scientific revolution is often described without mentioning its heavy dependence on major scientific advances made in the Islamic world over a period of several hundred years, following the foundation of Baghdad in 724. The golden age of science and literature under the Abbasid Caliphate was important for many reasons, but one was the sustained effort to collect books from all over the known world and translate then into Arabic, after which they were made available in many libraries throughout the Islamic empire. Without this, the works of Aristotle would not have become known in the West and the foundations for the scientific revolution there would not have existed. But Islamic scholars did far more than just transmit knowledge from earlier times. At around 1000, al-Biruni used Greek advances in geometry and trigonometry in an original way to measure the size of the earth to an accuracy of better than 1%, five hundred years before comparable accuracy was achieved in the West. Many other advances were made during this period, including the invention of algebra, but we will have to pass them by.

Apart from Copernicus, the leading figures in the scientific revolution of Christian Europe must include Brahe, Kepler, Galileo, Descartes, Newton, and Leibniz. But to restrict it to this short list does a major injustice to many others, including Torricelli, Boyle, Bacon, Hooke, and Huygens. If one includes the biological sciences the list expands even further. The causes and nature of the revolution have been debated for decades, and most of the explanations probably have some degree of truth. The development of printing, the telescope, the microscope, and the pendulum clock were surely important. So was the existence of a decentralized system of city states in Europe, whose wealthy rulers gained prestige by promoting the development of culture, both in the arts and sciences. The voyages of discovery encouraged individual enterprise, while the Reformation decreased the authority of the hierarchical Catholic church. But whatever range of factors was responsible, the development of science during the revolution changed the course of Western civilization profoundly.

Nicolaus Copernicus does not fit the conventional image of a revolutionary. Born in Torun, Poland in 1473, he became a canon at Frauenburg and gradually came to the attention of the Church authorities as an astronomer. But this was only one of many of his activities, which included reform of the coinage in Poland and other administrative, legal and diplomatic duties. In 1514 he was invited to participate in the reform of the calendar, but made little or no contribution. He communicated his idea that the Sun might be the centre of the world (the heliocentric theory) to a number of friends, but delayed publication of his famous book *De Revolutionibus Orbium Coelestium* (On the Revolutions of the Heavenly Spheres) until the year of his death, 1543. The book did not, initially, have a substantial impact. One reason for this was its massive break with accepted conventions. Copernicus proposed a completely new way of thinking about the planets, but it was not based on new observations and did not result in more accurate predictions of their movements in the heavens than did the well-established Ptolemaic system. It also conflicted with the Bible and with Church doctrine at a time when the Church was heavily involved with fighting the Protestant movement. His ideas were by no means ignored, but they did not attract enough support, even among astronomers, for the Church to bother to condemn them until 1616, when *De Revolutionibus* was put on their Index of Forbidden Books.

Tycho Brahe, the most important observational astronomer of the sixteenth century, was among those who did not accept the heliocentric theory of Copernicus. However, two of his discoveries tended to undermine the medieval picture of the heavens.[3] In November 1572 he was among the first to observe a supernova in the constellation Cassiopeia. His systematic observations of this, published a few years later, proved that the supernova was much further away than the moon, contradicting the scholastic view that all transient phenomena were confined to the sub-lunar sphere and that the heavens were perfect and unchangeable. (Note, however, that several previous supernovae had been observed and described in some detail by Chinese, Japanese and Arab astronomers.) His observations of a comet over a period of two months in 1577–78 led him to conclude that it was also considerably further away than the Moon. The movement of the comet through the heavens, watched by people throughout Europe, seemed to be unimpeded by the heavenly spheres, and Brahe came to doubt that the spheres existed.

Johannes Kepler, who was born in 1571 close to Stuttgart, was among the first to support Copernicus openly. In 1589 he went to the nearby University of Tübingen to study theology, but quickly established himself as a mathematician of unusual ability. Michael Mästlin, an astronomy professor in Tübingen, introduced Kepler to the Copernican theory; Mästlin was one of a fairly small number of astronomers who came to support the theory, although cautiously and away from the public eye. Kepler was bolder, and in 1596 published *Mysterium Cosmographicum* (The Cosmic Mystery), supporting the Copernican theory publicly. In 1600 he became an assistant of Brahe. The following year Brahe died rather suddenly, apparently of a urinary infection. However, a recent analysis of a sample of his hair has proved that his death was caused by massive mercury poisoning a day or so before his death. Recent speculations that he might have been murdered, even by Kepler, are almost certain to remain no more than that, because of the extreme unlikelihood of finding any corroborating evidence; Brahe might also have taken medicine containing excessive quantities of mercury. After his death Kepler inherited Brahe's position as Imperial Mathematician in Prague. Equally importantly he obtained full access to Brahe's observational data for the first time, and spent much of the next decade analyzing them.

Kepler's career over the next ten years owed a lot to the liberal attitudes of the Holy Roman Emperor, Rudolf II, in Prague. Although a Catholic, Rudolf tolerated Protestants and supported a wide range of arts and sciences. He also built up a spectacular collection of scientific instruments and other objects. He may have been inadequate politically, but he was a key figure in the Renaissance, allowing a degree of intellectual freedom in his court that was unthinkable in Rome. When Rudolf died in 1612, Kepler was forced to leave Prague and moved frequently from city to city in order to avoid religious persecution. He even had to spend time defending his mother against a charge of witchcraft.

In 1609 Kepler formulated the first ever unification law in physics. In his fundamental treatise *Astronomia Nova* (New Astronomy) he asserted that all bodies, earthly and heavenly, were of one kind, and that their motions should be described by the same laws of physics. He wrote:

> *Indeed all things are so interconnected, involved, and intertwined with one another that after trying many different approaches to the reform of astronomical calculations, some well trodden by the ancients and others constructed in emulation of them and by their example, none other could succeed than are founded upon the motions' physical causes themselves, which I establish in this work.*

This might seem obvious to us, because we have a mass of evidence to support it. Kepler and his contemporaries had almost none when *Astronomia Nova* appeared, and Copernicus had not addressed the issue at all. The prevailing view was that astronomy and mechanics were quite different subjects, which should not be confused with each other. The first described the mathematical form of the orbits of the planets in the sky, while the second attempted to describe the physical motions of bodies on the Earth. Nor was it clear what the laws of motion were, even when applied to earthly bodies. Nevertheless, Kepler used the notion of centre of gravity, taken from mechanics, in his discussion of the effects of gravity on the Moon and

Earth. Although he had no observational evidence to support his conclusions, they were qualitatively completely right.

> *If the Moon and the Earth were not each held back in its own circuit by an animate force or something else equivalent to it, the Earth would ascend towards the Moon by one fifty-fourth part of the interval, and the Moon would descend towards the Earth about fifty three parts of the interval, and there they would be joined together; provided, that is, that the substance of each is of the same density.*

It appears from these passages that he considered that an explanation of the orbits of the primary and secondary planets was needed, but he did not identify gravity as providing this. He supposed that the Sun emitted an immaterial species (somewhat like light) that was dispersed as it got further away from the Sun. This species rotated around the Sun as a result of the Sun's own rotation, and the planets were impelled by it to move in orbits around the Sun. He also argued that the species might well be magnetic in nature.

Kepler's ignorance of the laws of motion gave him no chance of reaching his goal, but he did formulate three rules, each of which made an important statement about planetary orbits. Two of his rules, only called laws much later, were accepted quite quickly, but the most famous one, stating that planets moved in elliptical orbits, was not. The problem was that ellipses had no other role in astronomy, and existing descriptions of the planetary orbits fitted the facts equally well. Moreover Kepler's claim that the Sun was at one focus of each planetary orbit, rather than at its centre, immediately led to questions about the role of the other focus, to which no answer was forthcoming.

Kepler's three rules did not explain the motion of the planets in terms of any laws of motion, but the rules were all eventually incorporated into Newton's theory of gravitation. Contrary to popular belief Newton did not base his theory on the ellipticity of the planetary orbits: he deduced the ellipticity from his theory. Kepler's vision, however, cannot be represented as just a lucky guess. It was based on a deeply felt conviction about the unity of the world and was the key to the Scientific Revolution in physics and astronomy.

The other important astronomer of this period was Galileo Galilei. Born in Pisa in 1564, he spent his adult life in Padua and later in Florence. All three cities were in the direct sphere of influence of Rome, which claimed the right to control what could be said about matters touching on religion; unfortunately Galileo had the courage, or possibly foolishness, to think that he could ignore this fact. He had known about the Copernican theory from quite early in his life, but he taught and defended the Ptolemaic system until after 1600. His public support for the Copernican theory followed the discoveries that he made with his new telescope from 1609 onwards, but a letter to Kepler shows that he was already privately convinced that the theory was correct in 1597.

Galileo's observations were of crucial importance in undermining the Ptolemaic theory. The existence of mountains and craters on the Moon soon came to be accepted, in spite of the very poor optics of the first telescopes. His discovery of sunspots was a further blow to the scholastic belief that heavenly objects were perfect and incorruptible. (Actually the Chinese had been recording sunspots systematically for more than one and a half millennia.) The observation of satellites orbiting around Jupiter, just as the Moon orbited around the Earth, suggested that the Earth and Jupiter might be the same kind of object. The strongest support for the Copernican theory was provided by observations of Venus. If this shone by its own light, as was wrongly thought by Kepler, then it should always appear as a full, circular disc. If, on the other hand, it shone by reflected light, then according to the Ptolemaic theory it would never appear as a full disc. According to the Copernican theory it should appear to be a small, full disc at superior conjunction, when it was close to the Sun in the sky, as a medium sized half disc when it had the greatest angular separation from the Sun in the sky and as a larger thin crescent at inferior conjunction. This is exactly what Galileo saw through his telescope. Interpreting the size of the disc as caused by the distance of Venus from the Earth, he concluded in letters written in December 1610 to Kepler and to Clavius, an elderly and respected German astronomer, that Venus orbited around the Sun.

Galileo's discoveries and his skillful self-promotion made him famous, but also brought his beliefs to the attention of the Church, with results that he did not anticipate. His advocacy was brilliant, but his arguments were regarded as indecisive by the Church because he was not able to provide a direct *physical* proof that the Earth rotated or that it moved around the Sun. Galileo tried hard to detect annual stellar parallaxes – small apparent shifts in the positions of the stars as the Earth moved around the Sun, but he failed – the effect existed but it was much too small to be detectable using the telescopes that he had. The fact that no parallaxes could be observed implied that the stars were *far more* distant than many people were willing to contemplate, if the heliocentric theory was correct. Feyerabend argued at length in *Against Method* that Galileo should not have convinced people according to the 'canons of scientific method' as they existed at that time.

Nevertheless by 1660 the Ptolemaic world-view had been abandoned by most serious astronomers, particularly those outside Italy. There were several reasons for this, one of which is described in more detail on page 22.

The to and fro swinging of a long pendulum actually provides a simple physical proof of the Earth's rotation, but its significance was not appreciated until 1851, when Foucault described the effect. He observed that the plane in which a pendulum swings turns slowly, the precise rate depending on the latitude at which the pendulum is swinging. The effect is perfectly described by Newton's laws of motion, which were not known to Galileo, provided the rotation of the Earth is taken into account. Another effect of the rotation of the Earth was first described by Coriolis in 1835 and was of importance in naval battles during the First World War. When firing shells distances of several kilometres, it was found that, unless adjustments for the Earth's rotation were made, they fell far enough away from the expected position that they missed their target. Whatever Feyerabend and the Church might have thought, the fact that the Earth rotated was believed by everyone long before this physical evidence was forthcoming; the *observational* evidence was regarded as overwhelming long before the nineteenth century.

Galileo made a fatal mistake when he employed his rhetorical skills to ridicule his opponents. Since these included important Jesuit figures and even Pope Urban VIII, his eventual fate was hardly surprising. The Catholic Church was more concerned with maintaining its authority during the Thirty Years War, which raged across Europe between 1618 and 1648, than with engaging in a theological debate with a troublemaker. Eventually the Peace of Westphalia in 1648 heralded the decline of the political influence of the papacy. The steady expansion of trade, newspapers and books made it easier for toleration to grow, particularly in Holland and England; both countries were major maritime trading nations with growing merchant classes. By 1670 it was possible for Newton, Huygens, Hooke, and others to discuss the Earth's motion around the Sun openly, without any fear of being persecuted. Indeed, John Wilkins, later to become one of the founders of the Royal Society and Bishop of Chester, had already published an introduction to the Copernican system in 1640 without affecting his close links with leading Republicans or Royalists.

The growth of religious toleration in England in the 1660s was aided by the fact that Charles II had liberal values and Catholic sympathies even though the country was officially Protestant. In 1656, Oliver Cromwell had decided to re-admit Jews (or at least rich Jewish merchants) into England more than three hundred years after they they had been banished by Edward I, and in 1664 Charles II affirmed their right to worship by exercising his royal prerogative. There were, however, limits to toleration even in England. In 1666 a House of Commons Bill against atheism specifically criticized Thomas Hobbes' book *Leviathan*, which expounded his secular political philosophy; Charles II interceded on his behalf, but Hobbes was forbidden from publishing any further work in England. More importantly the entire Quaker community was persecuted vigorously in England between its formation in the 1650s and the Act of Toleration in 1689.

Today the Catholic Church is usually criticized not for having disagreed with Galileo, but for forcibly preventing him from expressing his views on the Copernican theory; after his trial in 1633, he was confined to house arrest in his villa in Arcetri, near Florence, until his death in 1642. By comparison with the fate of Giordano Bruno, burned at the stake for his heretical religious beliefs rather than for his Copernicanism in 1600, this might be regarded as a moderate punishment. The Inquisition was a Catholic invention, but witches were being put to death in both Catholic and Protestant countries throughout the seventeenth century. We like to think of tolerance and free speech as basic human rights, but the twentieth century shows that these virtues are still practised less than they are preached even in Western democracies.

The treatment of Galileo is still a controversial matter. In 1990 Cardinal Ratzinger, now Pope Benedict XVI, quoted Paul Feyerabend as saying that the 'verdict against Galileo was rational and just'. This statement took a very narrow view of the trial and of the right of the Church to prevent people from expressing seriously held views. A pontifical commission set up by Pope John Paul II adopted a very different attitude from both Feyerabend and Ratzinger when Cardinal Poupard delivered its final report in 1992.

> *It is in that historical and cultural framework, far removed from our own times, that Galileo's judges, unable to dissociate faith from an age-old cosmology, believed quite wrongly that the adoption of the Copernican revolution, in fact not yet definitively proven, was such as to undermine Catholic tradition, and that it was their duty to forbid its being taught. This subjective error of judgment, so clear to us today, led them to a disciplinary measure from which Galileo had much to suffer. These mistakes must be frankly recognized, as you, Holy Father, have requested.*

Pope Benedict's retrogressive statements about a number of similar issues have been criticized widely, and in January 2008 his visit to La Sapienza University in Rome was cancelled as a result of strong protests about his anti-science attitudes by some of the academic staff and students. This prompted a backlash about the denial of free speech in the university. In

March 2008 the Vatican announced that it was to erect a statue of Galileo inside the Vatican walls, finally accepting a judgement that the rest of the world had made centuries before.

1.4 The Mechanical Philosophy

Although Copernicus initiated a new way of thinking about the Sun and planets, he did not contribute any ideas about the physics that maintained the planets in their orbits. On the other hand Galileo made fundamental advances in the new science of mechanics, but never integrated this into his advocacy of the Copernican system. Indeed, while promoting the idea that earthly bodies fell in parabolic paths under the influence of gravity, or moved in straight lines on a horizontal surface, he saw no need for an explanation of the approximately circular orbits of the planets around the Sun. In his view planets moved in circular orbits because circular motion was a natural form. Gravity was not involved. His consequent rejection of any influence of the Moon on the tides convinced almost nobody. Kepler was the first person to see that physics and astronomy should be integrated, but the time was not ripe for his ideas to be implemented.

The first person to make a serious attempt to do this was René Descartes. He was born near Tours in France in 1596 and educated at the Jesuit College of La Flèche in Anjou, but spent the later part of his life in Holland. One of his greatest achievements was to unify algebra and geometry, two subjects that had previously developed largely independently. This synthesis, often called coordinate geometry, would have assured his fame even if he had done nothing else. We have to pass this by and focus on his foundational contributions to philosophy and science. The condemnation of Galileo in 1633 led him to withdraw his treatise *The World* about physics and astronomy from publication. When his more ambitious book *Principles of Philosophy* appeared in 1644, he was careful not to claim that the Earth moved. All motion was relative to some body, so the Earth could be considered to be stationary in the relevant coordinates. But the Sun was also described as a fixed star.

Descartes' main philosophical works were published in the ten years before his death in 1650. These included his *Meditations*, which appeared in several editions. His work led to immediate objections in Holland as well as in France; it was criticized for undermining both the Aristotelean, scholastic philosophy and accepted Christian beliefs. In 1663 his work was put on the Catholic Index of Forbidden Books and in 1671 teaching his philosophy was banned throughout France by order of Louis XIV. In spite of this his ideas were discussed widely and were very influential in demolishing the scholastic system.

The starting point of Descartes' philosophy was his unshakeable conviction in his own existence, expressed in the immortal phrase 'cogito, ergo sum' (I think, therefore I am). From this minimalist position he tried to argue that true knowledge about the world could be obtained because of God's undeceitful nature.

> *Hence you see that once we have become aware that God exists it is necessary for us to imagine that he is a deceiver if we wish to cast doubt on what we clearly and distinctly perceive. And since it is impossible to imagine he is a deceiver, whatever we clearly and distinctly perceive must be completely accepted as true or certain.*

Leibniz was later to mock this claim by pointing out that Descartes' physics was so full of errors that his criterion for truth, 'clear and distinct perception', was, in practice, useless. Modern philosophers agree that this aspect of Descartes' philosophy cannot be taken seriously. In spite of this, his work was of tremendous importance, by posing many of the fundamental questions that were to occupy later generations of philosophers and scientists.

Descartes' mechanical philosophy was based on the idea that the behaviour of all physical bodies could be explained by analyzing them into very small and simple component parts, which moved and interacted according to physical laws. In particular he believed that almost all bodily functions of both animals and people were controlled by physical mechanisms that were capable of being investigated and explained without reference to final causes. These included the digestion of food, the processing of sensations, the formation of memories, even walking and singing when they occurred without the mind attending to them. His mechanical philosophy was to receive powerful support when Robert Hooke published his *Micrographia* in 1665. His microscopic observations revealed the cellular nature of cork, the compound eyes of insects and many other previously unsuspected structures in living beings.

In spite of the above, Descartes allowed one crucial exception. He contrasted the limited capacities of most bodily organs with the open-ended nature of our rational faculties. He considered that the latter could only be explained by our possession of an immaterial soul and supposed that this interacted with the body at the pineal gland, because of its location at the very centre of the brain.

> *Since reason is a universal instrument which can be used in all kinds of situations, whereas organs need some particular disposition for each*

particular action, it is morally impossible for a machine to have enough
different organs to make it act in all the contingencies of life in the way in
which our reason makes us act.[4]

It is easy to see flaws in his argument today. We know far more than
Descartes did about the incredible complexity of the brain, and have not
found any structure in it that might allow the 'soul' to influence its operation. Cartesian mind–body dualism might appear to have been abandoned
by modern philosophers, but many are still discussing the nature of subjective consciousness and what they called 'qualia' – the difference between
sense perceptions as described scientifically and as experienced.

In physics, Descartes proposed the important idea that all bodies continued in motion in a straight line unless acted on by an external force.
Circular motion was abolished as a natural kind, and had to be explained by
a particular cause. Kepler had said much the same, but both of them proposed explanations of the planetary orbits that only survived as long as they
did because nobody before Newton had any better theory. Descartes' laws
governing collisions between bodies were so far from the truth that he
could not have based them on experimental observations, but they spurred
the Dutch polymath Christiaan Huygens and the English mathematician
John Wallis to provide the correct laws some decades later.

The applicability of the laws of motion to the planets depended on the
gradually strengthening belief, and eventually the conviction, that the
celestial bodies were ordinary material objects. In 1672, Giovanni Cassini
(who had just become the director of the new Paris observatory) made a
major advance by using a parallax measurement of Mars to determine the
Earth–Sun distance as 140 million kilometres, tolerably close to the correct
value of 149.6 million kilometres; this distance is now called the
Astronomical Unit. He probably knew that John Flamsteed in England had
obtained a similar value in October 1672, but their relationship was always
strained, and he did not refer to this. By settling the absolute scale of the
Solar System, the measurements of Cassini and Flamsteed implied that
Venus and Mars were similar in size to the Earth, that Jupiter and Saturn
were much bigger, and that the Sun was enormous. After Cassini and
Hooke had observed the rotation of Jupiter in 1664–1665, it became easier
to believe that the Earth also rotated. Wallis regarded this as settled in 1666
and was confident enough to write the following:

Now supposing the Earth and Moon, jointly as one Body, carried about
by the Sun in the great Orb of the Annual motion; this motion is to be
estimated, (according to the Laws of Staticks, in other cases,) by the

motion of the common Center of Gravity of both Bodies. For we use in Staticks, to estimate a Body, or Aggregate of Bodies, to be moved upwards, downwards, or otherwise, so much as its Common Center of Gravity is so moved, howsoever the parts may change places amongst themselves.

In this passage Wallis was asserting that, as well as moving around the Sun, the Earth must be orbiting around the centre of gravity of the Earth–Moon system. Since he calculated that this centre of gravity was just outside the surface of the Earth, the Earth's monthly wobble would be small. Nevertheless the law of conservation of momentum, if it applied to heavenly bodies as it did to those on the Earth, implied that the wobble must exist. This prediction was particularly remarkable in the light of the fact that he admitted to having no idea what the cause of the constant association of the Earth and Moon might be, and no observational evidence that the conclusion was true.

Twenty-one years later Newton went even further, stating that the motion of the Earth around the centre of gravity of the Earth and Moon was 'sensible'. The fact that he made no attempt to demonstrate it suggests that he knew that it was actually too small to be observable with the telescopes of the day. Eventually they became accurate enough for the monthly wobble to be observed, but its existence had been regarded as settled long before that. A direct physical proof that the gravitation between pairs of astronomical bodies was mutual followed painstaking observations of the orbits of a steadily increasing number of visual binary stars in the nineteenth century, following the pioneering work of William Herschel.

1.5 The Impact of Technology

Christian theologians sometimes claim credit for the scientific revolution, on the grounds that the very notion of the world being governed by laws depends on the previous idea of God as a law-giver. While this has an element of truth, it is far from being the whole story. Historically, a large factor behind the revolution was the diffusion of Islamic scientific advances from Sicily and Andalusia in Spain into Christian Europe, starting in the twelfth century. The Islamic advances themselves depended on the insights of Plato, Socrates, Aristotle, Euclid, Archimedes, and others of the Greek classical period, which owed nothing to the Abrahamic God. One also has to remember the enormous influences of India and China on the development of mathematics and technology. In this section we present an alternative explanation of the scientific revolution; there are several others and their relative importance cannot be quantified in a simple formula.

Scientific advances are not always the result of asking new questions or thinking of new answers to old ones. They have frequently grown out of advances in technology – new instruments often reveal wholly unexpected aspects of the world. Indeed a case could be made that science has largely been a response to advances in technology, and that it only started driving technology in the twentieth century. Obvious examples are the telescope, first exploited by Galileo, and the microscope, by means of which Robert Hooke revealed the wholly unexpected existence of cells in cork and many other fascinating things. Much more recently the invention of photography has had a huge impact, for example by enabling scientists to observe processes that occur much too rapidly for the human eye to be able to follow them.

The Printing Press

The introduction of movable type printing into Europe is usually credited to one man, Johannes Gutenberg, but this is perhaps unfair to some of his contemporaries. The idea of printing had existed for centuries and was highly developed in China, where printers had normally used wooden blocks that were preserved for decades or even centuries. Gutenberg realized that the mass production of individual letters, cast in metal and then assembled into the desired text, would transform printing, and spent years perfecting the technique before he was ready to print the Gutenberg Bible in Mainz, Germany in 1455.

Gutenberg's printing process was soon copied throughout Europe and by the end of the fifteenth century there were about a thousand printing shops in Europe, and tens of thousands of different titles had been printed, each one with many copies; by 1600 it is estimated that about two hundred thousand different titles had been published. The invention steadily undermined the control of knowledge by the Catholic Church. Its response was typically authoritarian; the first Roman Index of Forbidden Books was produced in 1559 and banned the entire output of hundreds of authors as well as numerous individual books. In the event these attempts at control failed as authors with unwelcome ideas started to smuggle their manuscripts to other countries to be printed there. Nevertheless, the Index substantially reduced the freedom of expression, particularly in Italy.

The impact of printing steadily increased, and by the seventeenth century large numbers of pamphlets were already being circulated in the vernacular languages. Many of these were announcements of recent news stories, and in the seventeenth century the regular publication of newspapers started, initially under strict licences. The first scientific journals were the *Journal des Sçavans* followed closely by the *Philosophical Transactions of the Royal Society*, both of which started publication in 1665. These had an important effect on the development of science by expediting the publication of small additions to knowledge and allowing criticism of it by others. Of course this did not happen overnight; many scientists continued to keep their hard won expertise to themselves for many decades after that.

The effect of printing on the development of Western civilization, and in particular of science, was so great that one has to ask why the same did not happen in China, which was far in advance of Europe scientifically in the first half of the millennium. There must be many answers to such a complex question. One is that the Chinese writing system was not well adapted to movable type printing, while the small number of letters in European languages made movable type extremely easy to use once the technology had been developed. Another answer is that Chinese society was highly centralized around the court of the Emperor, while the fragmented city states of Europe encouraged entrepreneurial activity. Particular entrepreneurs were often ruined or cheated of their just rewards, as was Gutenberg, but his invention lived on after him to everyone's benefit.

The printing press affected the development of science because it increased the level of literacy, promoted independent thinking and facilitated general communication. The developments described below are more specifically scientific. Nevertheless, they have been important philosophically as well as scientifically, as we will explain at the end of this section.

Lenses

The development of the microscope disproves the frequent claims of philosophers that scientific research always proceeds in the context of some explanatory theory, which dictates experiments that might test it. It had been known for many centuries that glass of varying thickness could make objects behind it look larger, and spectacles with convex lenses exploiting this fact were being made in the thirteenth century. Early in the seventeenth century improvements in the manufacture of lenses and the crucial discovery of the effect of using two lenses together led to the first telescopes. These discoveries did not depend on a proper theory of lenses – the law governing the refraction of light at a surface was discovered some years later in 1621 by Willebrord Snell in Leiden and independently by Descartes in 1637. Terrestrial objects that one 'saw' using a telescope could be inspected at close quarters to confirm that they did have the stated features. The same applied to microscopes. With small magnifications it was obvious that the object seen through the lens was the same as one could see using one's bare eyes. There was no reason to doubt the existence of new structures that became visible as the magnification was slowly increased. The only 'theory' involved was the assumption that a continuous change of apparent size does not suddenly lead to the appearance of unreal objects, but we have always taken that for granted as we walk through the countryside. The subsequent history of the microscope has involved steadily more detailed attention to the laws of optics, but that is not how it started.

Logarithm Tables

We are now so accustomed to scientific calculators and computers that it is difficult to remember that astronomical calculations were all carried out by hand until the twentieth century. Even multiplying two numbers, a process that needed to be done thousands of times by astronomers when analyzing planetary orbits, was a time-consuming process requiring great care, because any error could propagate and render the rest of a lengthy calculation worthless.

The tedium of these calculations was greatly reduced when John Napier, Laird of Merchistoun near Edinburgh, introduced logarithms. In 1614, after years of work, he published a book called *Mirifici Logarithmorum Canonis Descriptio*, containing ninety pages of tables that made multiplication almost as simple as addition. Although he died in 1617 his achievement was recognized immediately. Henry Briggs, who had become the first Professor of Geometry at Gresham College, London in 1596, travelled from London to Edinburgh twice to discuss the tables with him, and in 1624 he published *Arithmetica Logarithmica*, which contained new and more extensive tables in a form that was more readily applicable.

Kepler realized the significance of Napier's tables very quickly and used them systematically to produce his important *Rudolphine Tables*, published after years of hard work in 1627. These were named after the Emperor Rudolf II, although he was by then long dead. The tables provided detailed positions of over a thousand stars based on Brahe's observations, but more importantly provided a procedure and the relevant data for calculating the positions of the planets at any chosen time. The Rudolphine tables were much more accurate than those in any previous publications. The calculations were carried out in the heliocentric framework, and this was undoubtedly a factor in the general acceptance of the latter by 1660.

Napier's tables and the earlier publication in 1585 by Simon Stevin of *The Tenth* both encouraged another computational revolution, the use of the decimal notation (for example the replacement of $14\frac{3}{8}$; by 14.375). This shift of notation took longer to complete, and Newton was still using both notations haphazardly when he wrote *The Principia* in 1687.

The tedium involved in producing log tables can hardly be imagined today. Briggs' *Arithmetica Logarithmica* tabulated the logarithms of 30,000 numbers, each result being accurate to 14 digits. A willingness to undertake such Herculean tasks remained necessary in astronomy and other areas of physics until the 1960s, when computers started to penetrate the industrial and university sectors. In the 1980s pocket calculators became cheap enough for children in Western countries to have one for their personal use. Books of log tables were removed from school classrooms, first to cupboards and then to dustbins. The revolution started by Napier was over.

Since the use of log tables has not been taught in schools or even universities for many years, two simple examples are given below. The accuracy obtained depends on the number of digits provided by the log tables. The calculation proceeds as suggested by the arrows.

Number		Logarithm
9.000123	→	0.9542484
8.000321	→	0.9031074
product = 72.00386	←	sum of above = 1.8573558

Number		Logarithm
16.00022	→	1.204126
square root = 4.000028	←	half of above = 0.602063

Time

In ancient times there were two methods of measuring time, sundials and water clocks. The first were much simpler but suffered the disadvantage of only working during the day and, even then, only if it was sunny. The second tended to be inaccurate or cumbersome, but they were developed to a high level of sophistication, particularly by the Chinese. They were widely used for many centuries, but were eventually superseded by the invention of the pendulum clock in the seventeenth century. Two people should be given the main credit for this. Galileo carried out extensive observations of pendulums, and proposed that they could be used as the basis for a clock. He produced a design for a pendulum clock in 1641, by which time he was blind, but it was never constructed. In 1657 Huygens actually manufactured a pendulum clock, and started a revolution in the measurement of time. The idea quickly spread around Europe, and many technical modifications and improvements were forthcoming. Huygens' first clock was *far* better than its predecessors, being accurate to a minute per day; he later improved this to ten seconds per day. By 1721 George Graham had achieved an accuracy of one second per day by using temperature compensation.

The pendulum clock brought the measurement of time to the same level of accuracy as measurements of length, mass (or weight) and of sidereal coordinates. By 1700 all of the fundamental quantities of physics could be measured to better than one part in a thousand, and the mathematization of the physical sciences became a real possibility. The immediate impact of this was in astronomy. As soon as it was possible to measure time with an accuracy comparable to that of sidereal latitude and longitude, Newton's theory could be tested in some detail. Its success came to be regarded as the standard to which other sciences should aspire.

The first pocket watches were made by Peter Henlein in the sixteenth century and were powered by coiled springs. They could not be regulated by pendulums and the first watch to use a spiral balance spring for this purpose was made for Huygens in 1675. Unfortunately the invention provoked claims by others that they had thought of a similar idea earlier, but the strongest was by Hooke. He had indeed demonstrated some such mechanism to the Royal Society in 1668, but the record is absent from the Society's minutes. The watch that he constructed did not function well and he did not pursue the idea. As happened on many other occasions, the demands on his time by his masters in the Royal Society prevented him from carrying the project through to fruition.

Huygens' ideas for regulating clocks were steadily refined until the twentieth century, when they were finally replaced by quartz clocks and watches for everyday use and atomic clocks when extreme accuracy was needed.

The Vacuum

Until the seventeenth century ideas about the vacuum depended more on the preconceptions of the philosophers involved than on experiment. Aristotle rejected the vacuum as inconsistent with his concept of place, and his views were adopted by the medieval scholastic philosophers. Although Descartes' approach to natural science was a decisive break from the scholastic school, to which he owed his education, he agreed with them in this respect. Space, even the parts of it that appeared empty, must be filled with some ethereal substance, because there could not be a vacuum. Descartes' grounds for this were philosophical and difficult to understand, because our thoughts are shaped by a quite different world-view. He delayed publication of his ideas until 1644 because of fears about the reaction of the Church. By this time his ideas had already been superseded by the invention of the barometer, which, for the first time, allowed the measurement of air pressure.

The person responsible was Evangelista Torricelli. Following Galileo's death in 1642, still under house arrest, Torricelli was offered the position of court mathematician to Grand Duke Ferdinand II of Tuscany. This was a natural choice: Torricelli was already an accomplished mathematician and had studied with Galileo for a few months before the latter's death. In 1643, he constructed the first barometer in Florence, creating a vacuum at the top of an eleven-metre column of water. He quickly switched to the much more practical mercury barometers, with a height of less than two metres. In 1644 he wrote to Michelangelo Ricci in Rome to tell him about his experiments, declaring 'we live submerged at the bottom of an ocean of the element air, that by unquestioned experiments is known to have weight.' He commented that his discoveries supported the observation that the atmosphere appeared to come to an end at a height of fifty miles (eighty kilometres) or less. Torricelli's work created considerable controversy, but in 1647, with the help of Perier, Pascal confirmed his ideas by showing that air pressure decreased as one goes up a mountain.

In 1660 Robert Boyle published his *New Experiments Physio-Mechanicall, Touching the Spring of the Air and its Effects*, describing a series of experiments performed in a 38 cm glass chamber that had been evacuated using an air pump designed by Robert Hooke, then his assistant. His discovery of the relationship between pressure and volume (Boyle's Law) reinforced the idea that air was a material substance that could be understood within the framework of the mechanical philosophy.

Philosophical Implications

Descartes argued that we could acquire true knowledge of the world because of God's undeceitful nature, but his argument was not accepted and the problem was put aside. It seemed evident that we did have such knowledge and an explanation of this was not the most pressing issue. It was much more interesting and productive to study the physical sciences by following his mechanical philosophy. Developments in experimental psychology over the last few decades have shown that Descartes' problem was far harder than he had appreciated. We now know that the stimuli that impact on our sense organs are analyzed at an unconscious level into fragments which are then combined in ways which depend, not only on what is there, but on our previous experiences and current preoccupations. It is amazing that the end result is the feeling that we are perceiving the real world as it actually is.

It can be argued that our scientific progress since the time of Galileo has depended on finding ways of reducing our dependence on our sense organs. The point of scientific instruments is that they replace our direct appreciation of the quantities in which we are interested by something else that we can observe with much greater reliability and accuracy. By virtue of the pendulum, measuring the passage of time was replaced by counting its swings to and fro. By virtue of the balance, weighing objects was reduced to observing whether a balance tipped one way or the other and counting the number of standard weights involved. By virtue of instruments with graded scales, measuring the size of objects or the angles between stars was again reduced to counting. In the process of reducing our reliance on our unaided senses we discovered that some measured quantities did not change over long periods of time, and that different methods of measuring quantities were often remarkably consistent with each other. The motions of the stars in the heavens, the flow of water in a water clock, the beat of a pendulum, and the mechanism of a spring-regulated watch give almost the same measures of time, and their deviations from complete consistency turned out to be explicable. Although we take this for granted, the world did not have to be like that. If it had not exhibited these long term regularities, mathematics could not have become one of our main methods of understanding it.

Our memories are as unreliable as our senses. When walking (or even driving!) along a familiar route one may literally have no memory of large sections of the journey, even at the moment of arrival. Controlled experiments show that long-term memory is a matter of creating a plausible story around a few essential details, and that people can create convincing false memories based on stories that they have been told about their childhood. By virtue of the development of writing and then printing and photography, our memories have been replaced by records that can be re-examined many years later. In a scientific context laboratory notebooks provide the best method of avoiding self-deception later in life.

Although there is no logical proof that we can escape from the subjectivity of our own sense impressions and memories, in fact we have done so, and the route was by finding many alternative ways of analyzing the world around us and discovering that they could be made consistent with each other. The world-view of physicists and chemists is now that dictated by their instruments, which reveal aspects of reality that we could not know about without them. The astonishing thing is that this process works. Eventually it led us to understand how limited our own sense organs and brains are, and how lucky we were to have found more reliable, although indirect, ways of understanding the world.

1.6   The Laws of Motion

As we have seen, Kepler insisted that earthly and heavenly bodies should obey the same laws of motion, whatever they were. The eventual elucidation of these laws is usually attributed to Newton, because of the Matthew effect. (The Gospel of Matthew Ch. 25, v. 29 says 'for unto every one that hath shall be given, and he shall have abundance; but from him that hath not, even that which he hath shall be taken away'.) In fact the history of the laws is much more complex and interesting.[5]

The law of conservation of momentum was formulated by Descartes in 1644. His laws describing the collisions of two bodies were, however, misconceived, and Huygens set to work to replace them. He completed his fundamental treatise *De motu corporum ex percussione* (On the Motion of Bodies as the Result of an Impact) laying out the final form of these laws in 1656, while still only 27 years old. At this point he seems to have lost his self-confidence: although the manuscript was circulated to a few chosen scientists, he never published *De motu*. However, he must surely have discussed his results with Wallis, Wren, Boyle, Hooke, and others during his visits to London in 1661 and 1663. Newton, still a very young man at that time, was not to meet Huygens until 1689, and his knowledge of Huygens' work on mechanics during the 1660s is not easy to determine. They did correspond to a limited extent about optics early in the 1670s and Huygens sent him a copy of his long delayed and very important *Horologium Oscillatorium* (The Pendulum Clock) when it was published in 1673.

In 1668 the Secretary of the Royal Society, Henry Oldenburg, invited Huygens, Wren and Wallis to submit articles about the laws of motion, which were published in the *Philosophical Transactions* in 1669. The first article, by Wallis, was excessively brief, but he was presumably too busy writing his magnum opus on the subject to want to make it longer. One has to infer his knowledge of the laws from detailed mathematical calculations involving a variety of examples. The article of Wallis was followed immediately by that of Wren, in which several of the key notions were not defined. However, it was agreed by all concerned that its contents agreed with the other two papers.

The publication of Huygens' article was preceded by several exchanges between him and Oldenburg. Huygens knew that he had scientific priority over Wren and Wallis, and was angry that his article was not published alongside the others. As a result he decided to submit a French version of his article to the *Journal des sçavans*. His article appeared a few months later in the *Philosophical Transactions*, and was preceded by a placatory statement by Oldenburg:

> Before these Rules of Motion be here deliver'd, 'tis necessary to preface something, whereby the worthy Author of them may receive what is unquestionably due to him, yet without derogating from others, with whom in substance he agreeth.

After a preamble describing the history of the Laws, Huygens listed the laws of motion, more or less as they were in *De Motu*. In our language these included laws for the conservation of momentum and of kinetic energy in elastic collisions. He also provided a graphical procedure for determining the outcome of a collision between two elastic bodies.

Wallis's magnum opus *Mechanica: sive De Motu, Tractatus Geometricus* was published in three parts, dated 1669, 1670 and 1671, and provided the first comprehensive account of the laws of motion, as well as illustrating their application in a variety of contexts. When Newton published *Principia* in 1687, he acknowledged the contributions of Wallis, Wren, and Huygens to the elucidation of the laws, and referred to their papers of 1668–9. However his own law governing the interactions of two bodies had one very significant novelty. His law of conservation of momentum stated:

> The quantity of motion, which is determined by adding the motions made in one direction and subtracting the motions made in the opposite direction, is not changed by the action of bodies on one another.

The use of the word 'action' implied the extension of the law to remotely acting forces – Wallis, Wren, and Huygens had only considered collisions. Newton was to apply his extended law to gravity, even though he had no direct evidence that this was appropriate. In the following pages of *Principia* he described experiments which confirmed that the law applied to magnets, which also interacted remotely. Nevertheless, his extraordinary attention to detail strongly suggests that he deliberately chose not to draw attention to his *assumption* that the law applied to gravity.

1.7 Universal Gravitation

Isaac Newton (1643–1727) is regularly voted one of the three most important scientists of all time, the others being Darwin and Einstein. Unfortunately he might also come near the top of a poll for sheer nastiness. Most of his crucial scientific discoveries were made at Trinity College, Cambridge, where he had few close relationships and often shunned contacts with the outside world. In later life he engaged in long and bitter disputes with Flamsteed and Leibniz, and almost succeeded in writing Hooke's existence out of the historical record. Only recently have Hooke's many important contributions to science been recognized.

Nevertheless, Newton's *Principia* is one of the most amazing and important books ever to have been written. Its central achievement was to lay out a Universal Law of Gravitation that was to survive unchanged for over two centuries. Indeed it is still used just as widely today in spite of Einstein's subsequent discoveries. Anyone who reads more than a few pages of *Principia* can only be astonished at the subtlety of its reasoning and the genius with which Newton resolved the many difficulties that he encountered. Unfortunately it is also very hard reading, except for a few sections near the start and end. The final section, at least in the second and third editions, is called the 'General Scholium' and is polemical in character. Moreover it does not represent the main body of the text accurately. It gives the impression that Newton followed the Baconian, or inductive, method throughout. (We discuss this further on page 35.) Historians and philosophers of science soon agreed that this was not the case, but they struggled to identify a 'Newtonian method' that would explain his success. In fact he used a great variety of methods, choosing the most appropriate one in each context. His success was a function of his genius and of being in the right place at the right time, not of having a special method.

It is difficult to absorb the fact that, without the intervention of Edmond Halley, *Principia* might well never have appeared in print, with unknowable consequences for the future development of science. Newton started working on the theory of gravitation seriously in 1684, as the result of questions about the motions of the planets put to him in Cambridge by Halley. Newton had written most of *Principia* in an astonishing burst of creative energy by 1686, but then a dispute relating to a much earlier suggestion by Hooke that gravity obeyed an inverse square law provoked Newton to threaten to withdraw his work. Although Halley eventually persuaded him to continue, Newton removed almost every reference to Hooke from his manuscript as a result. There were also financial troubles at the

PHILOSOPHIÆ

NATURALIS

PRINCIPIA

MATHEMATICA

Autore *J. S. NEWTON,* Trin. Coll. Cantab. Soc. Mathefeos
Profeffore *Lucafiono,* & Societatis Regalis Sodali.

IMPRIMATUR

S. PEPYS, *Reg. Soc.* PRÆSES.

Julii 5. 1686.

LONDINI,

Jussu *Societatis Regiæ* ac Typis *Jofephi Streater.* Proftat apud
plures Bibliopolas. *Anno* MDCLXXXVII.

Fig. 1.1 Title Page of Newton's *Principia*

Royal Society, which had committed itself to the publication of several
volumes of an expensively illustrated work on the *History of Fishes*, and in
the end Halley had to provide the resources to support its publication out of
his own, not very deep, pocket.

Book 1 of *Principia* lays down the laws of motion and then develops
their consequences in far greater depth than anyone had previously
attempted. In particular he uses a geometrical version of calculus to
determine the orbit of a body under a variety of *hypothetical* force laws.

This book is full of mathematical proofs and is the backbone of his analysis of the *actual* orbits of the planets in Book 3. One of the opening sections of this final book is entitled 'Phenomena'. Almost inevitably, the contents of this section are not actually phenomena; they are descriptions of the planetary motions that had been obtained before Newton started writing *Principia* by Brahe, Kepler, Cassini, Römer, Flamsteed, and other astronomers. In particular Kepler's formula relating the orbital period of a planet to its distance from the Sun would not have made sense to anyone before Copernicus, because the concept of an orbital radius did not exist. It is a derived concept rather than a measured phenomenon. Nevertheless Newton's judgement that the items in his list of phenomena were reliable has been amply justified by history. Now that we have space probes travelling around the Solar System on a regular basis, it has become impossible to think about the Solar System any other way.

A large part of Book 3 of *Principia* is devoted to the motions of the comets. Although many people had studied these previously and knew that their orbits were far from circular, nobody had a plausible method for computing the actual orbits. Newton's theory of gravitation suggested that the orbits were parabolic, and he was able to find the orbital parameters and confirm his parabolic assumption by a completely new and very difficult method. Although his analysis was later refined by Halley and others, Newton's solution of this problem was of major importance.

Newton infers his famous Universal Law of Gravitation by induction from the phenomena *provided* one accepts his starting point. The Law is obtained by combining a series of theorems, of which the following is typical:

> **Proposition 2** *The forces by which the primary planets are continually drawn away from rectilinear motions and are maintained in their respective orbits are directed to the sun and are inversely as the squares of their distances from its centre.*
>
> *The first part of the proposition is evident from phen. 5 and from prop. 2 of book 1, and the latter part from phen. 4 and from prop. 4 of the same book. But this second part of the proposition is proved with the greatest exactness from the fact that the aphelia are at rest. For the slightest departure from the ratio of the square would (by book 1, prop. 45, corol. 1) necessarily result in a noticeable motion of the apsides in a single revolution and an immense such motion in many revolutions.*

The fact that the aphelia – the points on their orbits at which the planets were furthest from the Sun – did not move sensibly over many orbits was of much greater importance in the deductive process than the ellipticity of the planetary orbits.

Newton took the Phenomena and Rules of Inference from the start of Book 3 and the laws of motion from the opening Axioms section of *Principia*. Almost nobody seems to have commented on Newton's claim in the General Scholium that the laws of motion *including their applicability to the heavenly bodies* had been obtained by induction from the phenomena. (The italicized part of the last sentence is not to be found in the General Scholium, but it was absolutely essential to Newton's application of the laws of motion in the main text.) Everyone at that time agreed that the laws of motion applied to the heavenly bodies, but there was *no evidence for this* before *Principia*.

One can resolve this problem by presenting the applicability of the laws of motion to the heavenly bodies and the Universal Law of Gravitation as a composite hypothesis, with all of the observational evidence that Newton used as evidence in support of it (or, as Popper would have said, failing to refute it). Newton would have disagreed with this. Everyone at that time took it for granted that the first issue had already been settled, not by quantitative evidence, but on general, intuitive grounds. The scholastic system was already dead and the mechanical philosophy had replaced it long before Newton started his investigations.

Newton did not confine himself to the inductive method. In fact he used a wide variety of different methods. For example, *Principia* describes a series of experiments that he performed to demonstrate that the inertial masses of a variety of substances were proportional to their gravitational masses. (He did not express it this way.) By showing that two pendulums of equal length but with bobs made of different materials swung next to each other with the same period, his experiment tested the above hypothesis in a truly Popperian fashion. In his account of the tides, he abandoned the precise language of the earlier text, and indulged in an entirely appropriate and open-ended discussion of the difficulties of taking account of the effects of coastal topography. *Principia* even contains a thought experiment as a part of the argument identifying the force acting on the Moon and planets with terrestrial gravity.

Newton's intellectual brilliance could not be challenged after the publication of *Principia*, but his theory was not accepted by everyone as a *physical* explanation of the motions of the planets. The criticisms of *Principia* by Huygens and Leibniz were based upon their allegation that he allowed interactions at a distance as a *fundamental ingredient* of his natural philosophy. This was the obvious conclusion to draw from the structure of the main body of *Principia*, but there is plenty of evidence that it was not his position, and that he tried hard to find a 'mechanical' cause for gravity. In the General Scholium, added when the second edition was published in 1713, he stated:

> *Thus far I have explained the phenomena of the heavens and of our sea by the force of gravity, but I have not yet assigned a cause to gravity. Indeed this force arises from some cause that penetrates as far as the centres of the sun and planets without any diminution of its power to act...I have not yet been able to deduce from phenomena the reason for these properties of gravity, and I do not feign hypotheses.*

Readers at that time would have understood that his unwillingness to feign hypotheses was a criticism of the Cartesian philosophy. Here and elsewhere Newton makes clear that when referring to the force of gravity he is interposing the notion of a mathematical explanation between the phenomena and an unknown physical explanation.[6]

Principia was an extraordinary advance on previous studies of the Solar System, and established that elucidating the laws of nature might need mathematics of a much more sophisticated character than anyone had previously tried to use in this context. But it was far from complete. Newton tried to explain the tides, and approached the problem correctly, but it was far too complex a phenomenon for him to succeed in his goal. His attempts to explain the anomalies in the orbit of the Moon were not successful because of his inadequate mathematical technique. In 1752, over sixty years after Principia was published, Alexis Clairaut eventually justified Newton's confidence that the anomalies could be explained by a careful analysis of the Earth–Moon–Sun three-body problem. By 1800 the mechanical philosophy was starting to be replaced by the mathematical philosophy, in which finding the equations that 'controlled' some phenomenon was considered to be the real goal. Maxwell's discovery of the equations governing electricity and magnetism in 1864 was a decisive step in this process. The failure of attempts to explain the propagation of these by the ether (in the same way as sound is propagated by the air) eventually led to people accepting that the ether did not exist. The new orthodoxy was that there was no mechanical explanation for electromagnetism – the fields existed in their own right, whatever that meant. We have now got to the position in which fundamental physics is entirely based on quantum fields and the mechanical philosophy is only relevant for bodies as large as molecules, which are huge by the standards of particle physicists.

The gradual mathematization of fundamental physics has been accompanied by the disappearance of the distinction between explanation and understanding in that field. Understanding the physics is more or less identified with understanding the mathematics, and this means having some intuitions about the form of the solutions of the relevant equations. This process has been taken to its logical conclusion in superstring theory, a subject disliked by some experimentally oriented physicists. We will discuss whether this is justified in Chapter 4.

1.8 Induction

In spite of David Hume's criticism of the logical flaw in the inductive law, it seems impossible to make progress in science without a belief in the uniformity of nature – that patterns in past events provide some guidance about what is likely to happen in the future. In my book *Science in the Looking Glass* I included a discussion of induction, concentrating on the period between Hume and Karl Popper, both of whom regarded it as logically unsound. Although they were right as far as *their own definition* of induction was concerned, Newton had already anticipated the difficulties that they pointed out. His formulation of the law of induction is not based on logical deduction and is difficult to fault. Once again, a careful analysis of what he wrote provides impressive evidence of the depth and subtlety of his thought.

Book 3 of *Principia* starts with a section entitled Rules for the Study of Natural Philosophy.[7] This section is methodological. Each of the rules refers to how one *should* behave as a scientist, not to how the world actually is or to any logical argument. Rule 1, for example, states:

No more causes of natural things should be admitted than are both true and sufficient to explain their phenomena.

This advice is sound even if the subject matter is extremely complicated, as biology is – deliberately seeking a complicated explanation of some phenomenon without a good reason is hardly sensible. Following his Rule 1, Newton then declares 'nature is simple'. This belief is shared by many physicists today, in spite of the advent of quantum theory, a subject so difficult that even the experts do not claim to understand it at an intuitive level; see page 130.

The most important of Newton's rules, Rule 4, states:

In experimental philosophy, propositions gathered from phenomena by induction should be considered either exactly or very nearly true notwithstanding any contrary hypotheses, until yet other phenomena make such propositions either more exact or liable to exceptions.

Note again the use of the word 'should'. Newton emphasizes that the conclusion is provisional – the phrase 'more exact' indicates that he is not using the word 'exact' in a logical sense. When discussing the orbit of the Moon, he argued that gravity obeyed an inverse square law in spite of the fact that the best match to the data was obtained by replacing the power 2 by $2\frac{4}{243}$. One might conclude that this indicates his preference for the 'exact' number 2 over the 'non-exact' number $2\frac{4}{243}$. However, his preference was justified. The power 2 gave a much better fit between theory and data for all bodies except the Moon, and in that case he was aware that the effect of the Sun on the orbit of the Moon around the Earth was important. In spite of much effort, he did not resolve this issue, but he was correct to believe that it would one day be resolved.

A fuller statement of Rule 4 may be found in the following extract from Query 31 of *Opticks*, published in 1704, seventeen years after *Principia*:

> *And although the arguing from Experiments and Observations by Induction be no Demonstration of general Conclusions; yet it is the best way of arguing which the Nature of Things admits of, and may be looked upon as so much the stronger, by how much the Induction is more general. And if no Exception occur from Phenomena, the Conclusion may be pronounced generally. But if at any time afterwards any Exception shall occur from Experiments, it may then begin to be pronounced with such exceptions as occur.*

This explicitly denies that induction provides a *logical proof*, or, in his words, a 'Demonstration', but argues that one should nevertheless use it, while accepting its provisional basis. Newton allows the possibility that the induction may have to be revised, and that the conclusion reached may turn out to be only approximate. He applies Rule 4 with these reservations in mind in the main body of *Principia*. The fact that he proves the inverse square law for two-body systems but applies it to planets in a multi-body Solar System does not invalidate the proof, because the derivation is stable under small perturbations. Popper and others could only accuse him of serious error because they they did not appreciate that his induction was not intended to be a logical proof.

The obsession with logic was characteristic of British philosophy in the middle of the twentieth century. Logical positivists and linguistic analysts were no doubt influenced by the rapid advances in mathematical logic that started with Frege towards the end of the nineteenth century. Other schools of philosophy always understood that logic cannot adjudicate between differences in world-views, and that human beliefs are influenced by a huge variety of experiences. This is not to say that logic is worthless, far from it, but it is only one among many considerations that scientists, like other human beings, use to create their theories.

Popper's charge could be made more fairly against Laplace, who rewrote *Principia* in the form of a mathematical treatise, but Laplace was also a creature of his time. By 1800 the successes of Newton's laws were so sweeping that everyone had come to believe that they represented the final truth about the world. Kant had the same problem as Laplace, with the consequence that a good part of what he wrote about science looked obviously foolish after Einstein. But Newton's caution in his Rule 4 provided him with a strong defence against such accusations. His laws, although approximate, are still much more widely used than Einstein's general relativity.

1.9   Conclusions

The Baconian account of scientific method had a metaphysical aspect – it suggested that human input into science could be minimized if one focused on the phenomena and used the method of induction. In the eighteenth century Hume correctly argued that induction, *as he understood the term*, had an unavoidable philosophical content, and could not be logically justified. Newton used induction, but his version drew people into the picture by formulating it as a regulative or methodological principle rather than as a rule of logic.

Popper did not understand, and probably had not read with any attention, what Newton had written about induction, and replaced it by his own theory, based solely on refutation.[8] This has substantial merits, but it disregards the initiative and imagination involved in scientific research. It also does not admit that certain theories have gone beyond any reasonable prospect of refutation. If the Copernican theory, atomic theory and the existence of viruses are to be regarded as provisional, perhaps our belief that the world is round is also provisional. Popper's philosophy does not give any account of major revolutions in scientific outlook, which sometimes occur long before significant supporting evidence is available. Nor does it mention the many important discoveries that have been direct consequences of the invention of new scientific instruments.

The unification of different theories has been a major goal in science, but neither Bacon nor Popper had any explanation for its successes, often after many decades of effort. During the seventeenth century, physical and mechanical explanations came to be regarded as superior to descriptions 'of the appearances' and the scholastic philosophy withered because it did not have the potential for providing the former. Definitive evidence for the correctness of Kepler's vision only appeared long after he had died, and by the time Newton provided a correct account of the planetary motions the philosophical issues about the form, and indeed nature, of the Solar System were already regarded as settled.

All of this supports Feyerabend's criticisms of the scientific method. However, his argument that science is no more than a cultural phenomenon is absurd. Newton's laws worked in the context that he discovered them, but they are also used in many other situations that he could not have imagined. A few centuries ago machines were designed by heuristic methods that did not owe much to scientific progress, but the huge range of sophisticated machines that are now a part of our lives only work as advertised because engineers have used scientific laws, *discovered in laboratories*, to design them. Ultimately, science is important because it works, not because it has advocates in high places.

Notes and References

[1] For a further discussion of world-views, see Ward, K. (2006), *Is Religion Dangerous?*, Chapter 4, Lion Hudson plc., Oxford.

[2] Feyerabend, Paul K. (1975). *Against Method, Outline of an Anarchistic Theory of Knowledge*, p.160. NLB, London.

[3] Astronomy in the medieval period was much more complex and fluid than this paragraph suggests. See Grant, E. (1994), *Planets, Stars and Orbs, the Medieval Cosmos 1200–1687*, Camb. Univ. Press.

[4] Cottingham, John (1992). Cartesian dualism: theology, metaphysics and science. In John Cottingham, ed. *The Cambridge Companion to Descartes*, p.249. Camb. Univ. Press.

[5] A detailed account of the material here appears in Davies, E. B. (2009), Reflections on Newton's 'Principia'. *British. J. Hist. Sci.* **42**, 211–24.

[6] Cohen, I. B. and Whitman, A. (1999). *Isaac Newton, The Principia, a New Translation*, pp. 408, 588, 943. Berkeley.

[7] A detailed discussion of the status of the rules may be found in Davies, E. B. (2003), The Newtonian myth. *Stud. Hist. Phil. Sci.* **34**, 763–80.

[8] See Davies (2003), *Stud. Hist. Phil. Sci.* **34**.

2
The Human Condition

Physics provides one type of understanding.
There are others.

2.1 Introduction

Human beings have been trying to understand the world we live in for at least five thousand years. The steady rotation of the heavens and the more irregular, but still predictable, motions of the planets have encouraged us to think that other aspects of nature may be governed by inviolable laws. As time has passed our knowledge of the world has deepened and also become more mathematical in character. Understanding why mathematics has such deep applicability is an enduring puzzle that we will discuss at length in Chapter 3.

Those who choose to devote their careers to mathematics or physics are particularly likely to forget that most aspects of our social and ethical worlds are wholly unamenable to mathematical analysis. This is liable to lead such people to a reductionist picture of reality in which the social and ethical worlds are only afterthoughts. In this chapter we advocate a more pluralistic account of the world, on the grounds that we cannot make sense of our own experiences any other way, whatever the world itself may really be like.

Mathematicians and physicists are by no means unique in viewing the world through the spectacles of their own subjects. Politicians, theologians and others exhibit similar behaviour. Philosophers of science are prone to keep re-analyzing old issues in ever increasing detail, disregarding new problems that are crying out for their attention. Scientists, on the other hand, often do not realize that their 'common sense realism' is a philosophical position, and that resolving a variety of serious criticisms of it is no small task. The solution to these problems involves serious engagement with what the other side is thinking, but this takes time and effort that few are willing to give.

This chapter presents a range of arguments that together strongly suggest that a logically straightforward, reductionist account of reality cannot enable us to say everything that we want to. Reductionism, defined below, has been an enormously successful scientific methodology, whose triumphs are by no means over, but that does not imply that it is the only valid way of looking at the world. In fact the richness of our experience and culture depends in large measure on the variety of different perspectives that are needed in different contexts.

It is easier to describe the limitations of the reductionist methodology than it is to propose an alternative that is not in obvious conflict with current scientific understanding. An excellent attempt was made by Edward Slingerland, whose expertise ranges over ancient Chinese culture, religion and philosophy.[1] The pluralist solution outlined here has a lot in common with his ideas.

We start with an observation:

> **Human behaviour does not always conform to the dictates of simplistic logical models, nor should it.**

The following game shows how difficult it is to separate 'simple' logical problems from human psychology. Similar puzzles are of increasing interest to economists, because of their repeated observation that people's economic behaviour does not conform to the dictates of the 'efficient market' hypothesis. This has recently led to the emergence of a discipline called economic psychology.

Two strangers in a casino play a game in which the winner receives a prize of $100 but neither player gets his previous payments to the casino back. They take it in turn to add to their total payments, initially zero. The person with the higher total payment wins when the other person refuses to add any more money. If they stop with equal total payments both lose.

One possibility is that player A puts in $1 and the other refuses to play, in which case player A wins a net $99. But if player B puts in $2 and player A stops, then player A loses $1 while player B wins a net $98. If both players continue in the game the total contribution of each escalates. To cut the analysis short suppose that player A has put in a total of $90 and player B has put in a total of $99. It seems to be logical for player A to put in an extra $10, so that he could break even instead of losing $90. But then it is logical for player B to put in an extra $2 so that he could lose only $1 instead of losing $99. The game could go on with each player losing more and more as it progresses.

Now suppose that at the start of the game player A realizes the problem and puts in $99 on his first move, hoping that player B will realize that he cannot possibly win anything in the game, and might well lose a lot, if he enters the competition. However, B might have taken an instant dislike to A and decided to put in $100, although he gets nothing out of it, because he makes A lose $99. Annoyed by this action A might well respond in kind.

If the game is played several times there is another possibility. Both players might realize that they should take it in turns to put in $1 while the other puts in nothing. Then they each walk off with a $99 profit alternately. But should B respond by 'punishing' A if A does not cooperate? How, indeed would he punish A without simultaneously punishing himself just as much?

A more sinister possibility is that one of the players is secretly in league with the casino owner, and might be deliberately encouraging the other to 'punish' him, because this increases the casino profits.

What we see from all these considerations is that treating the game as a purely logical puzzle imposes a structure that only reflects some of the issues that might be involved; unsurprisingly those that are neglected are not easy to treat scientifically. In real-life situations people do punish others for what they consider to be antisocial behaviour, even when it is personally disadvantageous. It is one form of altruistic behaviour, which benefits the community but not the individual involved. This is sometimes said to be irrational, but it helps to maintain the structure of our society and is a part of what makes us human. Or to put it another way, rationality should not be confused with behaviour that is wholly self-interested.

Let us turn to the notion of cause and effect, which has been the bane of philosophers since David Hume exposed the logical problems associated with the concept in the eighteenth century. I will not spell these out in detail.[2] Suffice it to say that the constant association between two phenomena in the past does not imply that this association will continue in the future. Indeed the thankfully rare supervolcano eruptions provide evidence that the sudden disappearance of human civilization is a real possibility. We assume that the laws of nature are inviolable, but all we know is that they have not changed significantly in the last thirteen billion years.

Hume was not the first to think about cause and effect. In the fourth century BC Aristotle classified causes into four types, which are conveniently explained by reference to the example of a pot:

- The material cause of a pot is the clay that it is made of;
- The formal cause is the description of its shape or form;
- The efficient cause is the process by which the potter made it;
- The final cause is the reason for which it was made, for example to hold grain.

These causes were of great significance in the scholastic philosophy, but it was not by chance that the scientific revolution in the seventeenth century coincided with the abandonment of the notion of final causes. The person most strongly associated with this was Descartes. His mechanical philosophy excluded final causes from physics, astronomy, anatomy and even mental processes, with the sole exception of the exercise of our rational faculties. In 1859 Darwin's theory of evolution eliminated final causes from the whole field of biology at a stroke. Identify 'final cause' with 'God' and one understands why Descartes' and later Darwin's theories encountered so much opposition.

There is a huge philosophical literature on the notion of causation, and it seems fair to say that no resolution of the disagreements between those involved is likely. It is impossible to compress hundreds of papers on the subject into a few pages, but the following examples illustrate a few of the problems. Such examples have led some philosophers to declare causation to be incoherent and others to call it a primitive notion that is not capable of analysis. Another widely supported argument is that the use of the word causation is context dependent. Until one has decided on the background facts that are to be regarded as fixed, it is not possible to decide whether one event should be regarded as the cause of another – the only thing that identifies one event as the 'real' cause rather than another is our interest, even if almost everybody is likely to have the same interest in some cases. The quest for an absolute, objective theory of causation may be a symptom of trying to apply the paradigm of physics to a context in which it is not appropriate.

Here are a few examples of events that would need to be explained by any general theory of causation:

- Sunburn can be caused by ultraviolet radiation emitted by the sun. This seems as clear an example of cause and effect as one can imagine, but in the next section we will see that some physicists deny that the notion of causation plays any role in physics. Although there is some basis for this, it is not clear how one could provide a useful or credible explanation of sunburn, without mentioning cause and effect.
- Consider a collision between a train and a car that has broken down on a level crossing. Most people would say that the car is the cause of the

collision, even though it is stationary. They are right to do so if they regard the regular passage of the train along the railway line as a part of the background context.

- Non-existent entities can cause things to happen.

> **When Jill arrived at the station she found that there was no train service on that day, and this led her to drive to her destination.**

The context in this case is Jill's determination to get to her destination, which preceded her discovery that there was no train service.

- In human interactions it can be almost impossible to disentangle causes from effects. For example, in an argument between a married couple each may genuinely believe that their own comments are reactions to provocations by the other. It is often pointless to follow the exchanges minute by minute, because they depend on deeper issues – the inability of each person to accept a compromise, for reasons that they may not be able to articulate and that may have a long history.

- It is well known to statisticians that the existence of a positive correlation between two types of event does not imply that either causes the other. There is, for example, a positive correlation between choosing to have your hair cut long and becoming pregnant, but neither causes the other. Both are associated with being female, but the relationship is only probabilistic in both cases. On the other hand, we do believe that the connection between taking antibiotics and recovering from bacterial infections is causal because of the substantial decrease in deaths among those given them for exactly this reason. Medical statisticians have been forced to recognize that taking placebos can have positive effects on one's health, but not because they contain any active ingredients. It is now well established that the belief that one will recover helps one to do so!

Whatever one thinks about the notions of multiple and final causes, both are regularly used in ordinary speech. The following quotation is typical of many that are appearing in popular articles written by biologists and physicists.

George Ellis is a cosmologist at the University of Cape Town; an active Quaker, he was awarded the Templeton Prize in 2004. His paper 'Science and the Real World', written in 2005, provides a wide variety of arguments in support of the notion of multiple causation in physics. Here is his answer to the question 'why is an aircraft flying?'

> *In bottom up terms: it flies because air molecules impinge against the wing with slower moving molecules below creating a higher pressure as against that due to faster moving molecules above, etc.*

In terms of same level explanation: it flies because the pilot is flying it, after a major process of training and testing that developed the necessary skills, etc.

In terms of top-down explanation: it flies because it is designed to fly! This was done by a team of engineers working in a historical context of the development of metallurgy, combustion, lubrication, etc.

These are somewhat analogous to the Aristotelean formal, efficient and final causes respectively. Almost any human action that involves planning can be analyzed in this way.

The idea that an event may have multiple causes, all equally valid from different points of view, is a form of pluralism,[3] and should not be confused with cultural relativism. The latter is often characterized as the (absurd) statement that all beliefs of all cultural groups are equally valid, period. The abolition of multiple causation has been such a successful strategy in the physical sciences that one needs to have very good grounds for rehabilitating it. In the following sections we will show that one cannot avoid referring to final causes in certain contexts, and the issue is not *whether* they have any relevance, but *when* they do. If some phenomenon is sufficiently simple that there is only one useful way of looking at it then one should expect that there is only one way of applying the notion of cause and effect to it. In more complex situations, which include most of those we encounter in ordinary life, an event may have several equally valid explanations.

There is an undeniable tension between pluralism and what is called ontology, the study of the ultimate nature of reality. Kant argued that we have little hope of understanding the latter, because our perception of the world is so strongly influenced by our human nature. Independently of this, it is perfectly legitimate to be as interested in what we can know about the world, given our limited intelligence, as in what the world itself is ultimately like.

Pluralism, as defended in this book, does not imply anything about how the world is in itself. Rather it is the claim that we, as human beings, need multiple, context-dependent viewpoints in order to understand the world as best we can.

For those who dislike the word pluralism, an alternative is the statement that there may be two, or even more, equally valid and complementary descriptions of the same phenomenon. This idea is of particular importance in quantum theory, in which wave–particle complementarity was crucial from the earliest days of the subject. Presumably this is because quantum phenomena are so far removed from our ordinary experience of the world.

The idea that pots have final causes is not particularly controversial, because pots are made by human beings, and we cannot understand our actions without reference to our own intentions. In other contexts much more care is needed. Biologists, for example, make a careful distinction between teleological and teleonomic explanations. A teleological explanation assumes the existence of an external purpose or design. On the other hand a teleonomic explanation is just a simplified form of words that we use when we find it useful. In biology any reference to the function of an organ is teleonomic; it does not involve a denial of Darwin's theory of evolution, even if the form of words appears to suggest this.

It is unreasonable to object to teleonomic language for the same reason that it is unreasonable to object to the statement that the Sun rises in the East. This does not imply a belief in the geocentric theory of the world. It is understood to be a contraction of the clumsy statement that the angle between the Sun and the Eastern horizon as viewed by a person on the surface of the Earth increases as a function of time in the morning because of the rotation of the Earth. Nobody says this, nor should they.

In everyday life it is not always easy to distinguish between explanation and understanding, and Ellis does not do so. Philosophers frequently conduct detailed analyses of distinctions of this type, sometimes illustrated by bizarre examples. The attempts by Oxford philosophers such as Ryle and Austin in a period centred around the 1950s to reduce all aspects of philosophy to the analysis of ordinary language did not succeed in spite of a sustained effort over many years. The philosophers involved revelled in their discussions, but eventually their students moved away from what had become a sterile activity. The philosopher Bryan Magee, who was studying in Oxford at the time but had no sympathy for the prevailing attitudes, later wrote the following about the atmosphere there:

> The way these philosophers conducted themselves sowed a lasting hostility towards philosophy among gifted people in other disciplines, many of whom either saw or suspected – accurately, to my mind – that the philosophers were self-deluded and that most of their work was superficial and irrelevant; that all this capering about was more a matter of public preening than anything else, and that it left serious problems untouched. It is not going too far to say that the philosophers of that day made themselves hated in parts of their own university.[4]

Recognizing the dangerous fascination of such discussions, we will avoid word games whenever possible. However, in some cases ambiguities and unstated associations cause real confusion and have to be addressed. I will use the word explanation to refer to a description or account of an event or phenomenon that allows the person who uses it to make some type of predictions about what will happen *in a range of similar situations*, or to relate it to other similar events in the past. Explanations in this sense may provide very accurate predictions in tightly specified situations, particularly when they are mathematical; they may have more limited accuracy in a wide range of circumstances, as in studies of biodiversity; finally they may be completely wrong, as with early ideas that comets were portents. One of the tasks of scientists is to try to discriminate between explanations, and to eliminate those that have little value.

This use of the word 'explanation' emphasizes its role in providing some degree of unification of disparate phenomena and breaks the link between explanation and causation. This is particularly important in physics because nobody has succeeded in providing a causal link between the solution of some sets of equations and the behaviour of physical bodies. They are different *types* of entity and it is difficult to see how one could influence the other. Platonism appears to do this, but on closer inspection it becomes apparent that it does not.

Ptolemy's explanation of the motions of the planets was, indeed, an explanation, in spite of the fact that we now know that it was physically wrong, and we would not use it in any circumstances. Much more recently, chemists use the, ball and stick model of molecules instead of the full quantum mechanical theory, in spite of its physical inadequacy but because it is extremely simple and yields reasonably good answers when used appropriately. As we shall see below, in biology the value of multiple, context-dependent explanations is undeniable; no single theoretical account of the biological world could provide the variety of insights that biologists need.

In the *Novum Organum*, published in 1620, Francis Bacon explained the heat in a body as being the result of the motion of invisible small corpuscles that made up the body. This was a speculative theory based on a variety of forms of evidence, but the idea eventually led James Clerk Maxwell to a quantitative and highly mathematical kinetic theory of gases, in the second half of the nineteenth century, when many scientists still did not believe that atoms were more than a convenient fiction. Today nobody doubts that this theory is correct, because of the host of successful predictions that flow from it.

Newton's laws of motion and of gravitation provided wonderfully accurate predictions in a wide range of contexts, but left open the question of whether the laws *caused* the motion or merely *described* it. Newton was careful not to claim that his laws provided a complete physical (i.e. causative) explanation of the motion of the planets, but was nevertheless criticized as though he had. By the nineteenth century the earlier reservations about his laws were generally forgotten and mathematical (i.e. descriptive) explanations were all that people sought. After the advent of general relativity the situation changed; now the motion of the planets was caused by the curvature of space-time, and action at a distance became as unacceptable as it had been in the middle of the seventeenth century. Our next step along the path of unification may well abolish space and time as we currently understand them.

Quantum theory is much more peculiar than general relativity. It explains everything about the motion of atoms, in the sense that if one solves the relevant equations the results are always confirmed by experiment. One the other hand everyone agrees that it is impossible to understand what is really going on. Some people feel that this means that it must be incorrect, while others believe that the problem lies in the inadequacies of our mental processes.

Explanations in the above sense are not mental states; they may be written down on paper and read by another person years later. They are often said to provide understanding, which involves a mental state and also a truth claim. The latter causes philosophers problems, because it is never possible to be *certain* that one's understanding of anything is correct. While this is inevitable, it is no harder in this case than for all other claims to knowledge. One has to accept that every time one says one understands something, one might turn out to be wrong.

Multiple explanations of events are commonplace in biology. Consider the response of an animal (or human) to signs of danger. This may cause the production of certain hormones by the hypothalamus and then the pituitary gland; this stimulates the adrenal medulla to produce adrenalin, which causes the heart to beat harder and hence increases blood flow to the muscles and brain. (This description of the relationship between the activity of the organs concerned is highly simplified, but it will suffice.) As described above, each event in the chain causes the next one, and no reference to the overall function is needed. For someone investigating physiology or medical pathology this may well be the right level of explanation. However, if one says that the function of the system is to allow the animal to escape from a threat to its survival, then one would correctly predict that if any step in the chain fails, its life would be threatened. Any reference to the overall function of a process involves a high level teleonomic explanation, which does not require a detailed knowledge of the biochemical processes and does not imply that the system was designed by some external agency such as God.

In an article written in 2004, criticizing anthropocentric explanations, the botanist David Hanke rightly draws attention to the dangers of assigning functions to the behaviour of plants. He states that 'all too often, explanations in biology that feel right intuitively do so because they reflect human values'.[5] However, even he refers to a 'pigment, phytochrome, [that is] yoked to a biological clock in a system that measures the duration of the night with surprising accuracy'. By using the term 'biological clock' he is assigning a function to the cellular processes which he describes. The lesson is that one must be constantly alert to the possibility of being led astray by anthropocentric prejudices, not that one can dispense with the notion of function.

In practice it is impossible to avoid interpreting biological processes in this way. Transplant surgery depends on the belief that bodily organs have functions and may be replaced by similar, but healthier, organs with suitable precautions. One does not assign a function to hepatocellular carcinoma (liver cancer) although its growth can be analyzed perfectly well in terms of the physiological and biochemical processes involved. By calling it a pathological process we make a judgement that its consequences are not conducive to the health of the whole organism, and commit ourselves to the idea that the notion of health is meaningful. We simply cannot live our lives without such judgements: they infect every aspect of our language and our thought processes.

If one wants to understand why the level of CFCs in the Earth's atmosphere increased steadily until about 1990, after which it stabilized and started gradually to decrease again, physics and chemistry provide a very limited insight, even though everything that happened during this period was in conformity with physical laws.[6] One must instead make reference to the Montreal Protocol of 1987, the political process associated with it, and the intentions of those signing the Protocol, all of which are well documented as politico-historical events. The gradual and legally enforced replacement of CFCs by HFCs in refrigeration plants can only be explained by reference to scientists' pressure on governments, which was the result of their fears of the consequences of not doing this. This is not an exceptional case, but the norm for most of what happens around us.

One might also ask why CFCs were replaced by HFCs rather than by anything else, and here physics and chemistry are important. (Chemists will have to forgive my simplification of a subject that involves a range of related compounds.) The CFCs were reacting with ozone in the upper atmosphere and this was damaging the ozone layer, which protects us against harmful ultraviolet radiation. HFCs replaced them in many applications because, although not completely harmless, they did not have the same chemical effect on ozone and could be used as refrigerants without any great commercial losses. Note that even at this level one needs to refer to public health issues and economics in order to understand atmospheric events – physics and chemistry are not enough.

In theory one might argue that there is a complete, reductionist explanation of the CFC phenomenon. The entire world, including the atmosphere, the chemical manufacturing plants, the observational equipment and computers of the climatologists, and the brains of the politicians and those who implement their decisions, is a collection of atoms that interact according to the laws of quantum mechanics. It could be claimed that if one were to solve the relevant equations with the correct initial conditions by brute force, one should be able to predict that the level of CFCs would vary in time exactly as observed. However, such a reductionist analysis of the phenomenon is a fantasy, rather than a serious possibility: the computations involved are *far beyond* anything that we can imagine. In particular, nobody has any idea how the part relating to the political negotiations, which involved thousands of people from all over the world, could be understood by any process of scientific analysis.

The claim that there are limits to what computers can analyze needs a gloss. There is a mathematical theorem that any universal Turing machine can simulate the performance of any other such machine, irrespective of the size and complexity of the two machines. (A Turing machine is an abstract specification of a computer, and is said to be universal if it has a certain minimum list of properties.) The critical proviso is that one ignores the time taken by the computation. A computation that will only finish after trillions of years have passed is of no conceivable relevance to us. Mathematical theorems that ignore such issues provide little help when discussing problems in the real world.

Chess provides another example of the limitations of mathematical analyses. Let us call a position winning if the next player can force a win against any possible response. Call it losing if, whatever the next player does, his opponent can force a win. Call all other positions open: depending on the moves that the players make it might turn into a winning or losing position or end in a draw. In principle two inhumanly intelligent players can survey all possible games at the very start. Having done so, one or other should resign without moving a single piece, or they should immediately agree a draw. Chess is only a viable game because of the fatal words 'in principle'. There is no realistic way of recognizing winning positions early in the game. Even the best players adopt an entirely different strategy from that outlined above. They assess positions by using informal methods based on experience and intuition. These include 'rules of thumb' such as 'if you are a queen down then you will almost surely lose unless you have a clever series of forcing moves or your opponent's queen is severely restricted in its movements'. Such rules would not always yield victory against a supernaturally intelligent opponent following the 'proper' analysis, but neither we nor any computers that we can imagine could implement the proper analysis. The existence of such computers poses no philosophical problems in principle, but, as with so many arguments about principles, this is entirely irrelevant *as far as we are concerned*.

2.2   The Arrow of Time

In 1913 Bertrand Russell wrote an essay 'On the Notion of Cause', in which he argued that science made no use of the concept, which should be abandoned.

> *To me it seems that philosophy ought not to assume such legislative func-*
> *tions, and that the reason why physics has ceased to look for causes is*
> *that, in fact, there are no such things. The law of causality, I believe, like*
> *much that passes muster among philosophers, is a relic of a bygone age,*
> *surviving, like the monarchy, only because it is erroneously supposed to*
> *do no harm.*

Russell described science as providing objective descriptions, which are to be preferred to the anthropocentric notions that are used in other areas of life. This all sounds very logical, and Russell was a leading logician at a time when this subject was considered to be of great foundational importance. However, his words fell on deaf ears, and over the last century scientists of all persuasions have continued to use the language of cause and effect, and not only in their everyday lives. In 2007 Ross and Spurrett observed that in recent years the word 'cause' is being used in about 90 documents per month in the journal *Science* alone. I checked their conclusion by using Google. When I typed 'the purpose of this study was' into it I obtained 1,850,000 hits.

The physicist John Norton is among those who have argued that the notion of cause and effect does not play any fundamental role in science, although he accepts that it might be convenient to use it in appropriate scientific contexts.[7] He mentions the Kantian account of causation, but in a rather negative manner. I will argue that:

whether or not the equations of fundamental physics justify the use of the notion of cause and effect, as human beings we cannot understand most of what is happening around us without using it.

The arguments of Russell and Norton presuppose that reality can be identified with physics and that physics can be equated with the mathematical equations that describe the fundamental entities, be they fields or particles. This is a very narrow view even of physics. Theories in the physical sciences contain the following elements:

- the mathematical equations that describe the general theory;
- the interpretation of the theory, including the types of instrument that are used to relate the variables in the equations to the real world;
- the domain of applicability of the theory;
- the particular solutions of the general equations (or the initial data) that enable one to relate the general theory to the situation in which it is being applied.

Polyani and Polkinghorne[8] have emphasized that all except the first of these depend upon the judgement and expertise of physicists, transmitted from one generation to the next. As a human activity, science is much more than a set of equations. A distinction between past and future certainly enters at some point – one sets up one's apparatus before doing an experiment and looks at the spectral characteristics of a star after the light has been emitted by it. The comet Shoemaker–Levy collided with Jupiter in July 1994, but nobody believes that a comet could suddenly emerge from a planet and shoot off into space.

Einstein's concentration on general equations, as opposed to particular solutions, was his great strength – but also his fatal weakness. He discovered the general theory of relativity, but always dismissed the solution describing black holes as irrelevant to his vision of the subject. As it turned out, the analysis of black holes has provided more insight into general relativity than anything else over the last forty years. After 1920 he spent much of his time trying to construct a unified field theory, with no success. Meanwhile those applying the new quantum theory were making steady progress which was to transform science. Unfortunately many theoretical physicists of the present generation seem to regard Einstein as their role model, rather than Newton, who was fully engaged with observational data when writing *Principia*.

The domain of applicability of a theory may involve specifying the range of values of some parameters for which the theory provides sufficiently accurate predictions. Chemistry as we now understand it is more or less defined by its domain: it is the study of collections of atoms for which the interatomic spacing is a few Angstroms and the temperature no more than a few thousand degrees Celsius. Newtonian physics was originally the study of bodies whose sizes varied from a centimetre up to the size of the Solar System. Astonishingly, its actual domain of applicability ranges from a millionth of a metre up to many multiples of the size of our galaxy. Its domain of applicability in time goes back over a billion years. The domains of general relativity and quantum theory overlap that of Newtonian mechanics, and allow us to make accurate predictions where the older theory fails. The domain of applicability of the biological sciences is less easy to specify, but it does not include matters relating to ethics, law or money; how much of the study of consciousness and free will it includes remains to be determined.

When we look at the physical world we see that the past and future look quite different – this fact is often referred to as the 'arrow of time'. In astronomy, for example, the amount of hydrogen in a star is a decreasing function of time, because hydrogen is the fuel that keep the star shining. The universe is not symmetric with respect to time reversal, and the explanation of this fact almost surely involves its origins, in other words, the Big Bang. This is generally regarded as the explanation of the second law of thermodynamics, which states that, appropriately measured, the disorder of a system must increase with time unless there is an external reason to prevent this, for example the constant flow of energy from the Sun. The second law provides the theoretical underpinning for the existence of an arrow of time. It is one of the few scientific laws that are embedded into a legal code: the United States Patent Office rejects applications for perpetual motion machines without consideration. If the arrow does not appear in the fundamental equations of physics, then it must be a consequence of the initial conditions or of the types of solution of those equations that are physically relevant.

The arrow of time has a major effect on living organisms. Every animal starts life as a single cell and ends it as a large number of cells, often being eaten by other organisms. A tree may fall down and then rot, but the reverse process never happens. We are taught to read and write at the start of our life, not at the end. These facts condition our existence and every aspect of our language.

The existence of an arrow of time does not directly justify the use of terms such as cause and effect. One solution to this further problem appeals to ideas of Kant that are discussed later in this chapter. It may seem surprising to jump from irreversible dynamics to one of the most obscure philosophers of all time. Many of his ideas about science were completely wrong, but he had something of real importance to contribute to this question.

Even if one concedes the existence of an arrow (i.e. direction) of time, this does not explain why we have the impression that time is something that passes. We feel embedded in the present, which changes without our having to do anything. Our perception of time is quite different from that of space, although the theory of relativity tells us that they are the same type of thing. It is the biggest mystery about the nature of reality, or possibly about our own nature. If the nature of time could be explained, perhaps we would have a much clearer idea of the nature of our subjective consciousness.

2.3   Reductionism

It is not easy to describe reductionism in a few words because it has so many aspects, but it involves trying to explain the behaviour of a complex entity in terms of (or by assuming the existence of) much smaller and simpler components that can be fully analyzed. When successful, the theory describing the behaviour of the components is regarded as more fundamental than that of the original entity. Eventually the components may be decomposed into even smaller entities, leading to a hierarchy of increasingly

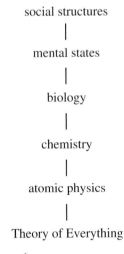

Fig. 2.1 A Reductionist Hierarchy

fundamental theories. Figure 2.1 shows a typical hierarchy, in which the currently non-existent Theory of Everything is at the bottom and mental states are near the top. A vital part of reductionism is the claim that causation is a one way process, from the more fundamental to the less fundamental descriptions, which are sometimes dismissed as epiphenomena, being 'nothing but' the consequences of the 'true' underlying causes.

We next list a few of the objections to the above reductionist position. They will be explored in greater depth below.

- There is a fundamental aspect of reality that relates to God, the human soul, and life after death.
- Even if questions relating to ethics, purposes, and meaning only arise out of our nature as intelligent, social animals, we can only address them on their own terms.
- The reductionist programme takes a simplistic attitude towards cause and effect. High level entities do often cause lower level entities to behave in a particular manner.
- The fact that reductionism has been an enormously successful scientific methodology, particularly in the physical sciences, does not imply that it is the only valuable way of looking at the world.

It is important to distinguish between reductionism as a philosophical position (or world-view) and as a methodology. Reductionism in the former sense is now regarded as the antithesis of religious belief, so it is rather ironic that it owes its origins to the mechanical philosophy of René Descartes, who was a devout Catholic. In the middle of the twentieth century Skinner took the reductionist philosophy to its logical limits, adopting what is called the behaviourist position. He tried to find direct connections between stimuli and responses without any reference to the possible mental states of his experimental animals. His belief that *all* animal and human behaviour could be reduced to perhaps quite complicated series of conditioned reflexes was even more extreme than that of Descartes, who had admitted the soul to explain those human actions that involved rational thought. Skinner's programme was rejected by many as being spiritually bankrupt, but the story that he kept one of his daughters in a 'Skinner box' for more than a year, depriving her of normal human contact, is a myth. His theories are now regarded as giving a hopelessly inadequate account of normal human behaviour, although they have some value when treating people with certain psychological problems, such as phobias.

When physicists say that they believe that a Theory of Everything exists, as Stephen Hawking used to, they are expressing their conviction that they will eventually discover a theory that will never need to be revised. This may involve elementary particles, strings, or something that has not yet been imagined, but almost surely it will be described in mathematical terms. It would not herald the end of physics, because developing the applications of these equations would be a Herculean task. Our current understanding of quantum theory suggests that a Theory of Everything would be probabilistic, and so would not fully determine the behaviour of the fundamental entities in the theory, whether or not these are elementary particles. There is no logical necessity to believe that there is such a theory: one can hope to make a contribution, even a fundamental contribution, to human knowledge without having any commitment about where the scientific enterprise will eventually lead.

There are many books studying the relationship between reductionism, emergent phenomena, and complexity. Emergence is a dangerous word because it has two significantly different meanings. Some accounts claim that a new phenomenon genuinely comes into existence (emerges) when a large enough number of simple entities such as atoms, ants, neurons, or computer components interact in ways that do not seem to be implicit in their individual natures. Others imply that, although nothing new has really appeared, it becomes more convenient or even necessary for us to use a different type of language to describe complex entities because of the way our minds work. When discussing the nature of subjective consciousness this distinction is of particular importance.

The classification of substances into solids, liquids, and gases is a typical emergent phenomenon, because it does not refer to properties of the constituent molecules of the substances. There are good reasons for claiming that the existence of three phases is real: to a good approximation, solids have fixed sizes and shapes, liquids have fixed densities but variable shapes, while gases have variable densities and shapes. However, if one examines the phase diagram of a typical substance, shown in Figure 2.2, one discovers that the situation is not as simple as it seems. In the diagram we have marked a 'critical point', which refers to a particular temperature and pressure of the substance in question. If one stays well to the left of the critical point in the diagram (i.e. only considers temperatures significantly below the critical temperature), the distinction between liquid and gas is clear. However, to the right of the critical point (i.e. at higher temperatures) one cannot sensibly divide fluids into liquids and gases. The existence of the critical point is not a mathematical or linguistic convention. As the temperature and pressure get closer to the critical values fluids steadily lose their transparency to light, a phenomenon called critical opalescence. This

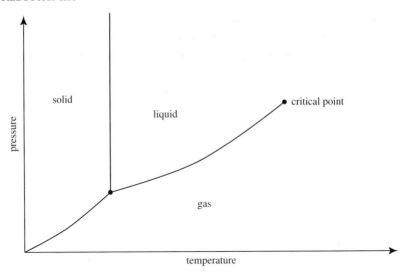

Fig. 2.2 A Generic Phase Diagram

is explained at our level by increasing fluctuations in the body of the fluid between the liquid and the gaseous states, and at the molecular level by the rapid increase in long range interatomic correlations near the critical point.

It is highly surprising that a wide variety of completely different chemical substances – for example water, alcohol, and mercury – all exhibit very similar macroscopic features in spite of the fact that they have little in common at the atomic level. Liquids all obey the same equations of motion and these equations are the key to understanding many of their properties. Explaining this is a major technical challenge in statistical mechanics. Experts agree that the properties of individual solids, liquids, and gases can, with great technical effort, be deduced from those of their component atoms by using the techniques of statistical mechanics, but this does not settle the philosophical question about the ultimate reality of the three phases of matter. A (hypothetical, intelligent) virus might have a different view about the nature of liquids, but we are not viruses. Our language and concepts are justifiably adapted to help us understand our own experiences as medium-sized entities that live at intermediate temperatures and pressures.

The notion of a species in biology is another example of a concept that is useful in spite of not having a sharp definition. Indeed Darwin devoted Chapter 2 of *On the Origin of Species* to explaining that the difference between species and variety was arbitrary. Recent discoveries about the transference of genes between bacteria only serve to emphasize this point. If one takes a long enough view, a single species may gradually split into two or more, and there is no point in time at which the division take place. The same imprecision confronts us when we try to describe quantum mechanical processes in ordinary language. Unstable elementary particles do not decay suddenly; if one examines their decay mathematically at a short enough time scale one discovers that the process is continuous, with no sharp beginning or end. It only seems sharp because we normally look at such things on our own time scale.

The relationship between chemistry and physics may be used to illustrate the successes and limitations of the reductionist world-view. In 1970 computer calculations of the properties of molecules were only possible if they were extremely simple. Many chemists did not believe that this new way of studying their subject had any serious contribution to make. Slowly but steadily the models became more sophisticated and computers became more powerful, with the result that today, university chemistry laboratories use computer modelling as a routine tool. In 1998, Walter Kohn and John Pople were awarded Nobel prizes for their pioneering work developing this field. It is now agreed that chemistry is fully reducible to physics in this sense.

On the other hand, the Nobel prize awarded to Curl, Kroto, and Smalley in 1996 shows one of the limitations of the reductionist programme. They established that there was a completely new class of compounds composed entirely of carbon, the first of which, C_{60}, was called buckminsterfullerene (buckyball for short) in honour of the architect Buckminster Fuller. The buckyball, shown in Figure 2.3, is not new in itself. It was known to Archimedes as the icosidodecahedron, and to most people today as the arrangement of panels used when constructing a football.

Although the existence of C_{60} was easy to confirm *after the event* using computer modelling, it could not have been predicted by a truly ab initio calculation of the lowest energy state of 60 carbon atoms. The number of possible configurations of 60 atoms is so vast that one has to specify fairly precisely what type of configuration one is interesting in before the calculation can proceed. Historically, the actual discovery of the structure of C_{60} depended on using the much more primitive ball and sticks models, based on old-fashioned chemical and geometrical intuition. This objection could be dismissed with the claim that the *ab initio* computations could have been carried out 'in principle', weasel words discussed further below.

Fig. 2.3 The Buckyball Molecule C_{60}

Nancy Cartwright and others have criticized reductionism, and indeed the entire status of science, by claiming that it is a social construct which depends on conventions about how experiments are set up, passed from teacher to pupil: according to her there is no justification for believing that they have any significance outside a laboratory. Logical justification there may not be, but logic is not everything. Indeed it is only a small part of the overall structure of science.

> **If it had not been found again and again that phenomena discovered in laboratories apply in a wide variety of other circumstances, science would be no more than an intellectual game.**

In particular Newton's theory of gravitation explains not only the orbits of the planets, but those of thousands of asteroids, optical binary stars, and even galaxies, all quite unknown in the seventeenth century. Atomic fusion explains the power of hydrogen bombs, the radiation of energy by the Sun and the proportions of the various elements in the universe. Nobody could have known that science would be so effective, but we have found that it is and our confidence in it has grown as its scope has expanded.

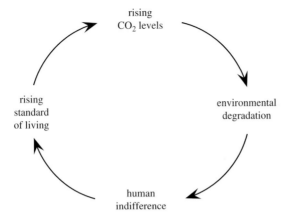

Fig. 2.4 The Environmental Problem

Laboratory experiments lead to principles that can be applied in a wide variety of other situations, and in that sense they provide objective knowledge. That does not imply that other forms of understanding are worthless, or that they will eventually be superseded. Figure 2.4 shows the approaching world environmental disaster schematically. Avoiding it depends on our determination to persuade those who have political and industrial power to create a social order in which our children will be able to enjoy something like the lifestyle that we ourselves have had. Our intervention must be based on social considerations, but its consequences will be entirely physical, a reduction in the amount of CO_2 in the atmosphere. Whether or not we collectively have the moral strength and sense of community to do something before it is too late remains to be seen, but philosophical arguments that our concerns are 'no more than' consequences of the interactions of the atoms in our brains provide no useful insights.

2.4 Determinism

Reductionism and determinism are regularly confused. Reductionists seek to *understand* what governs the behaviour of the world. Determinists make the much stronger claim that one could 'in principle' *predict* the exact future behaviour of any body given a knowledge of the relevant laws and exact data about the entire state of the universe at some time. This idea was promoted by Laplace at around 1800 as a result of the astonishing success of the Newtonian programme.

If a determinist wishes to predict the course of a forest fire a day in advance, he might need to know precisely where a bolt of lightning will strike. This would necessitate unbelievably detailed knowledge of the wind speed, vapour density, temperature, and electric charge distribution throughout a huge volume of the atmosphere. He would also have to know the precise distribution and moisture content of combustible material in the forest. There is no realistic possibility of collecting all this information, let alone using it appropriately. Indeed it is not clear that the exact values of the various quantities involved exist, except in the narrow context of the mathematical model used, because the chaotic nature of atmospheric dynamics implies that one cannot ignore the influence of effects at the atomic level. As standardly understood quantum theory is intrinsically probabilistic and undermines the Laplacian argument; a determinist must therefore believe that it is wrong (as Einstein did), or adopt an unconventional interpretation of it.

It is a pretty safe bet that people who are fond of asserting that things are possible 'in principle' are trying to persuade you, and genuinely believe, that their theoretical arguments take priority over the properties of the real world. Replacing the phrase 'in principle' by 'not' often makes a sentence correspond more closely with reality. This does not imply that theoretical considerations can throw no light on discussions. Often they do, but one has to consider each one on its merits, and judge whether the conclusion reached by using a particular mathematical model is really relevant to the original problem. In everyday contexts erroneous conclusions are not usually the result of failures of logic. They are built into the way the problem is formulated.

While some continue to anguish about such issues, the world moves on. Bradley Efron, a distinguished statistician, has pointed out that physicists are having to consult statisticians steadily more frequently because the problems that they are facing are increasingly complicated and messy. Estimating the mass of the neutrino or the distribution of galaxies in the universe are not problems that can be resolved easily. Probability and statistics permeate every aspect of physical science today, both practically and theoretically, and we need to adjust our attitudes to that fact.

The gravitational effects of small, unknown, remote bodies might seem to be of no significance when studying terrestrial events, because of the extraordinary weakness of gravitational forces. This is wrong. The ultimate reason is the extraordinary instability of the laws governing molecular motion and fluid dynamics. According to the physicist Michael Berry, the gravitational field due a single extra electron at the limits of the known universe has substantial effects on the motion of gas molecules in a box within a fraction of a second; successive collisions between molecules amplify the extremely slight perturbation in the initial conditions caused by the electron, and the effect builds up exponentially. These effects are not measurable because nobody could compute where the molecules would have been if the electron responsible did not exist. David Ruelle estimated that within a day or so one might expect this to affect the shapes of clouds and the location of gusts of wind. Within a few weeks the global weather pattern would probably be affected.

These estimates are very rough, but the conclusions are probably within a few orders of magnitude. Computer based weather forecasts confirm the theoretical conclusions: the effects of tiny changes in initial data accumulate rapidly and render forecasts useless after a surprisingly short period. References to the 'butterfly effect' draw attention away from a problem that is far worse than it appears at first sight. There are billions of flying insects, each of which moves around erratically in a way that depends on its own environment. External events, including the weather, affect their movements, just as their movements affect the weather.

It is simply not possible to construct an information-processing system that could collect and make use of all the relevant data about every flying insect, let alone every particle in the universe, including every particle in the system itself. This would be true even if Newton's laws were exactly true, and one did not have to contend with the extra indeterminacy due to quantum theory. Even if it were somehow possible for an entity outside the universe to do the relevant calculations and to store all of the relevant information, it could not obtain the information because of the uncertainty principle in quantum theory. Obtaining the information would cause changes in the quantum state of the universe that would render the calculations worthless. We are forced to the conclusion that, if the physical laws that we know are indeed true, they cannot be used to provide long-term weather forecasts, *even in principle.*

Of course the physical laws that we know at present are not true in any final sense. They are not even consistent with each other in certain extreme situations, and physicists are still looking for their Theory of Everything. However, quantum theory is so accurate in the type of circumstances being considered above, that nobody believes that the conclusions about weather forecasts will be overturned by future developments.

The behaviour of human beings is impossible to predict over very short periods of time. Indeed our actions just one minute ahead might depend on whether anyone else in the world is about to make an unexpected telephone call – even by mistake. Predictions of such matters would depend on having so much knowledge about external factors, in this case the intentions of a large number of other people at remote locations, that the relevant information could not possibly be collected. We conclude that the applicability of determinism to human actions is a metaphysical belief that is incapable of being tested.

In spite of the above, there are many situations in which one can use a computer to predict the behaviour of a moderately complicated system with high accuracy, given sufficient data. Even in such cases this is not an adequate substitute for understanding what is going on. A serious weakness of numerical simulations is that, if one changes the data or the design parameters of a system, one has to repeat the calculation all over again. Understanding allows us to short-circuit this process and make rough and ready judgements of the likely effects of some design change. At present only a person can understand something, and a reference to understanding is an admission that the deterministic philosophy is not enough for us, even in those cases when it is enough for nature and our computers.

2.5 The Mind-Body Problem

Generations of philosophers have argued about the relationship between the conscious mind and the brain. In recent years they have been joined by an army of neuroscientists, aided by a variety of sophisticated scanners, which reveal something of what is happening inside our brains as we perform various mental tasks. In spite of all this research, the method by which the neurons, synapses, glial cells, and other 'wetware' in our brains generate our conscious thoughts remains largely unresolved. We know that what seem to be clear memories of past events are imaginative reconstructions based on context and a few snippets of fact, but the details still elude us. The 'savants' who can memorize entire scenes accurately and later describe minute details in them are extremely rare, and often suffer cognitive problems in other directions. The fact that many of our conscious thoughts depend on our use of language should not lead us to suppose that our brains work by storing and manipulating logical or linguistic symbols, as early AI researchers imagined. The fact that our brains have much in common with those of other animals makes it unlikely that this is so.

In this situation, it is hardly surprising that there is an astonishing variety of theories about the nature of human consciousness. A recent debate between Maxwell Bennett, Daniel Dennett, Peter Hacker, and John Searle about the correct framework for discussing recent developments in neuroscience has entrenched their disagreements rather than helping to resolve them.[9] Their essays concentrate on whether it is legitimate to use words such as memory, information, belief, decisions etc. when describing the behaviour of assemblies of neurons in the brain; we will discuss the possibility of machine intelligence on page 173, but focus on the nature of our own consciousness for the time being. Although Hacker provides numerous examples that demonstrate that there are real dangers here, avoiding them will not solve the main problem.

Eliminative materialists argue that discussions about subjective consciousness arise from a primitive and radically false theory of the world which they call 'folk psychology'. This is supposedly destined to be replaced by a much deeper and reductionist explanation of brain states in terms of the functioning of neurons alone. One can illustrate the difference between eliminative and straight materialism as follows. One can explain the functioning of a mechanical clock in purely materialistic terms by describing the arrangement of the wheels inside the case. A statement that its hands turn as the result of the activity of an army of ants inside the case is also materialistic, but radically false. There are no ants, nor, eliminative materialists would claim, does folk psychology have any relevance to the functioning of the brain.

Francis Crick, who won the Nobel Prize for his discovery of the genetic code, supports eliminative materialism. In his book *The Astonishing Hypothesis* he states:

> '*You,' your joys and your sorrows, your memories and your ambitions, your sense of personal identity and free will, are in fact no more than the behaviour of a vast assembly of nerve cells and their associated molecules. As Lewis Carroll's Alice might have phrased: 'You're nothing but a pack of neurons.' This hypothesis is so alien to the ideas of most people today that it can truly be called astonishing.*

If we return to the analogy with a clock, it may be seen that what may be a complete description from one point of view can be wholly inadequate from another. A mechanical description of the components and how they interact with each other is exactly what a clock repairer needs. However for those who use clocks it is fatally incomplete. They are mainly interested in the cultural context – the fact that clocks may be used to organize their lives because they are designed to measure an abstract notion called the passage of time. While both descriptions are useful in the appropriate context, the phrase 'nothing but' suggests that the cultural context is secondary to the reductionist description, whereas actually it is the only reason for the existence of clocks.

The philosopher Mary Midgley regards Crick's attitude as absurd. Born in 1919, she was educated at Somerville College, Oxford, as were many other British women of her age who became eminent in later life. She published her first book at the age of 59 and has by now written many incisive philosophical articles and reviews. She has a very wide range of knowledge and is particularly critical of all forms of scientism. In a recent book she has criticized Crick's extreme form of reductionism (which she downgrades from a philosophy to a myth) as rendering our conversations meaningless.[10] It is difficult to disagree.

Midgley considers it obvious that one cannot understand normal conversations without reference to social factors. In her entertaining article 'Reductive Megalomania' she commented on the sentence 'George was allowed home from prison at last on Sunday' as follows:

> *The sentence as it stands does not refer only to the physical items involved. Indeed most of the physical details are irrelevant to it. (It does not matter, for instance, where the prison is or by what transport or what route George came home.) What the sentence describes is a symbolic transaction between an individual and a huge social background of penal justice, power structures, legislation and human decisions. The words it uses are suited to fill in that historical and social background. Without such concepts, the whole meaning of the sentence would vanish.*[11]

If one disregards Crick's philosophical gloss, his 'nothing but' statement might be no more than the now well accepted statement that there is no vital spirit that differentiates animate objects from inanimate ones; the difference lies only in the organization of their atoms. He may simply be claiming that the programme to unravel the workings of the brain will not eventually encounter an insuperable barrier. Success in the endeavour would be established if it became possible to make a computer model of a human brain that shows how a generic person would respond in a variety of situations. It would also be necessary that this model copies the structures in our brains as opposed to the concepts that we use when thinking. We would then understand how we think and might be able to use this knowledge to great benefit. However,

Understanding how the brain works would not invalidate our thoughts and ideas any more than understanding the physiology of our kidneys invalidates discussions of their role in maintaining our vital functions.

We do not need to make a choice between two different types of description of the same entity, be it a kidney or a brain, because both can provide valuable insights. In his book *Consilience*, the Harvard biologist Edward O. Wilson emphasizes the *pragmatic* limitations of determinism as applied to human thought. He argues that the brain is so complex and the neural patterns in its cells are so open to modification by unpredictable external stimuli that:

> there can be no simple determinism of human thought, at least not in obedience to causation in the way physical laws describe the motion of bodies and the atomic assembly of molecules.... Thus in organismic time and space, in every operational sense that applies to the knowable self, the mind does have free will.[12]

George Ellis starts by saying much the same thing in *Physics and the Real World* but he draws a stronger conclusion:

> You can't predict the future on the basis of the lower level structures alone, you have to also include the effects of causally relevant higher level structures; but unless you understand those structures at their own level, you don't know what aspects of the lower level variables are relevant.... Physics by itself cannot causally account for any animal behaviour that is adaptive and depends on context, for example beaver dam-building, bird nest-building, or cooperative hunting by whales. These too emerge as higher level autonomous behaviours of biological structures, made possible but not causally determined by the workings of the underlying physics and chemistry. Indeed physics and chemistry by themselves cannot even determine the development or functioning of a single living cell, for that depends on its biological context, etc.

Although Wilson and Ellis agree that free will exists, one does so 'in every operational sense', while the other appears to take it literally. The difference between them is perhaps explained by the fact that the former is a secular humanist, while the latter is a Quaker. Each has a world-view and chooses an interpretation of the facts about complex systems that fits in with his own beliefs. It is, perhaps, worth mentioning that Polkinghorne also argues that Newtonian dynamics is rendered irrelevant by chaos.[13] He calls this ontological openness.

Debates about the existence of free will cause endless confusion because of the lack of agreement about what the phrase means. One may *define* it to be our ability to make choices when presented with a range of conflicting evidence and/or goals. Freedom in this sense should be contrasted with compulsion by other human beings or society, rather than with dependence on the action of the laws of physics, or mere randomness. This resolution of the problem is simply by fiat: it follows Hume in adopting a definition that is not philosophically troublesome, as well as corresponding fairly well to the way the the term is normally used. Of course it evades another problem, that for many people the phrase 'free will' really stands in for a dualistic world-view incorporating immaterial souls.

Agreement about this problem is impeded by the fact that people's beliefs about their thought processes are almost always based on intuition rather than knowledge. We manage our thoughts without knowing how our brains provide the desired results.

> **Scientific research demonstrates that we are only consciously aware of a tiny proportion of what is going on in our heads.**

As we get older many of us find that we take longer and longer to remember the names of people whom we recognize immediately. In my own case, I occasionally wait minutes before my brain delivers up the name of someone whom I have not seen for some time, *and I have no idea how it eventually obtains the answer.* Oliver Sacks' wonderful books, *The Man who Mistook His Wife for a Hat* and *Musicophilia, Tales of Music and the Brain*, show that our whole view of reality relies on the normal functioning of machinery in our brains of which we have no awareness. People with brain damage can develop bizarre beliefs about the world and even about parts of their own bodies.

Many mathematicians of great eminence have attested to the fact that, after days or weeks of intense thought on a mathematical problem an idea may come to their conscious attention, quite suddenly, from a part of their brains to which they have no direct access. These ideas are often quite simple, a suggestion that the problem is connected to another one or that a certain way of looking at it might be fruitful. They are correct surprisingly often, but unfortunately not always. Subsequent checking of the intuition is essential and must be carried out consciously. Often this leads to another barrier that the unconscious mind 'examines' at its leisure. This does not imply that the unconscious mind is thinking logically or that the 'real' mathematician is hiding there: it seems to be functioning in an intuitive and non-logical manner, seeking a partial match between the problem and other things that have been committed to memory.

It is very plausible that similar considerations apply to free will. The gap between consciously weighing up alternatives and coming to a decision seems mysterious, because we do not have access to the part of the brain that 'makes the choice'. Hume expressed it as follows:

> *The command of the mind over itself is limited, as well as its command over the body; and these limits are not known by reason, or any*

acquaintance with the nature of cause and effect, but only by experience and observation, as in all other natural events and in the operation of external objects. Our authority over our sentiments and passions is much weaker than that over our ideas; and even the latter authority is circumscribed within very narrow boundaries.[14]

The really troublesome philosophical problem is subjective consciousness. One can be aware of this when sitting quietly, not attempting to make any decisions at all. I do not understand why I feel that I might inhabit someone else's body rather than my own, at the same time as I think that this notion is nonsensical. It might be a by-product of modules in my brain dealing with empathy, but we do not know nearly enough to give sensible answers to such questions. My subjective awareness of myself is the only thing that might conceivably persuade me into some form of religious belief. Hundreds of books have been written about the relationship between subjective and objective consciousness, and whether the former is a proper subject for scientific analysis, but they throw little light on it. Understanding objective consciousness is already a hard enough problem, and its solution will at least make much clearer what the nature of the other problem really is.

One might make an analogy between the conscious mind and the Chair of a large company. The Chair communicates with the CEO and a few of the senior directors, formulating medium-and long-term goals and occasionally dealing with immediate problems. He (or equally she) is aware that there is a large body of staff implementing the ideas and producing the paperwork, although he never sees them. He tries to make sensible decisions but discovers that he is not always in control, because unexpected events in the outside world may need to be dealt with immediately at a lower level, and also because his perceptions about the capacities of the company are sometimes wrong. At the bottom end of the hierarchy the staff struggle to do what they can, but may feel frustrated at not understanding or being able to influence higher levels of management. The system works, but nobody is fully in control in spite of the fact that the paperwork may all be in order.

2.6 The Blank Slate Theory

The steadily increasing successes of the reductionist methodology, and the possibility that it would start invading the study of the human mind, led to considerable unease, particularly among those in the humanities. Eventually it could not be ignored, and one reaction was the rise of postmodernism. In a recent book, Edward Slingerland claims that postmodernists can be recognized by their acceptance of Locke's blank slate theory, whatever they say about their beliefs. (In 1690 Locke had argued that the new-born human mind was a blank slate, onto which almost *any* ideas could be impressed, depending on the culture in which the child was raised. The blank slate idea goes back to Aristotle, but Locke's contribution was of major importance.) According to postmodernists science is just another belief system, of no more significance than any other.

It is difficult to discuss postmodernism, because its adherents are a very heterogeneous group and seem to revel in obscurity. This is not surprising because they want people to agree that all belief systems are socially conditioned *without applying this conclusion to postmodernism itself*. The logical trap is finessed by the use of language that is so convoluted that no outsider can understand it. The postmodern movement has been particularly strong in France and was given a boost there by the student revolution of 1968. Paul Feyerabend adopted its values, but Thomas Kuhn's attitudes towards it were more complex. His arguments about the incommensurability of different scientific paradigms were quite justifiably taken as endorsement by an important figure, but he was not happy with this and later tried to dissociate himself from the theory.

Slingerland provides lengthy arguments, drawn from the scientific literature, to show that the blank slate theory is simply wrong. The book proposes a way out of the need to choose between reductionist objectivity and postmodernism.

> *Against postmodern relativism, we can maintain that there are structures of cognition common to all human beings regardless of their culture, language, or particular history. Against objectivism, we can argue that these commonalities are not reflections of some a priori order existing independently of humans, and necessarily true for any conceivable rational being, but rather arise out of the interactions of biological systems with a fairly stable physical world over the course of both evolutionary and personal time, which makes the presence of certain cognitive structures inevitable for creatures such as ourselves.*[15]

In other words, human cognitive structures depend on our *particular nature* as biological organisms. We will provide a little of the evidence for this below, and more in Section 3.6, but it is worth pointing out that Steven Pinker has written an entire book discussing many people's opposition to suggestions that our genetic endowment might have any effect on our mental capacities.[16]

We next turn to Emmanuel Kant's criticism of the blank slate theory, which influenced much of the subsequent development of philosophy. Kant was one of the greatest and most impenetrable of philosophers. Born in 1724 in Königsberg, Prussia, he lived his whole life in the same city. His greatest work, *Critique of Pure Reason*, published in 1781, is now regarded as one of the most important works in philosophy. Unfortunately it is almost unreadable, as well as being over eight hundred pages long in the German edition. (Obscurity is a real asset for philosophers, because it gives future generations so much to argue about.) It was not well received, and in 1783 he wrote the much shorter *Prolegomena to any Future Metaphysics* to explain the main ideas. The name given to his philosophical system, 'transcendental idealism', is meaningless unless one is an academic philosopher.

Kant claimed that mathematics provided synthetic a-priori knowledge; in other words mathematics is not based on logic alone, nor is it based on experience. Unfortunately Kant's belief that human beings are forced by their own natures to interpret the world via Euclidean geometry and Newtonian mechanics turned out to be completely false. Both were superseded by general relativity. They are now regarded as approximations to the truth, still extremely useful but in no way the necessary bases of our thoughts. Nevertheless something remains, after one has eliminated his errors and translated (some of) his ideas into modern terminology.

Henri Poincaré, (1854–1912), was one of the towering mathematical figures of his era, and had firm views about the nature of mathematics.[17] He followed Kant in believing that, when doing mathematics humans relied on intuitions that could not be reduced to logic. These were much more limited than those Kant (wrongly) assumed, but included a limited notion of infinity, as applied to the integers, and the geometric notion of the continuum. The most basic of our intuitions is that of the passage of time, closely associated with our notion of cause and effect. However, he rejected Cantor's Platonistic set theory on the grounds that it purported to assign meaning to statements that we, as finite beings, had no means of verifying, even in principle.

Poincaré argued that our notion of natural numbers is based upon our intuition about counting upwards one at a time without ever coming to an end. Once one has this intuition one can try to find a precise logical formulation of it, but the formulation is only acceptable to the extent that it matches our intuition sufficiently closely. The logical formulation cannot be the real thing, because there is always a faint possibility that we might find some lack of correspondence between it and our intuition, and replace it by a more sophisticated formulation.

Poincaré's notion of the continuum is not easy to understand.[18] For most of his life he seems to have believed that the physical world was necessarily described in continuous terms; the advent of quantum theory makes this much less clear to us, as he recognized in the last year of his life. However, the peculiarities of quantum theory do not invalidate the fact that our perception of the world, as mediated by our eyes, is naturally expressed in terms of a continuum. The continuous line is not a part of mathematics, but embodies two intuitions, that any part of it can be subdivided into smaller parts indefinitely, and that there are no gaps between one place on it and another. Real numbers were invented to give a precise mathematical expression to these intuitions. For this reason Poincaré believed that although, in a narrow logical sense, the real number system can be defined without reference to our physical nature, this disregards the profound reasons that lie behind its introduction.

Over the last century, the ideas of Kant and Poincaré have been further developed by locating our synthetic a-priori intuitions in the innate biological structure of the human brain. This further modification of Kant's ideas should be contrasted with the blank slate theory and is often called the 'evolutionary Kantian position'. For the sake of brevity, I will call it Kantian, because of his key role in starting the line of thought.[19] From now on we will avoid the awkward term 'synthetic a-priori knowledge' by referring to 'innate predispositions of the human mind' or, equivalently, 'inherited biological characteristics of the brain'. By avoiding the use of the word 'knowledge', we remove any implication that what is innate must be a true representation of the world in itself.

The existence of innate mental capacities in mammals is demonstrated by the annual migration of millions of wildebeest in Africa. The vast herds are relentlessly pursued by predators, but new-born calves get to their feet and walk within a few minutes of birth and can run as fast as their mothers within two days of their birth. Evidently their vision must be fully operative almost immediately. The relevance of this to human beings is hard to demonstrate, because newborn babies are so helpless. However, the attention that extremely young babies give to human faces is evidence of an enormous degree of programming in their brains. Depending on the position and distance of the parent the retinal image of a face can have a wide variety of shapes and sizes. Babies have to be disposed to link all of these images together into a single gestalt, and later learn *not* to regard all faces as manifestations of a single individual. Finally children develop the belief that other individuals have minds, that different individuals have different knowledge about the world, and that deliberate deceit is possible. Almost all human beings in all societies negotiate their way through these complex problems to the same conclusion; the few who fail, do so because of anatomical or biochemical abnormalities in their brains, not because they have different cultural backgrounds.

Human beings are unique in having well developed languages. There is abundant evidence that our language instinct (as Steven Pinker calls it) is innate: we acquire language with an ease that far exceeds that of chimpanzees or the famous African grey parrot Alex. Recent scientific research demonstrates that language is not just a function of our general intelligence. It depends on specific circuits in our brains that other animals do not have or only have in a rudimentary form. Nevertheless, there are many different languages, and the differences between them are undoubtedly the result of historical processes.

The neural mechanisms that underlie mental capacities were illuminated by Eric Kandel, who was awarded a Nobel Prize in 2000 for his research in this field, particularly on the giant marine snail *Aplysia*. This has only 20,000 nerve cells, but they have no fundamental functional or biochemical differences from those of human beings. Along with many others, he found that *Aplysia* have fundamental reflexes that are based on the inherited and invariant synaptic connections between its nerve cells. In addition, new long-term memories (i.e. permanent modifications of its behaviour) are made possible by changes in the strengths of synaptic connections that involve the synthesis of new proteins. These discoveries are directly relevant to studies of the far more complex neural structures in the brains of higher animals, including human beings. Our innate capacities are the result of the particular neural wiring and synaptic connections present at birth, and subsequent learning is associated with changes in both. The research studies of Kandel and others are in their infancy, but it is reasonable to expect that they will eventually reveal many of the mechanisms that govern our own thinking. They will not, however, solve our ethical problems.

Experimental psychology has advanced to the point at which we can now say with some confidence that the blank slate theory is no longer tenable, unless one rejects the naturalistic approach to knowledge entirely. Nevertheless, the extreme plasticity of the human mind must not be forgotten. People can acquire an astonishing variety of skills, ranging from mathematics and ballet dancing to haute cuisine and impromptu comedy. These show how much our cultural environment can affect our brains by the time we reach adulthood.

According to Kant, one should distinguish between the world in itself (Kant's noumena) and our perceptions of it (his phenomena). The following proposition might be regarded as an updated version of one of Kant's central claims:

We interpret the world by using our innate capacities and in particular our strong disposition to interpret events in terms of causes and effects. We project these notions onto the world, and have no choice but to do so, because of our own natures.

The fact that these projections work well in many circumstances does not imply that they provide a full understanding of the world in itself. We may employ several complementary descriptions of a particular phenomenon to help us to understand it. For example, tables appear solid and continuous to us, but we also believe that they are composed of atoms and that their apparent colours are to a large extent creations of our visual system; we keep both of these pictures in our minds and use whichever is more appropriate. We manage to survive because our innate capacities have a positive relationship to the world in itself. It would be surprising if they did not!

2.7 Plato, Popper, Penrose

The next three chapters will show that Platonism still has a substantial influence on three areas of human thought: pure mathematics, fundamental physics, and theology. One need not agree that this is a desirable and justifiable state of affairs in order to wish to understand why it is the case. It is worth sparing a few pages describing its historical origins. We start with Pythagoras, who was born on the Greek island of Samos more than a hundred years before Plato and studied mathematics under Thales in Miletus. He spent periods in Egypt and Babylon, but eventually settled in Croton, southern Italy, where he founded a school of followers who called themselves Pythagoreans. Accounts of his life are far from reliable, perhaps little more than myths, but his school, which could also be called a religious cult, placed mathematics at the core of reality. The following was one of their beliefs:

> 'The inhalation of the apeiron' [or perhaps 'the appearance of structure in the boundless cosmic chaos'] is also what makes the world mathematical, not just possible to describe using maths, but truly mathematical since it shows numbers and reality to be upheld by the same principle.

The Greek philosopher Plato spent most of his life in Athens, where he opened an Academy devoted to philosophical thinking in 386 BC. Many of his books survive and reveal a fully worked out philosophy. His *Republic* is admirably clear, but *Timaeus*, in which he set out his cosmogony and religious views, is incomprehensible without expert interpretation. His Platonism developed into neo-Platonism over the centuries, and this had a significant influence on the early Christian Church. The Platonic Demiurge, a single creator outside space and time, has much in common with the Christian God, but lacks the personal characteristics of the latter.

Plato's notion of ideal forms, explained in *Republic*, was central to his philosophy. He considered that Beauty, Truth, Justice, and other forms were more real than the particular instances of them that we encounter in our ordinary lives. Through Socrates, he expresses his contempt for those who believed that the material world was real, preferring to describe it as a weak shadow of the ultimate reality of the ideal forms. These forms were by no means restricted to abstract entities:

> *God created only one essential Form of Bed in the ultimate nature of things, either because he wanted to or because some necessity prevented him from making more than one; at any rate he didn't produce more than one, and more than one could not possibly be produced...And I suppose that God knew it, and as he wanted to be the creator of a real Bed, and not just a carpenter making a particular bed, decided to make the ultimate reality unique.*[20]

All of his forms existed in an ideal world outside space and time, and philosophers could catch glimpses of them, or possibly remember them from an earlier existence, with sufficient effort. Plato was strongly influenced by the older Socrates and by the Pythagoreans, but accorded mathematics a lower status than the study of intelligible reality, although both dealt with ideal forms. Mathematics (by which he meant arithmetic and geometry) was concerned with reasoning *from* assumptions and not *to* first principles, and so could never finally understand its subject matter. Plato had little interest in what we call physics, believing that philosophers should focus their attention on reality, and not on the imperfect approximations to it that the physical world provided.

There are real differences between ideal forms as conceived by Plato and what we call concepts. Concepts are mental states; they depend on our existence and may be vague. They may be modified or develop as time passes. Ideal forms, on the other hand, exist in their own right and would do so even if human beings had never existed. Plato thought that each ideal form was unique, but this causes tremendous problems. How could the angles of an ideal triangle add up to 180° unless each of them has a determinate value? The obvious resolution of this problem is to have a different ideal triangle for every size and shape, but this would suggest that there should be a huge variety of ideal beds for similar reasons. Even if one accepts this, one still has problems in situations that involve several identical triangles in different positions, as in Figure 2.5.

Aristotle studied at Plato's Academy, but came to disagree with much of what Plato wrote about the philosophy of mathematics. Aristotle's attitude towards the world was more experimental and empirical. In particular he made a distinction between physics and mathematics, and considered physics to be the more fundamental. Although we have no systematic account of Aristotle's philosophy of mathematics, it appears that he regarded mathematics as arising by a process of abstraction from the physical world. The meaning that Aristotle associates with the word 'form' – he also used the word 'essence' – is substantially different from that of Plato:

> *The mathematician theorizes about abstractions, for he theorizes having removed all sensibles such as weight and lightness, hardness and its opposite, heat and cold, and the other sensible opposites. He leaves only the quantitative and continuous in one, two, or three [dimensions], and the properties of these as quantitative and continuous, not considering them in any other respect.*[21]

Aristotle took it for granted that the proper abstraction of the geometrical aspects of the world was Euclidean geometry – not, as we now know, something close to, but in certain contexts quite different from Euclidean geometry. He was therefore willing to conclude that the properties of Euclidean geometry, in particular the continuity of space, were necessarily mirrored in the physical world. Modern experimental science follows Aristotle's

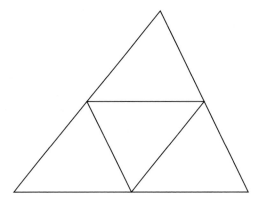

Fig. 2.5 Four Identical Triangles

philosophy more than that of Plato, but Platonism lingers on in pure mathematics and theology.

Plato's and Aristotle's accounts of the human soul are difficult to explain, because in each case different texts are not consistent with each other. Perhaps it suffices to say that their notions of soul differ in much the same way as their notions of form. We will therefore not attempt to describe in any detail their influences on later philosophers, such as Augustine and Descartes, even though those influences were of great importance.

The survival of Platonism to the present day owes more to the Neoplatonist Plotinus (204–70 AD) and St. Augustine (354–430 AD) than to anyone else. Let us take them in reverse order. Augustine spent his life in North Africa, apart from a few years in Rome and Milan, and was Bishop of Hippo Regius (Annaba, in Algeria) for his last 35 years. A large number of his works have survived to the present day and reveal his subtle and important contributions to Christian thought. He divided reality into the transitory world of sensible, or physical, entities and the eternal spiritual realm, God being the ultimate source of both. Human beings were supposed to be composed of two substances, their material bodies and their souls. Augustine took it for granted that the soul was the superior partner and that it was both immaterial and immortal. He argued that people could directly perceive the absolute truths of mathematics and logic with the active support of God, a process that he called illumination. In his later years he became increasingly fatalistic, i.e. committed to the doctrine of predestination, which was never accepted by the Catholic Church. We will say more about his influence on Christian thought in Chapter 5.

Augustine was more important than Plotinus in that his synthesis of Plotinus's ideas with early Christian traditions underlies much of present day theology. Augustine's God is a development of what Plotinus calls the One. The One is the ultimate, self-caused first principle, the origin of the world of Platonic forms, simple in nature but not itself describable; it is more abstract than Augustine's notion of God and lacks the element of creative love. Augustine commented that he read the Scriptures, and in particular the teaching of the apostle Paul, *after* becoming familiar with the books of the Platonists, and emphasized the absence in these books of any mention of charity, love, sacrifice, redemption, salvation, and other specifically Christian doctrines.[22]

In spite of the efforts of Plato, Aristotle, Augustine, the medieval philosophers, Descartes, and later figures, philosophers still argue about the nature of reality, particularly in connection with human consciousness. Recapitulating the historical development of this subject would involve explaining concepts such as substance, essence, simple natures, and other categories that are largely forgotten in today's world. Instead of doing this we will jump directly to the anti-Platonist philosophical views of Karl Popper, one of the most famous philosophers of science in the twentieth century.

Popper spent the early part of his career in Vienna and was associated with the so-called Vienna Circle of philosophers. His Jewish ancestry and the rise of Nazism forced him to emigrate to New Zealand in 1937. He spent much of his later life at the London School of Economics, but was responsible for a bitter dispute with his one-time student Imre Lakatos there soon after his retirement in 1969. Lakatos was not the only person with whom he had profound disagreements; the list included Ludwig Wittgenstein and the Oxford philosophers. He once described the latter as 'people who are always compulsively cleaning their spectacles instead of looking through them at the world'. Bryan Magee, who knew him well, wrote that he pursued arguments relentlessly, beyond the acceptable limits of aggression, and that he seemed unable to accept the existence of different points of view.

In his book *The Self and Its Brain* Popper proposed that reality has three aspects. His World 1, the universe of physical entities, includes material bodies, forces, and fields. In particular it includes the brain considered as a physical entity. World 1 is better understood than either of the other worlds, and all of our highly developed mathematical theories refer to its behaviour.

Popper admits that his World 2, the world of mental states, is more controversial. The division of the world into physical and mental needs no explanation if one is a mind–body dualist. If one is a reductionist one may justify it by reference to the extraordinary character of the mental world, which lies near the top of the reductionist's hierarchy. The depth and complexity of our thought processes have no parallel anywhere else in our world, and maybe in the universe. If any aspect of the reductionist's world merits special attention our mental powers must be the choice. Popper continues:

> By World 3 I mean the world of products of the human mind, such as stories, explanatory myths, tools, scientific theories (whether true or false), scientific problems, social institutions, and works of art. World 3 objects are of our own making, although they are not always the result of planned production by individual men.[23]

Popper explains that, although a book belongs to World 1, its contents, which remain invariant over different copies, belong to World 3 as the result of an agreement about the interpretation of the words on the pages. He also refers to certain material objects, such as a painting or sculpture, as lying in both World 1 and World 3; the World 3 aspect is what makes the object significant to human beings. For this reason he regards entities in World 3 as *abstract and public*, or at least potentially public. They may reside in the mind of only one person, as with a mathematical theorem that has not yet been communicated to anyone else. He insists that entities in World 3 are real because they may induce people to act on World 1 in a way that they would not do otherwise – this is, indeed, his criterion of reality. In particular, a law about the proper punishment for murder may lead to a person being executed, even though the law is a non-material entity belonging to society as a whole.

Figure 2.6 shows the relationships between Popper's three worlds. Popper states that there is no direct connection between his Worlds 1 and 3; entities in World 3 can affect the mental states of people, and these in turn can affect their actions, and hence World 1.

| World 1 | World 2 | World 3 |
| (physical) | (mental) | (cultural) |

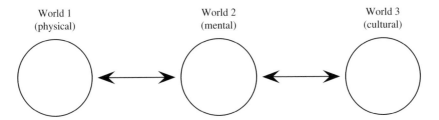

Fig. 2.6 Popper's Three Worlds

I have described World 3 as consisting of the products of the human mind. But human minds react, in their turn, to those products: there is a feedback. The mind of a painter, for example, or of an engineer, is greatly influenced by the very objects on which he is working. And he is also influenced by the work of others, predecessors as well as contemporaries. This influence is both conscious and unconscious. It bears upon expectations, upon preferences, upon programmes. In so far as we are the product of other minds, and of our own minds, we ourselves may be said to belong to World 3.[24]

Popper contrasts his World 3 with Plato's eternal world of ideal forms in the following words:

I am an opponent of what I have called 'essentialism'. Thus, in my opinion, Plato's ideal essences play no role in World 3. (That is, Plato's World 3, though clearly in some sense an anticipation of my World 3, seems to

me a mistaken construction.) On the other hand, Plato would never have
admitted such entities as problems or conjectures – especially false con-
jectures – into his world of intelligible objects.[25]

Popper states that a story that is repeated orally within a prehistoric
tribe and eventually forgotten appears in World 3 but then 'in a sense disap-
pears'.[26] More radically, it follows from Popper's account of World 3 that,
if the human race along with all of our cultural products were to perish in
an environmental disaster, then Worlds 2 and 3 would disappear in toto. In
spite of their time-dependent status they are all equally real now.

His failure to fully resolve the difference between World 3 and the
Platonic world is evident in his treatment of musical compositions:

One might even say that the whole depth of [Mozart's Jupiter Symphony]
cannot be captured by any single performance, but only by hearing it
again and again, in different interpretations. In that sense the World 3
object is a real ideal object which exists, but exists nowhere, and whose
existence is somehow the possibility of its being reinterpreted by human
beings.[27]

He goes on to suggest that his 'World 3 is perhaps best conceived along
Platonic lines', before repeating the differences between the two notions.
He could (and should) have maintained the distinction by declaring that
'Mozart's Jupiter Symphony' is a blanket term referring to a variety of different entities in World 3, characterized by their relationship to the original
score. Using a single word to refer to all of them does not create an ideal
entity out of nothing.

In a physical or historical context distinguishing between truth and
knowledge about the truth is not usually considered to raise philosophical
issues. Consider the question about whether the one-thousandth ancestor in
the male line of the British prime minister was born in Egypt. We consider
this to be true or false in spite of the fact that no evidence either way now
exists, *because* we regard historical events as real. We do so because we
have plenty of supporting evidence for the more general statement; the fact
that the evidence does not include the answer to the particular question is
not regarded as important.

However, one is not forced to take the same view about entities in
World 3. Unicorns exist within World 3 even though they do not exist
in World 1. My impression is that they are generally white, but this is not a
question that has an objective answer. If a story about a black unicorn were
to be written – inevitably I later found out that one had – I would broaden
my views about the possible colours of unicorns without thinking that I had

discovered a fact about unicorns that I had not previously known. This example suggests that the extent to which a World 3 entity has definite properties may vary from case to case.

In a mathematical context, one may take the view that claiming that theorems are true before they have been proved is a quibble about when it is appropriate to use the word 'true' with reference to cultural creations – and Popper was very intolerant of verbal quibbles. If we only use the word 'true' with respect to a mathematical statement when some human being has proved it to be true and the proof has been checked carefully by the community, then the true statements about a mathematical entity will be time-dependent, as well as the entity itself. (In other words one can refuse to accept that there is a distinction between the ontology and epistemology of mathematical entities.) This has the consequence that as we prove more about a mathematical concept, the concept itself becomes sharper, or fuller, in our minds. This *modification* of Popper's account of World 3 is easier to defend than his own, in which the properties of a mathematical entity are 'objectively there' the moment the entity has been constructed. It is not far from the position of Wittgenstein, who regarded mathematical proofs as creating new connections in the language that did not exist until it made them.

The above description of World 3 is close to that of Popper, but one can approach it from a much less philosophical perspective, that of the evolution of the structures – libraries, museums, professions, governments, religions, sciences, etc. – that define our civilization.[28] Until the last ten thousand years human culture was largely transmitted orally and was limited by the size and imperfections of our memories. The transition to the Neolithic age made possible the accumulation of ever increasing numbers of art objects and also led to the development of written literature, historical and commercial records, musical scores, money, and many other cultural artifacts. From this point of view the use of the phrase, World 3, is simply a way of drawing our attention to the fact that most of our civilization is embedded in and dependent on material objects, which may be appreciated by people whom we have never met. Many of these objects were produced by who are people long dead and will affect the lives of others who are not yet born. They provide a major external enhancement of our ability to make mental representations of the world, and to transform our nature as a species. If one accepts the identification of World 3 with human civilization, then its reality can hardly be denied. Mathematical statements that may or may not be proved some time in the future are called conjectures, and, as such, are a part of World 3. They only join World 3 as theorems once they have been proved.

In *Shadows of the Mind* Roger Penrose radically modifies some of Popper's ideas, replacing Popper's World 3 by the world of Platonic forms. He also places his three worlds in a triangle and joins then by arrows.

The interpretation of his arrow from the mental world to the Platonic world is not obvious, because the Platonic world exists independently of human beings and cannot be influenced by them. Indeed Penrose admits that such an arrow fits better into the Kantian (and Popperian) framework. He then seems to retract his own suggestion that the connections should have directions. The role of the arrow from the Platonic world to the physical world (which has no analogue in the Popperian figure) is also not clear: the mechanism by which mathematical equations could influence the behaviour of physical objects has never been explained, and Penrose does not even try to do this. Plato himself said that physical objects were no more than partial and imperfect copies of the corresponding Platonic forms, which exist at the apex of Plato's philosophical scheme. Penrose's problems with explaining his own diagram illustrate the difficulty of relating Platonism to other things that we now believe about the world.

George Ellis also argues in support of the physical effectiveness of human cultural institutions. Many of his examples in *Physics and the Real World* – plans for a Jumbo jet, housing policy, rules of football, money, thermostats – fit Popper's criteria for World 3 objects exactly. In his 2004 Templeton Foundation Lecture 'Science, Complexity and the Nature of Existence' he

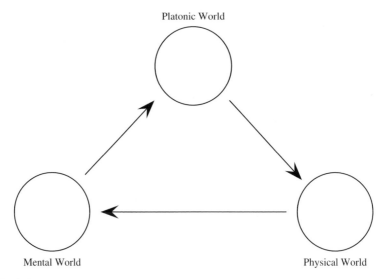

Fig. 2.7 Penrose's Three Worlds

makes no distinction between the theories of Popper and Penrose; his text follows Popper closely, but he refers to Penrose. He also proposes a further world of physical and biological possibilities. It is not clear from the lecture whether he considers that this further world is a concept introduced to help us to understand a reality that is too complex to grasp without its help, or whether it is supposed to have an independent existence; however, elsewhere he reveals himself to be a strong Platonist. He assigns existence to any kind of entity that can be demonstrated to have a measurable effect on physical matter, exactly as Popper did, and then writes:

> There is a reality to the possibility space that determines what is and is not possible (at the lower end of the hierarchy, this is characterized by inviolable physical laws, whose ontological status is however unclear).

The interpretation of this curiously phrased sentence is difficult. The possibility space for Newtonian mechanics is completely different, not just in detail but in its entire mathematical structure, from that for quantum mechanics. By saying that the ontological status of physical laws is unclear Ellis seems to be withholding any claim about their truth, although the first part of the sentence seems to assign reality to their possibility spaces. This must be a central issue in a lecture about the nature of existence, but its resolution depends heavily on whether he wishes to adopt a Platonic or Popperian position – Popper allows false theories into his World 3, but Penrose and Plato surely cannot.

There are people who believe that each possible universe really exists, in the same way as ours, but saying that a possibility space is real is not the same as saying that each possibility in it is physically realized. The same issue is the source of much disagreement in quantum theory. Some people say that an observation forces the world into one of two possible states, while others say that there are two equally real outcomes, although we are only aware of one. To confuse things even more, yet others say that the only thing that changes in an observation is our knowledge of the world, rather than the world itself. The quantum version of the multiverse theory involves a superposition of a vast array of equally real worlds. Such questions give rise to real passions, but there seems to be no way of choosing between them apart from expressing one's personal preference. The difference between them is metaphysical rather than scientific; all of them yield the same predictions in actual experiments, because they depend on solving the same mathematical equations.

Popper and Penrose illustrate two views about the nature of human culture. A number of scientists seek to explain it in biological terms. Among these is Edward Wilson. In 1975 he wrote a book on the genetic control of behaviour in animals, and in its final chapter dared to suggest that some central aspects of the behaviour of the human species could also be explained in the light of Darwin's theory of evolution.[29] This drew fierce criticisms because of its lack of political correctness – it was regarded as the first step towards admitting that different people might have different genetic endowments, and then possibly to using this as a justification for treating some worse than others. The problem was that his research might be used by people who had quite different agendas from his own – this was exactly what had happened with Darwin's theory many decades earlier. Eventually this conflict was defused to some extent by a shift of emphasis in which Wilson's label 'sociobiology' was replaced by 'evolutionary psychology'.

The ideas in Wilson's book were developed by a number of biologists, and led to the concept of gene–culture coevolution, a term coined by Charles Lumsden and Wilson in 1981. It is amusing that, although Popper's three worlds were described by him as embodying a pluralist philosophy, Wilson uses a similar division in support of his notion of consilience, the unity of all human knowledge.[30] Surprisingly he does not mention Popper in *Consilience* and only mentions Penrose once, and then negatively. He envisages genes and human nature both changing slowly over time, each influencing the way in which the other develops. Human nature also influences and is influenced by culture, but genes and culture are only connected indirectly. However, as our understanding of the genetic code increases, gene therapy is beginning to provide a direct link from culture to genes. So far there have been no attempts to interfere with the germ cells, but this may be only a matter of time. Some religious authorities are already warning that this is interfering in matters that only God should control.

Human culture differs both quantitatively and qualitatively from the complex, but genetically determined, patterns of behaviour of other animals, resulting, for example, in ants' nests, spiders' webs, and beavers' dams. Our own species has developed hundreds of complex types of behaviour – dancing, singing, tool-making, cooking, building shelters, religious rituals, decorating the body, and making clothes, to name just a few. Many of these have been transmitted within individual tribes and communities over many generations, but they are often very different from one region to another. The overarching characteristic of our species, language, also varies enormously from one place and time to another.

Wilson does not question the reality of human culture, and one guesses that he would regard a discussion about this as bizarre. He emphasizes that the interactions of genes, human nature, and culture can be investigated scientifically. The question that interests him as a scientist is how biology and culture interact across all societies to create the commonalities of human nature. This is an interesting question, but one must emphasize that it is still in its infancy, and only addresses a tiny fraction of the things we find interesting about human societies. One of these is incest, banned by law in many societies but also inhibited by unconscious, inborn traits. Another is altruism, apparently in conflict with Darwinian theory, but actually not, if one takes a wide enough view. One can pursue such studies without believing that they provide the only, or even the most important, approach to the mysteries of our nature.

Richard Dawkins went one step further than Wilson by introducing the ideas of memes in his book *The Selfish Gene*, in 1976. These are putative units of cultural inheritance, transmitted socially rather than physically, and subject to occasional mutations, just as are genes. In a characteristically outspoken manner he describes religion as a meme, something like a 'cultural virus', whose existence and development can be studied in a scientific manner. The meme concept has been promoted by a small number of people, including the philosopher Daniel Dennett, and Dawkins lists his responses to some of the objections in Chapter 5 of his book 'The God Delusion'. An objection to the meme concept is that it is simply a picturesque analogy; it does little more than encapsulate the fact that some ideas can be transmitted with few changes from one person to another and can affect their behaviour. The idea that one might be able to reduce the rich variety of our traditions and beliefs to discrete, replicable units *looks* as though it might be the starting point for a reductionist scientific investigation of human culture, but those pressing the merits of this idea have not come up with much that compels attention, after thirty years. A possible exception is the description of words as discrete, culturally transmitted memes that are remarkably stable over long periods of time.

The Christian view of our human nature and culture is more Platonic in character. Christian theologians inevitably reject Dawkins' meme-based account of culture and religion. In 2007 the Archbishop of Canterbury, Rowan Williams devoted a substantial part of a lecture in Swansea to explaining why it was wholly inadequate, even crass, from his point of view.[31] He sees religion as a valid response to the nature of God, rather than as a meaningless cultural relic. God as the 'ground of being' is the explanation of rationality itself, rather than something to be explained rationally. He is approached via contemplation of the ultimate truths, rather than by scientific analysis.

Williams repeatedly said in his lecture that Dawkins reduced religion to being in some sense a survival strategy. Several people have remarked that this is almost the exact opposite of Dawkins' views as expressed in *The God Delusion*. Dawkins explained at length that he believed that religion was an accidental by-product of something else, a cultural virus which reproduces *in spite of deleterious effects on the host*.[32] The journalist John Cornwell, also a strong critic of Dawkins, did not make this mistake in his recent book.[33] Williams surely disagrees with the cultural virus theory as well, but as a theologian he had a particular responsibility to criticize what Dawkins actually wrote, *and had said so himself in that very speech*. However, this blunder on Williams' part does not affect the fact that the two have irreconcilable differences concerning the validity of religious belief and the nature of reality.

2.8 Conclusion

Science has progressed as far as it has because of the extraordinary degree of regularity in the natural world. We can only understand this regularity to the extent that we are capable of formulating it in our own terms. Mathematics is one ingredient in this understanding, but it cannot be the only one. Indeed, in the biological sciences it does not have anything like the same importance as it does in the physical sciences.

Some people claim that fundamental physics is the ultimate reality and that everything else is of secondary importance. This is an extremely tempting idea for those who have spent their lives studying the subject and who would like to believe that their efforts have greater significance than those of other mortals. However, even if a final Theory of Everything eventually appears, we will only be able to use it if we, the scientific community, understand what the equations mean. Every physicist may agree about the meaning of E (energy) in Einstein's famous equation $E = mc^2$, but it would take many pages to explain it adequately. Without interpretation equations are meaningless, no more than patterns of ink on a piece of paper.

We know that our mental state can influence the physical world. We can even affect the behaviour of elementary particles by building suitable accelerators. There is no evidence that we will ever be able to describe our actions without reference to our mental state, and we might as well accept this. Such facts may not matter to those working in the physical sciences, but the rest of us should not heed the claim of some that they have the only proper way of describing the world. This is merely a statement about their personal world-view, and need not be taken seriously.

Notes and References

[1] Slingerland, Edward (2008). *What Science Offers the Humanities.* Camb. Univ. Press.

[2] Davies, E.B. (2003). *Science in the Looking Glass*, Chapter 10. Oxford Univ. Press.

[3] Nancy Cartwright's 2007 book, *Hunting Causes and Using Them: Approaches in Philosophy and Economics*, Camb. Univ. Press, focuses on different meanings of the word 'cause' rather than different contexts in which the word might be used.

[4] Magee, Bryan. (1997). *Confessions of a Philosopher*, p.83. Phoenix, Orion Books Ltd.

[5] Henke, D. (2004). Teleology: the explanation that bedevils biology. In John Cornwell ed. *Explanations*, p.151. Oxford Univ. Press.

[6] Davies, E.B. (2008). In Vincent F. Hendricks and Hannes Leitgeb eds. *Philosophy of Mathematics, Five Questions*, Chapter 8. Automatic Press, VIP.

[7] Norton, J. D. (2003). Causation as Folk Science, *Philosophers' Imprint*, **3**, 22pp.

[8] Polkinghorne, J. (1996). *Beyond Science*, p.17. Camb. Univ. Press.

[9] Bennett, Maxwell *et al.* (2007). *Neuroscience and Philosophy.* Columbia Univ. Press, New York.

[10] Midgley, M. (2003). *The Myths We Live By*. Routledge.

[11] Midgley, M. (1995). In J. Cornwell ed. *Nature's Imagination: the Frontiers of Scientific Vision*. Oxford Univ. Press, USA.

[12] Wilson, E.O. (1998). *Consilience, The Unity of Knowledge*, p.132. Little, Brown and Co., London.

[13] Polkinghorne, J. (1996). *Beyond Science*, pp.71, 72. Camb. Univ. Press.

[14] Hume, David (1748). *An Enquiry Concerning Human Understanding*, Section VII.

[15] Slingerland, Edward (2008). *What Science Offers the Humanities*, p.24. Camb. Univ. Press.

[16] Pinker, Steven (2002). *The Blank Slate*. Penguin Books, London.

[17] Folina, J. (1992). *Poincaré and the Philosophy of Mathematics*. Macmillan Press Ltd., London.

[18] Folina (1992), Chapter 6.

[19] Slingerland (2008), pp.117–19.

[20] Plato. *The Republic, Book Ten, Theory of Art.*

[21] Aristotle. *Metaphysics XI*, 1061a29.

[22] Saint Augustine. *Confessions, Book VII*, Chapters 20, 21.

[23] Popper, K.R. and Eccles, J.C. (1977). *The Self and Its Brain, An Argument for Interactionism*, Chapter P2 and p.38. Routledge, London.

[24] Popper and Eccles (1977), pp.144, 145.

[25] Popper and Eccles (1977), p.43.

[26] Popper and Eccles (1977), p.449.

[27] Popper and Eccles (1977), p.450.

[28] The following was influenced by private communications with Petros Gelepithis.

[29] Wilson, Edward O. (1975). *Sociobiology: The New Synthesis.* Harvard Univ. Press, Cambridge, Mass.

[30] Wilson, Edward O. (1998). *Consilience*, pp.182–99. Lillian, Brown, and Co., London.

[31] *How to Misunderstand Religion*, lecture in the University of Swansea, 13 Oct. 2007, available at the Archbishop of Canterbury's official web site.

[32] Dawkins, Richard (2006). *The God Delusion*, Chapter 5, pp.200, 218. Bantam Press, London.

[33] Cornwell, J. (2007). *Darwin's Angel, An Angelic Riposte to 'The God Delusion'*, Chapter 19. Profile Books, London.

3
The Nature of Mathematics

Science has taught us that our intuition
is often wrong.

3.1 An Early Influence

Many people can remember some event early in their careers that had a
major influence on their development. In my case it was reading a book that
I mentioned to hardly anyone for thirty years. The year was 1967; I was just
finishing my DPhil thesis at Oxford and was hungry for new ideas. The
book was called *Foundations of Constructive Analysis*, and was written by
the eminent American mathematician, Errett Bishop. For most of his career
he had published high quality papers of an entirely conventional type, but
eventually he became dissatisfied.

Bishop's book re-opened a debate that most people thought had been
settled in the 1930s. Two famous mathematicians, David Hilbert and
L. E. J. Brouwer, had been in open conflict about the right foundations for
mathematics. Hilbert advocated what is now called 'formalism', a programme in which the symbols of mathematics were emptied of meaning,
so that the correctness of proofs could be verified by purely formal procedures; in present day terms this would amount to manipulating mathematical expressions as a computer might. (This did not mean that Hilbert
believed that the symbols were indeed meaningless.) On the other hand
Brouwer advocated an 'intuitionist' programme, in which meaning stood at
the centre of the stage. He required existence proofs to provide a method of
constructing any object that was supposed to exist. Their conflict spilled
over into other matters and came to a head when Hilbert forced Brouwer's
removal from the editorial board of the journal *Mathematische Annalen*, in
1928. Brouwer never recovered from this blow to his esteem.

The stories of the mathematical conflict between Brouwer and Hilbert and of the discoveries of Kurt Gödel in the 1930s have been told many times, so I will be brief. Hilbert's goal was to find a formal approach to the foundations of mathematics that would establish for all time its truth and objectivity. Brouwer believed that this was misguided: mathematics needed radical changes to eliminate the temptation to use ideas that were, in the last resort, devoid of real meaning. Hermann Weyl, one of the most outstanding mathematicians of his era, gave his moral support to Brouwer's intuitionistic programme over many years, even though he realized how seriously it affected the body of mathematics. Unfortunately for Brouwer, its consequences were regarded as unacceptable by the mathematical community. Hilbert's formalist programme also failed, for reasons described below, but for some reason his general views about the nature of mathematics survived. His comment, 'no one shall drive us out of the paradise which Cantor has created for us' eventually led the philosopher Wittgenstein to write:

> I would say 'I wouldn't dream of trying to drive anyone out of this paradise'. I would try to do something quite different: I would try to show you that it is not a paradise – so that you'll leave of your own accord. I would say, 'You're welcome to this, just look about you.'

Gödel was only 25 years old when he made the first of his shattering discoveries in 1931. He proved that in any sufficiently complex formal system, such as ordinary arithmetic, there must exist statements that make sense but can neither be proved nor disproved within the system. This was *interpreted* by many people, including Gödel himself in later life, as meaning that there were mathematical results that were true, but not accessible to human reason. Gödel never abandoned his belief that such a thing as absolute truth did exist in mathematics, and that intuition might somehow bridge the gap that reason could not fill. Today many mathematicians are equivocal about this. They use set theory, one of the greatest sources of controversy, as a builder uses a spade (they regard it as a useful tool, but no more basic than other parts of mathematics) and carefully avoid the more abstract aspects of the subject.

One of the issues relating to set theory is illustrated in Figure 3.1. Classical mathematicians are willing to contemplate the entire set (by which we always mean collection) of regions in the plane as a single entity, in spite of the fact that the variety of such regions is literally beyond imagination. When they say that all regions have some property, they imagine selecting one of them arbitrarily out of the set of all regions, and being able to assert with certainty that it has the property.

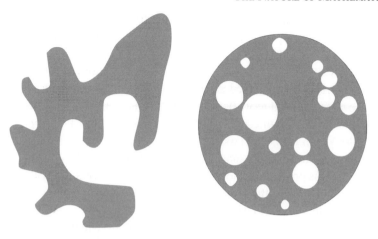

Fig. 3.1 Two Regions in the Plane

Constructivist mathematicians avoid references to the set of all regions and interpret the same statement as follows. If one specifies a particular region constructively, then there is a *known procedure* for proving that the region has the required property. They would not use, as a classical mathematician would, existence theorems that give no information about the entity that is supposed to exist. In ordinary conversation both mathematicians might use exactly the same form of words, but there will nevertheless be a real difference between what they mean by them.

Let us reduce the level of abstraction by discussing jewellery instead of regions in the plane. An expert in this field will be familiar with a very wide range of jewellery, and might have been involved in making or designing it. He might have a through knowledge of the different types of jewellery that have been worn at different periods and in different cultures. There is no need for him to believe that there exists an abstract set of all possible jewellery, including jewellery that could be designed but never will be. Such ideas are extraneous to the field and add nothing to it. One need not be quite as negative about set theory in mathematics, but it is reasonable to regard it as an organizing device, rather than as the description of a Platonic reality.

By the 1960s most mathematicians believed that the foundational debate was over and that Gödel's lessons had been absorbed into their culture. It was therefore a considerable surprise when Bishop showed, in 1967, that in one of the main fields of mathematics the sacrifices needed to carry out a constructivist programme were really quite small, and that constructive proofs of theorems need involve only normal, straightforward mathematics. He showed how to construct the real and complex number systems and developed a substantial part of mathematics using entirely constructive methods that any mathematician could accept. This distinguished his approach to constructivism from that of Brouwer, whose intuitionist mathematics contained theorems that were classically false.

One does not need to work through its formal details in order to understand the broad significance of Bishop's programme. Every proof in Bishop's system is also a classical proof, so every theorem that has a constructive proof in Bishop's sense is also true classically. Understanding the character of his programme does not depend on any familiarity with formal logic or philosophy – the issue is whether the advantages of pursuing his programme are judged to be worthwhile, at least in some situations.

The difference between classical and constructive mathematics can be illustrated as follows. Suppose that you recently put your mobile phone down but cannot remember where. A classical mathematician might reassure you that it must still exist and that you will eventually come across it. A constructive mathematician would say that the issue is to find it and suggest that you should call its number using another phone and listen for the ring tone. The classical mathematician might object that this is a very special procedure, only applicable to mobile phones, while they were making use of the *general principle* that solid objects do not simply stop existing for no reason.

The above analogy has its faults, but its moral is correct: constructive mathematics requires more ingenuity and constructive solutions are often of limited applicability. However, the difference can be important. Some of the standard theorems taught in universities assert that a certain type of equation always has a solution. (The intermediate value theorem is one such.) Such a theorem may only be constructively true in the sense of Bishop, subject to a further condition that allows a numerical analyst to write down a procedure for finding the solution. Without the extra condition, a numerical procedure may fail to find the solution or may even find something that appears to be the solution but actually is not even close to it. Classical mathematicians may not care about such issues, but some of us do.

This may have given the impression that there are just two types of mathematics, classical and constructive, but that is far from being the case. Some, like the nineteenth century mathematician Leopold Kronecker, are strict finitists and do not accept the existence of irrational numbers, such as the square root of 2 or $\pi = 3.14159\ldots$. Bishop did not take either of these positions. He was perfectly happy to assert that π existed, because for him, this *meant* that there is *at the present time* a procedure for working out as many digits of π as one likes.

Bishop had strong philosophical reasons for developing his theory. He wrote:

> With the constructive definition of the integers, we have begun our study of the technical implementation of the constructivist philosophy. Our point of view is to describe the mathematical operations that can be carried out by finite beings, men's mathematics for short. In contrast, classical mathematics concerns itself with operations that can be carried out by God... You may think that I am making a joke, or attempting to put down classical mathematics, by bringing God into the discussion. This is not true. I am doing my best to develop a secure philosophical foundation, based on meaning rather than formalistics, for current classical practice.

Helen Billinge has argued that Bishop did not develop a systematic philosophy of constructive mathematics. True, but he was not addressing philosophers. His goal was to persuade *mathematicians* of the merits of his approach by working out the details, and in this he had more success than may have been apparent in his lifetime. In 1973 he was invited by the American Mathematical Society to give a series of four lectures, entitled 'Schizophrenia in Modern Mathematics', but in spite of this he felt that the general response to his ideas was indifferent or hostile, and that it had contributed to a heart attack.

The issues involved may be illustrated by examining the first 501 digits of π:

$$\pi \sim 3.14159265358979323846264338327950288419716939937510$$
$$58209749445923078164062862089986280348253421170679$$
$$82148086513282306647093844609550582231725359408128$$
$$48111745028410270193852110\underline{555}964462294895493038196$$
$$44288109756659334461284756482337867831652712019091$$
$$45648566923460348610454326648213393607260249141273$$
$$72458700660631558817488152092096282925409171536436$$
$$78925903600113305305488204665213841469519415116094$$
$$33057270365759595195309218611738193261179310511854 8$$
$$07446237996274956735188575272489122793818301194912$$

Consider the question 'do there exist arbitrarily long sequences of consecutive 5s in the decimal expansion of π?' Most mathematicians would guess that the answer is yes, but all one can see by looking at the digits presented above is that there is a sequence of three consecutive 5s, underlined above. Current technology for computing the digits of π probably allows one to find a sequence of ten consecutive 5s, but clearly this makes no contribution to answering the question. There is no conceivable purely computational procedure that would find the first occurrence of a million consecutive 5s (if there is one). A supernatural being might be able to contemplate the infinite set of all digits of π at a glance and immediately answer the question. A Platonist would say that the set of all digits of π exists and therefore the answer is either yes or no. Bishop would have answered that neither of these responses is useful because we do not have access to God. (I am confusing God with Platonism here, but that is because Bishop mentioned God.)

A mathematician who is asked whether a set of entities is finite or infinite might give the answer, 'yes', 'no', or 'we do not know at present'. Platonists would say that this is unsatisfactory because it inserts mathematicians into problems that do not mention them, but Bishop considered that the state of mathematical knowledge does change with time, and that he was merely acknowledging that fact. In their formal publications constructive mathematicians simply stay silent when faced with uncertainty, rather than asserting that every meaningful statement must be true or false. In philosophical language, they consider that mathematics should not be invaded by ontological commitments: quasi-religious beliefs about the true nature of things.

My own reaction to Bishop's book was two-fold. I was greatly attracted to his view of mathematics, but also saw that openly supporting it might not do my career any good. Some of my best early research papers were responses to his influence, but I cast them in a classical form and made no mention of this fact. His ideas gave me a perspective on mathematics that was to affect me and some others of my generation for the rest of our lives. As time passed, I realized that I was not being intellectually honest and came to classify myself as a pluralist.

3.2 Pluralism in Mathematics

Human beings have been fascinated by mathematics throughout recorded history. Indeed, once civilization got to the point where bureaucracy, accountancy, and taxation became important, arithmetic quickly followed. The Babylonian, Egyptian, Chinese, Indian, and Arab mathematicians all developed systematic ways of doing calculations in arithmetic, and the answers that they obtained are as true today as they were at that time. They also introduced the idea of formulating practical problems as equations involving unknown quantities, and developed systematic ways of solving the equations. On the other hand, Euclid's Elements, published in thirteen books around 300 BC, provided a connected body of geometric theorems with general proofs, and became the model for all modern mathematics. All of these developments were brought together during the flowering of scholarship called the Islamic Golden age, which followed the foundation of Baghdad in 762 AD.

Philosophers down the ages have found mathematics fascinating, because it seems to provide the only body of certain knowledge. Almost everything else appears to depend on judgements that people can and do argue about. If one disregards a few deficiencies revealed by Hilbert at around 1900, Euclid's proofs are accepted and admired as much today as they were two and a half thousand years ago. No other field of knowledge can make such claims, and this needs to be explained. Nevertheless, our *attitude* towards Euclidean geometry has changed dramatically. Until the last two hundred years it was regarded as providing an exact description of the physical world; now it is seen as an abstract axiomatic system, which fits the world quite accurately, although it is definitely wrong in situations where special or general relativity are relevant. Mathematical certainty has been preserved by the device of denying any necessary relationship between mathematics and the nature of the external world. The certainty is therefore relative to the assumptions, or axioms, chosen. Make different assumptions and one gets hyperbolic geometry instead of Euclidean geometry. For a mathematician it now makes no sense to ask which one, if either, is *right*; the two co-exist and are equally valid.

There is another sphere of activity in which there is no scope for disagreement about the facts, the many and varied games that people play. A common response to this – that mathematics is a serious subject, not to be compared with frivolous pastimes – is not justified, because *all* analogies between two different subjects are bound to have limitations. David Wells has pointed out that many famous mathematicians have been interested in games and that the connections are wide-ranging and deep.[1] Games, geometrical puzzles, and codes turn imperceptibly into problems in combinatorics, graph theory, and number theory as the context widens. Tic-tac-toe (also called noughts and crosses) is a game, at least until one has learned the strategy for avoiding defeat, but determining the optimal strategy for the many more complex variations of the game is highly non-trivial. The fact that there is an optimal strategy in each case follows from the finite length of the games, but the number of different ways of playing a complex game is so huge that one cannot hope to find it by enumeration, and has to resort to theoretical, i.e. mathematical, methods.

A variety of approaches to the foundations of mathematics started to surface late in the nineteenth century, and the issues involved became steadily more pressing in the first half of the twentieth century – we described some of these in the last section. By 1940 all of the ideas had failed and it seemed that the search for secure foundations could not succeed. The current situation may be understood by reference to the notion of a (metaphysical, theoretical, or linguistic) framework.[2] According to this one cannot talk about the truth of a statement or the existence of an abstract entity until one has chosen the framework within which the assertion is made. The choice of framework is based on its fruitfulness in a particular context.

According to Wittgenstein human social interactions are based on a wide variety of 'language games', each with its own rules and conventions. (The term 'language game' gives an unfortunate impression of frivolity, but it is well-established.) The meanings of words can only be understood by examining their use, which may vary from one social context to another, or from one language game to another; many philosophical disagreements arise by not recognizing this fact. Wittgenstein's only published book, *Tractatus Logico-Philosophicus*, appeared in 1921 and marked him out as a philosophical genius, but he changed his views substantially in later life. In spite of an enormous literature published by others about his later work, there are still disagreements about his philosophical beliefs.

Classical mathematicians and constructivists both believe that the merits of their own mathematical framework are so great that the other should be abandoned. A pluralist, on the other hand, can switch from one to the other depending on the context. Taking pluralism seriously imposes an extra burden on mathematicians – one must remember which theorems have constructive proofs, which currently do not and which are unlikely ever to have. A classical mathematician might ask why one should take on the extra burden of remembering which part of the subject can be implemented in a constructive framework. One answer is purely aesthetic: if one enjoys the views from the tops of two different mountains why should one have to make a choice between them? Another is that mathematics is about more than whether certain statements can be proved. Every new proof of a theorem involves different insights: the details of a constructive proof tell one something interesting even if one does not accept constructivism as a philosophy. When a classical theorem is false constructively, it often has a constructive analogue, and the difference between the two tells one something about the issues involved in the proofs.[3]

Constructive methods may not have any contribution to make in some contexts. These include parts of algebra, geometry, and the higher reaches of set theory. Although parts of analytic topology have constructive versions, it is not clear that the advantages outweigh the disadvantages. However, in fields that involve quantitative bounds, one can obtain a fuller understanding of the relationships between the various results by keeping track of which are constructive and which are not. This is not only relevant to numerical analysis, although it is particularly important in that context.

In 1997 the eminent logician Solomon Feferman gave a detailed logical analysis of Bishop's system and concluded that it provided a viable alternative to the scientifically applicable parts of classical mathematics.[4] In spite of (or more likely in ignorance of) this, some eminent mathematicians, including Fields medal winners, adopt very hostile attitudes towards anyone who does not fully accept the consensus as they perceive it: I have experienced it myself in a public meeting. It is interesting that, although mathematicians are generally extremely mild, they are so unused to dealing with differences of opinion that their reactions in such a context can be very immature.

Carnap's ideas about linguistic frameworks were criticized in the 1950s by the American philosopher Willard van Orman Quine, who tried to rescue mathematical realism by means of the 'indispensability argument'. Putnam later explained it as follows. Since the use of mathematical entities is indispensable for science and we adopt a realistic attitude towards science, it is intellectually dishonest to argue that mathematical entities are mere fictions.[5] A strength of Quinean realism is that it avoids any appeal to the Platonic realm. A weakness is that it makes the truth of the equation $2 + 2 = 4$ appear to depend upon the nature of the physical universe, whereas any mathematician would say that it is a logical truth. Whether the numbers 2 and 4 would still exist as logical constructs if there were no universe is one of those questions that fascinate same people while leaving others completely cold. Another problem with Quinean realism is that it does not provide any justification for those parts of pure mathematics which physics does not use.

An important weakness of Quinean realism is that it makes the false assumption that the mathematics of mathematicians is essentially the same as the mathematics of typical physicists. (I speak of a generic theoretical physicist here: the spectrum of attitudes towards mathematics between them and pure mathematicians is continuous.) In fact the goal of physicists is to obtain formulae that can be checked against the results of experiments; whether such a formula has been derived by a procedure that a pure mathematician regards as rigorous is of no interest to them. A famous physicist, who had better remain nameless, once said that he knew why something was a theorem and considered that providing a rigorous proof or even a logically precise statement would be a waste of effort, in spite of being presented with a series of counterexamples that he considered 'pathological'.

Quantum electrodynamics (QED) illustrates the chasm between pure mathematics and theoretical physics very clearly. The quantities of interest are the sums of an infinite number of terms, each of which is associated with what is called a Feynman diagram. Unfortunately each diagram represents an integral whose value is infinite, and a procedure called renormalization has to be carried out to obtain a finite number. Even then the sum of the infinite series is expected to diverge, so a further ad hoc procedure to by-pass this problem is added. From a physicist's point of view QED is an extremely successful theory that has allowed the computation of the anomalous magnetic moment of the electron to more than ten significant figures. Rigorous mathematicians consider that QED does not exist in any meaningful sense – it is a set of recipes that look like mathematics at a superficial level, but actually do not relate to any coherent mathematical structure. Indeed it is accepted that as a mathematical structure QED is internally inconsistent, but, fortunately, the inconsistencies are hidden for the experimental regimes that are of concern.

During the late 1960s and 1970s a group of mathematical physicists, most of whom were at American Ivy League universities, made a major effort to resolve these problems. After ten years' work they were able to establish a consistent way of removing all the infinities for a variety of 'super-renormalizable' models in two space-time dimensions and a few in three space-time dimensions. As some people in the theoretical physics community had predicted, they were not able to produce a single model exhibiting genuine particle interactions in four space-time dimensions, the only case of physical importance.

In other cases a theory may be reasonably well-defined but solving the relevant equations from first principles is not possible. Physicists frequently assume that the solution may be approximated by a simple expression involving a few parameters and then carry out calculations based on this, using experimental information to determine the values of the parameters. The difference between this type of theoretical calculation and a pure mathematician's rigorous derivation of the solution is well recognized. In the worst cases the two groups do not communicate and have no mutual respect. Occasionally mathematicians may take physicists' 'solutions' as conjectures that they then try to prove 'properly'.

Since applied mathematicians and physicists are more interested in obtaining useable formulae than in rigorous proofs that their equations have solutions, they should prefer constructive mathematics, which yields both. In practice their arguments are equally valid (or invalid) irrespective of whether they are regarded as being classical or constructive. Peter Lax is one of the most distinguished applied mathematicians of the last few decades, and knows very well what rigorous mathematical proofs are. He has pointed out that in fluid mechanics people regularly have to cope with problems which are not known to have solutions. According to Lax they may then 'use several different numerical methods to calculate approximate solutions and compare the results. If they are in reasonable agreement, [mathematicians] can be reasonably sure of the results.'[6] In such situations the difference between classical and constructive mathematics is again irrelevant.

Some pure mathematicians regard the way that physicists use 'their' subject as close to prostitution. This is quite wrong. Pure mathematicians do not own mathematics, which has a much greater variety than the rigid axiomatic consensus of the twentieth century would lead one to believe. What applied mathematicians and physicists are doing is perfectly appropriate in their context.

3.3 Mathematical Platonism

From this point onwards **Platonism will be taken to mean mathematical Platonism**, as now described. Theorems are supposed to be true statements about timeless entities, and to be true whether or not they have ever been or will ever be formulated by human beings, and whether or not they have proofs. Platonists believe that the infinite set of all natural numbers actually exists and has objective properties. This is quite different from adding the existence of this set to one's mathematical framework as a deliberate choice; the latter makes the existence of the set a convention rather than an independent truth.

The above definition of Platonism is sometimes challenged by mathematicians, but it is the one accepted in philosophical circles.

> *For the platonist, mathematical statements are true or false independently of our knowledge of their truth-values: they are rendered true or false by how things are in the mathematical realm. And this can be so only because, in turn, their meanings are not given by reference to our knowledge of mathematical truth, but by how things are in the realm of*

mathematical entities...The mathematician is, therefore, concerned, on this view, with the correct description of a special realm of reality, comparable to the physical realms described by the geographer and the astronomer.[7]

Platonism fits in well with most mathematicians' feelings about their subject. Different mathematicians agree about what is true and false to an extent that may not be matched in any other subject, and this agreement often persists over hundreds of years. Moreover, they feel constrained by their formulae in a way that suggests that they are examining something objective. The issue is, perhaps, whether this something is to be found in nature, logic, or the characteristics of the human brain.

The difference between Platonists and non-Platonists is not just a philosophical quibble. There is a remote possibility that basic arithmetic as we presently understand it is not internally consistent. Platonists generally deny this because they believe that the infinite set of all natural numbers exists in an objective sense, and claim that the axioms that we use to study it are obvious properties of it. Gödel proved that the consistency of arithmetic cannot be established without introducing further assumptions which might, in turn, be questioned; he left open the remote possibility that its consistency might be disproved one day, possibly by a fairly elementary argument. Some eminent mathematicians, including Jack Schwartz, consider that the consistency of arithmetic is not obvious, because of the fact that some long-held beliefs in other branches of mathematics later turned out to be wrong.[8] The obvious example is the parallel postulate of Euclidean geometry (Euclid's fifth postulate). For many centuries most mathematicians believed that this could be proved from the other axioms of Euclidean geometry, even though they were unable to do so. Between 1800 and 1850 attitudes changed completely; it was seen that there were many equally interesting types of geometry, only one of which obeyed the parallel postulate.

There are some very eminent mathematicians who are seriously committed to the type of Platonism that I described above, and whose beliefs contain recognizable elements of what Plato himself taught. Here, for example, is a quotation from Roger Penrose:

When mathematicians communicate, this is made possible by each one having a direct route to truth, the consciousness of each being in a position to perceive mathematical truths directly, through this process of 'seeing'...Since each can make contact with Plato's world directly, they can more readily communicate with each other than one might have expected. The mental images each one has, when making this Platonic contact, might be rather different in each case, but communication is possible because each is directly in contact with the same externally existing Platonic world![9]

Alain Connes, another extremely eminent mathematician, expressed his Platonism in the following terms:

> *I maintain that mathematics has an object that is just as real as that of the sciences I mentioned above, but this object is not material, and it is located in neither space nor time. Nevertheless the object has an existence that is every bit as solid as external reality, and mathematicians bump up against it in somewhat the same way as one bumps into a material object in external reality... In fact there will always be a property that holds for primordial [mathematical] reality but which escapes the mode of exploration afforded by axiomatic, logico-deductive methods.*[10]

From the point of view of most mathematicians, Platonism is a convenient belief, whose content is usually not formulated in any detail. The conviction that your question already has an objective answer, which resides in a Platonic realm of an unspecified nature, provides a strong incentive for trying to find it. The mathematician Paul Erdös, a convinced Platonist, even referred (jokingly?) to God's book, in which the best possible proofs of all theorems were to be found. Gödel, and later Turing, altered our conception of what is provable in mathematics, but Platonists cling to the hope that a better world exists, in which the limits that Gödel discovered can be transcended. To assert that Platonism is obviously correct, and that to deny it is simply ridiculous, is to commit oneself to a quasi-religious world-view. It is fairly harmless within pure mathematics, but it impoverishes mathematicians' understanding of the rest of the world. The geocentric theory of the world is also harmless for almost all everyday purposes, but we are surely right to have abandoned it.

Many mathematicians who claim to be Platonists have little interest in the historical or philosophical studies of the subject; their belief in Platonism is based on its intuitive plausibility, which is known to be a very unreliable basis for judging scientific truth. The result is depressingly familiar in other spheres of life, particularly religion; someone tells you that they believe X, but under cross-examination reveals that they do not subscribe to most of the tenets generally associated with X. If one takes the trouble to show that one version of Platonism has little substance, one is likely to be confronted some time later with a modified version, and later yet another.

The last defence of such people is to withdraw to what is called formalism, the claim that mathematical arguments are no more than the manipulation of meaningless symbols according to certain formal rules. This is indeed what computers do when they are used to verify that mathematical proofs are correct, but it bears no resemblance to the thought processes of mathematicians. We know that we have *ideas*, whatever they are, and think about them in a very general and intuitive way, checking and modifying our intuition by repeated calculations until we feel that the imagined structure has an intellectual integrity. Then we submit our work for others to decide whether they agree with our judgements.

However, rejecting formalism by no means forces one to accept Platonism. The variety of beliefs associated with the latter is now so great that Mark Balaguer has written a book cataloguing, comparing, and assessing them.[11] He concludes that 'Platonism and anti-Platonism are both perfectly workable philosophies of mathematics'. However, the fact that the two positions are both internally consistent from a logical point of view, does not mean that both fit other things that we believe about the world equally well. Balaguer does not raise such questions.

One only has to peruse a recent volume of opinion pieces to realize that many philosophers are not impressed by the supposed merits of Platonism.[12] Phrases like 'disease' (Bell) and 'muddying the waters' (Tait) feature. One of the leading logicians with an interest in philosophical issues, Solomon Feferman, has written many technical papers exploring what can and cannot be proved in different axiom systems in logic. His conclusion is as follows:

> Though [platonism] accords with the mental practice of the working mathematician, I find the viewpoint philosophically preposterous ... set-theoretic platonism is the medieval metaphysics of mathematics.[13]

However, I must emphasize that:

Platonism is ultimately a world-view, and cannot be proved to be true or false by a logical argument. Its plausibility is another matter.

Supporters of Platonism often argue that alternative world-views such as materialism and reductionism also involve metaphysical commitments. I agree with them. Rather than simply criticizing Platonism, I will describe an alternative way of looking at mathematics. Those who are not already committed to Platonism may see merits in the alternative, particularly its capacity for relating to other things that we believe about the world. This alternative synthesis is not totally new: it borrows ideas from Aristotle, Kant, Poincaré and Popper, but does not follow any of them exactly. I will explain it by means of examples as well as abstract arguments.

Philip Davis and Reuben Hersh were probably the first mathematicians to take Popper's approach to the nature of mathematics seriously.[14] The philosophical position laid out in their fascinating and insightful book has much in common with mine, in spite of their negative attitude towards Kant. They say nothing about Poincaré in this context, but he argued that Kant's ideas contained important truths, after certain errors were removed; subsequent research has amply confirmed this.

Nomenclature

In recent years there has been a regrettable tendency to call mathematical Platonists *realists*, presumably on the grounds that they claim that numbers are real. In the philosophical study of fairies this would force us to use the word realists to refer to true believers, whom most of us would call fantasists. It ignores the fact that Popper claimed that his World 3 was real, although he regarded mathematics as a human creation. Bishop also called his constructive version of mathematics realistic.

3.4 What is Mathematics?

Since Platonism is familiar to most mathematicians, I devote the rest of this chapter to arguing that a biologically and culturally based description of mathematics provides a coherent alternative. Readers will have to decide for themselves whether it connects better with other beliefs that they may hold about the world. The following assertion summarizes what follows:

> **Mathematics is an aspect of human culture, just as are language, law, music, and architecture. Its vocabulary is highly specialized and its domain of applicability excludes much of what we care about in our everyday lives.**[15]

Mathematics is by no means unique in combining abstract concepts with relevance to the outside world. Consider the fact that, as the eldest son of the reigning monarch Queen Elizabeth II, Prince Charles is the heir to the British throne. In spite of the undeniable, objective truth of the statement, the concept of hereditary monarchy is an abstract human creation.

The same applies when referring to the distant past. Given our ability to agree about the meanings of the various terms we are correct to say that the diplodocus had four legs. We are also correct to say that no diplodocus had a sense of humour or a good command of English, even though the notions of a sense of humour and a good command of English were meaningless at the relevant time. This type of example does not force one to be a Platonist for the number four any more than it forces one to be a Platonist for legs, a sense of humour, or the English language.

The status of mathematics is brought out by making an analogy with a school timetable. If this is done by a person, as it always used to be, his or her starting point may be to impose some structure on the desired solution, in the hope that this will simplify the task. As more and more entries are added the timetable becomes clearer and clearer, and the constraints on further entries become sharper. Occasionally, one may find inconsistencies and have to go back and change some of the entries, or one may find that the imposed structure must be modified or abandoned. It may even be found impossible to complete the timetable without deleting some combination of optional subjects (this corresponds to imposing an unexpected extra condition in a theorem in order to rule out a counterexample). In the end the internal consistency of the final timetable is an objective fact that may be confirmed without reference to the way in which it was produced.

Mathematics has changed over time in a way that can be elucidated by historical research, and one can have varying views about its most important features. We have seen that communication between classical pure mathematicians, constructive mathematicians, applied mathematicians, and physicists is difficult and sometimes unproductive. All of these features are commonplace in other aspects of human culture.

In a recent essay, the Harvard mathematician Barry Mazur states that arguments about the historical and cultural development of mathematics or the mental processes of mathematicians are entirely irrelevant to 'the Question' – whether mathematics is invented or discovered – and implies that this must be addressed by focussing on what *mathematics itself is about*:

> For me, at least, the anchor of any conversation about these matters is the experience of doing mathematics, and of groping for mathematical ideas. When I read literature that is ostensibly about The Question, I ask myself whether or not it connects in any way with my felt experience, and even better, whether it reveals something about it. I'm often – perhaps always – disappointed. The bizarre aspect of the mathematical experience – and this is what gives such fierce energy to The Question – is that one feels (I feel) that mathematical ideas can be hunted down, and in a way that is essentially different from, say, the way I am currently hunting the next word to write to finish this sentence. One can be a hunter and gatherer of mathematical concepts, but one has no ready words for the location of the hunting grounds. Of course we humans are beset with illusions, and the feeling just described could be yet another. There may be no location.[16]

Mazur describes Platonism as a 'fully-fledged theistic position' and continues:

the only way one can hope to persuade others of its truth is by abandoning the arsenal of rationality, and relying on the resources of the prophets.

Nowhere in his article does he reveal whether or not he is an adherent to the belief. Indeed he seems to have given a description of Platonism and anti-Platonism in which no sensible choice between the two possibilities could possibly be made.

People frequently talk about invention and discovery as though they are diametrically opposed concepts, but actually the same event may often be described in both ways. For example, one might say that stone-age axes were *invented* many millennia ago, or that our distant ancestors *discovered* that stones with sharp edges could be used for a variety of purposes, and, possibly much later, *discovered* that they could be made by hitting one stone with another. The discovery/invention could only have been made in the last few million years, because only we have the type of hands that can manipulate stones with sufficient precision. Before that the abstract concept of a stone axe could not have existed – unless in the mind of God.

Galileo's idea of using a pendulum as the regulator of a weight-driven clock was an act of genius. The need to have more accurate clocks already existed, but the idea that the goal could be achieved by such a method was his. Although he never constructed a pendulum clock, he started a line of development that was to last for more than two centuries, as others elaborated his basic idea. One could say either that he invented the pendulum clock or that he *realized the possibility* of using pendulums to regulate clocks, and that this possibility had already existed before he discovered it. Once again the distinction between invention and discovery seems unclear.

The following two examples show that the same issue arises in mathematics. There are many stories of mathematicians who have had sudden insights into the solution of a problem while doing something quite different. Typically they have been studying a very hard problem for months or even years and have tried a number of different ideas, none of which has led to a solution. These efforts might be described as preparing the ground for further analysis by a part of the mind whose operations are not under our conscious control.

One such story relates to the Irish mathematician William Rowan Hamilton. Complex numbers had been used since the second half of the sixteenth century, but nobody had been able to come to terms with the results that they provided. It gave the right answers to a variety of problems, and this could not be by chance, but nobody was able to provide a convincing explanation. In 1833 Hamilton solved this problem by constructing complex numbers from real numbers, rather than by trying to find them in some Platonic heaven. In 1843 he used the same method to construct what he called quaternions, and opened up the idea that number systems did not simply exist; new systems with strange properties could be *invented* and could then fight for survival on the basis of their usefulness. He later described his sudden insight into how to produce this new type of number in a letter to P. G. Tait.

> *[Quaternions] started into life, or light, full grown, on [Monday] the 16th of October, 1843, as I was walking with Lady Hamilton to Dublin, and came up to Brougham Bridge, which my boys have since called the Quaternion Bridge. That is to say, I then and there felt the galvanic circuit of thought close; and the sparks which fell from it were the fundamental equations between i, j, k; exactly such as I have used them ever since. I pulled out on the spot a pocket-book, which still exists, and made an entry, on which, at the very moment, I felt that it might be worth my while to expend the labour of at least ten (or it might be fifteen) years to come. But then it is fair to say that this was because I felt a problem to have been at that moment solved – an intellectual want relieved – which had haunted me for at least fifteen years before. Less than an hour elapsed before I had asked and obtained leave of the Council of the Royal Irish Academy, of which Society I was, at that time, the President – to read at the next General Meeting a Paper on Quaternions; which I accordingly did, on November 13, 1843.*

Similar stories have been told by Poincaré and many other mathematicians. Of course, the process of developing a new mathematical idea varies greatly from one instance to another, and it may be worthwhile to recount one of my own experiences. The story starts in 1958, when the mathematical genius John Nash proved some fundamental results on parabolic partial differential equations. Unfortunately he was to suffer a serious psychotic breakdown the following year, and this effectively terminated his mathematical career. His ideas were not fully understood because of their excessive brevity and an alternative, but more complicated, approach to the problems was devised by others during the 1960s.

In 1958 I was still a teenager. By the mid 1980s I became interested in the proof of Gaussian heat kernel bounds for second-order parabolic equations. I had read the existing literature and skimmed through Nash's work, but found both very hard to follow; the context and statements of the main results were quite simple, but the proofs were extremely devious, even by the standards of the subject. I felt crushed by this and decided that I had to try to find a simpler approach that was within my grasp. After some effort I was able to do this by using ideas that had been developed in a different context over the intervening thirty years. This is the point at which the tale becomes interesting, because it developed in a way that I had not envisaged as a possibility, let alone intended.

My new approach was considerably simpler, and as it happens also more constructive, than the original one, but it was messy. I felt that for the sake of a clean exposition I should optimize the choices of various constants that appeared in the argument. This took several months because there were quite a number of constants and they interacted with each other. As I progressed I gradually realized that not only was I beginning to understand my own arguments better, but the result that I was obtaining was moving steadily beyond my original goal. By the time I had finished my heat kernel bound was far stronger than the original version of Nash and others. In addition it applied to operators on manifolds and to difference operators in a discrete setting, rather than merely in the context of the original results. It took me five years to develop all of the implications, but they opened up a new and productive line of development in the subject.

An interesting feature of this research was that there was no Eureka moment. My goal was modest and I achieved a clumsy version of it relatively early in the research. I had not been struggling to prove a new result but merely to find a new proof of an old one. The apparently routine process of writing out the details of the proof in the best possible manner led me to the realization that I had achieved far more than I had ever intended. The fact that such things happen is, perhaps, a warning against the familiar story that major progress necessarily involves flashes of inspiration coming out of the blue. Such phenomena do occur, but they are not the only way in which mathematics progresses.

Let us return to the issue of invention versus discovery. In the case of the quaternions one could equally say that Hamilton invented them or that he discovered that his problem could be solved by introducing a new type of algebraic system. In my own work, I felt that I had *invented* a new method of proving heat kernel bounds, but then that I *discovered* that it allowed a much more powerful insight into the subject. It appears that Mazur's question does not have a useful answer: one can *always* say that an entity can only be invented if the possibility of inventing it already existed, and it is impossible to provide a purely logical argument that distinguishes between the possibility of inventing something and the prior Platonic existence of the entity itself. Most people are, and should be, straightforward realists with respect to the existence of physical objects, but there is nothing that forces one to take the same attitude towards abstract entities, let alone towards possibilities that are not yet actualized and may never be.

I can at least try to respond to one issue that Mazur raises. There are many different types of answer to the question 'What is X ultimately about?' In some cases the answer is straightforward, but in others it is not. Physics is concerned with understanding the rules governing the motion and interactions of bodies in the external world. Religion is about understanding our spiritual place in the world; I will have more to say about this topic in Chapter 5. Novels are controlled exercises of the imagination; in one sense they are fantasies about non-existent people, but at a deeper level they are explorations of human relationships. Music involves the creation and appreciation of complex patterns of sound, but it stimulates deep emotional and spiritual feelings in a way that is hard to explain. Chess appears to be about capturing the opponent's King, but at the grand-master level it is also the struggle for dominance between two individuals. I will leave the reader to think about what the word 'money' is ultimately about, as distinct from what it is used for; it is not at all clear that such a distinction makes sense. Mathematics might be about revealing the properties of entities in a Platonic realm, but it might equally be about developing certain capacities of our own minds. The noted Oxford philosopher Michael Dummett put it as follows:

> *Intuitionists differ from platonists not over whether mathematical statements are about anything, but over the kind of thing that they are about; for platonists, they are about abstract structures, existing independently of our knowledge of them; for intuitionists they are about the free products of human thought.*[17]

One has to decide which of these alternatives fits in better with other things that we know about the world. The *scientific* answer is clear: the Platonistic view makes no contact with our current knowledge about the natural world, or the functioning of our minds.

Discovering a new property of a mathematical entity gives mathematicians a feeling of the intense beauty of our subject. Indeed for many of us this is why we put so much of our souls into it. We use the language of discovery because we have little access to the part of our brain that creates new ideas and links between apparently unrelated concepts. It is hardly surprising that insights seem to come from outside ourselves, because we naturally identify ourselves with the parts of our minds of which we are conscious. We should celebrate the intuitive capacities of our unconscious minds, which go far beyond what our more rational and conscious selves are capable of. This has been a painful lesson for those working in artificial intelligence, and it is only slowly percolating into our general culture. We should also celebrate the achievement of the classical Greeks when they invented the notion of mathematical proof, which provided an independent arbiter of the validity of our intuitions.

Mathematics is often described as the systematic study of patterns, symmetries, structures, and regularities using abstract, symbolic methods. The wonderful patterns to be found on the walls of many mosques provide source material for mathematics but do not qualify as mathematics themselves, because they are not abstract and are not studied by symbolic methods. Although the artists found all of the repeating planar patterns, they did not try to prove that there were no others. In pure mathematics patterns

Fig. 3.2 St Paul's Cathedral, London

often arise from number theory, geometry, or algebra. In applied mathematics they are obtained by abstracting from some feature of the external world; examples are snail shells, the rings of Saturn, sand ripples on beaches and in deserts, and the shapes of many types of cactus. In fact patterns seem to surround us everywhere we look, many being embedded in the objects that we ourselves have created.

Some of the earliest megalithic sites were built out of irregular stones, cut into shape on site, a type of construction that has analogies to the way that birds make their nests. It was soon realized that it was more efficient to use standardized blocks made of stone, or later brick, and that the most useful shape for such blocks was rectangular (i.e. cuboidal). It is almost impossible to avoid laying these in repeating patterns, and to experiment with variations. In addition to patterns that are consequences of industrialization, there are others that have been created for their own sake. Many of the greatest buildings in the world, such as St Paul's Cathedral in London, are celebrations of the sheer beauty of symmetry. Recently the wheel has turned full circle: a small number of architects, such as Frank Gehry, have started designing highly irregular buildings, which ostentatiously accept the cost of having to design every component individually. These buildings are disturbing precisely because of their rejection of the concept of pattern.

It should be emphasized that patterns are not always geometrical. The sequence

$$110111011110111111101111111111101111111111111110\ldots$$

might be ideal for convincing remote alien intelligences of our existence. The strings of ones have lengths 2, 3, 5, 7, 11, 13, ... which match the prime numbers and are exceedingly unlikely to be produced by any natural process.

Mathematicians have been particularly intrigued by the following apparent pattern:

$$2 + 2 = 4$$
$$3 + 3 = 6$$
$$3 + 5 = 8$$
$$3 + 7 = 10$$
$$5 + 7 = 12$$
$$7 + 7 = 14$$
$$3 + 13 = 16$$
$$\ldots$$

Goldbach's conjecture, that every even number greater than 2 is the sum of two prime numbers, has been verified for all even numbers up a thousand trillion, and almost every mathematician believes that it is true. However, if it turns out to be false and the smallest counterexample has a million digits or more, it would be impossible to check this fact by writing out all the relevant sums – there would be too many to make this feasible. The statement that there exists a counterexample to Goldbach's conjecture with exactly a million digits could in practice only be established by a proof, even though in principle it only involves checking a finite number of sums. In spite of all the 'experimental' evidence, and a lot more that I have not mentioned, almost nobody believes that a proof is likely to be found in the near future.

Although mathematicians study patterns wherever they find them, they also have to adapt their intuition to what they are studying. One of the hardest aspects of research is that it is *different* from what is already known; old ideas have to be combined in new ways or new ideas created to achieve understanding. Some of this process is conscious, but once learned the part of the brain that carries the intuition changes permanently, so that the idea, once so difficult to grasp, comes to seem inevitable. The task is a bit like learning to ride a bicycle, at first so hard as to seem impossible, and later so easy that one cannot imagine not being able to do it.

If one regards the ability to do mathematics as a skill, this does not imply that the unconscious part of the brain is using the kind of rational processes that we follow when we test the ideas that it presents to us. We do not know how our brains work, but the analogy with bicycling may well be relevant. In that case we learn by trial and error to make the kind of movements that lead to ordered motion along the road and avoid the kind that lead to our falling over. Surely nobody thinks that Newton's laws of motion have anything to do with how we learn to ride bicycles, even though it is possible to use them to explain why the right kind of movements do, in fact, work. Similarly with mathematics. We need not believe that our unconscious minds are operating some superior mathematical algorithm when presenting us with ideas, many of which are quickly seen to be wrong. Our mathematical skills are partly innate, but they are developed over years of conscious effort and vary widely from one person to another. They include the ability to argue logically, but it is remarkable that most mathematicians do not use any of the advances in formal logic of the twentieth century, have never attended any courses in formal logic, and do not feel that they are missing anything as a result. Imagination and persistence are much more important for mathematical success.

On rare occasions mathematicians appear who can create fundamentally new types of structure, whose study illuminates, indeed may create, entirely new branches of mathematics. How they achieve their insights is impossible for the rest of us to understand, but it usually happens when they are in their twenties or thirties. Whether such achievements are regarded as inventions or discoveries, they are among the towering achievements of the human species, and show that, occasionally, we can achieve insights that go far beyond anything that we can explain. Such people stand alongside the great composers, even though their subject leads to their being far less well known to the general public.

The distinction between knowledge and truth is evident when one is talking about material objects, but that does not imply that it is appropriate in abstract situations. Some abstract entities, such as a bishop in the game of chess, only have definite properties because we adopt certain conventions: it is simply impossible to declare that your bishop can take your opponent's queen if there is something on the diagonal between them, because it would not then be a bishop. Once the rules of the game are agreed, certain consequences follow. In the case of mathematics the specification of what counts as a proof is very narrow and detailed, so one should not be surprised about the high level of agreement concerning the truth of theorems. However, as Lakatos pointed out, the background assumptions of theorems are often not fully explained, with the result that they might later have to be reformulated.

> **Invented entities, even abstract ones, should not be regarded as mere fictions: the more precisely they are specified the more conclusions we can expect to be able to draw about them.**

There are two views about what it means to say that a theorem is true. For Platonists a theorem refers to an actual property of a Platonic entity, and it is true if the entity does indeed have that property. An alternative view is that we are only entitled to call a theorem true if it has a proof. Gödel showed that one must be extremely careful not to take it for granted that these two statements are equivalent. One may fall into all sorts of trap when discussing his actual results, but they do not refer to Platonic truth, even though he himself was a Platonist. The two views might be called the ontological and epistemological aspects of mathematics. These refer respectively to what is actually true and what we know to be true. But this distinction begs the question – assuming that there is an important distinction is already conceding the Platonist position.

Dummett's approach to this issue concentrates on the notion of meaning. Platonism declares that the truth of a mathematical statement is not dependent on whether that truth can be reliably communicated from one person to another:

> But to suppose this is to make meaning ineffable, that is, in principle incommunicable...A notion of meaning so private to the individual is one that has become completely irrelevant to mathematics as it is actually practised, namely as a body of theory on which many individuals are corporately engaged, an enquiry within which each can communicate his results to others.[18]

Many people find the very high consensus in mathematics difficult to reconcile with the fierce debates in almost all other disciplines. This is achieved in spite of mathematicians' wide variety of personalities and approaches to the subject. The consensus is not a miracle: it depends on the extremely demanding standards for accepting proofs and the fact that they do not depend on facts about the physical world. The syllabuses of university mathematics courses are remarkably similar throughout the world, so the basis for agreement is very high. One sees again and again that partly worked out arguments are not accepted, no matter how eminent the person making them, and that a new result is only accepted by the community when it can be written down in a form that all sufficiently well trained people can understand. (Perelman's proof of the Poincaré conjecture is just the latest example.) Even Ramanujan, one of the most creative and incomprehensible of mathematicians, who seemed to have mystical insights, occasionally wrote down identities that proved completely wrong. The process of sorting through his claims had to be carried out using the normal assessment procedures.

It is a truism that a theorem can only be proved if the possibility of proving it already existed, but this need not lead to Platonism. One could equally say that since a novel could have been written a year earlier than it actually was, it already existed *as a possibility* before it was written. Similar remarks apply to almost every artistic and technological product. To pin one's Platonism to a platitude about possibilities that has no specifically mathematical content is an act of desperation, unless one accepts Plato's entire system.

There is an argument that reducing mathematical truth to the existence of a proof is letting Platonism in by the back door. (The unqualified existence of a proof requires that an unspecified member of the *infinite set* of potential proofs is an actual proof.) One can resolve this problem by requiring that a proof must exist in a material form, so that it may be inspected in detail to see whether it conforms to the accepted criteria for proofs. If one accepts this, then a proof only comes into existence when some mathematician has succeeded in producing it, and the extent of mathematics depends on time. Mathematicians spend their professional lives expanding the range of proven theorems, not the range of 'true' theorems.

David Deutsch has proposed that we should extend the notion of proof to include what can be achieved by using quantum computers.[19] The logic of my position dictates that I do not think that there is an important distinction between a computation by a classical computer that could be repeated by human beings in principle but not in practice, and a computation by a quantum computer that could not be carried out by a human being even in principle. However, there is no hurry to decide this issue. Quantum computers do not yet exist and we can wait until the problem arises before deciding the merits of such an extension.

In the end, debates about the objective truth of mathematics often lead to questions about the consistency of arithmetic, taken for granted in all serious mathematics. If I declare that I believe that arithmetic is consistent, I seem to be assigning it an independent existence, even if I accept that human beings will never be able to prove that it is consistent. However, for me the statement *means no more* than that I would be extremely surprised if someone were to produce a fundamental contradiction using only standard arithmetic. Beliefs may have varying strengths, and for that reason are generally more relevant than claims to knowledge, to which our finite species has limited access. We can perhaps know in a sense that is close to absolute that the proofs of some theorems are correct, and in that sense the said theorems are true within the framework supplied by the axioms of the theory concerned, but with the deepest theorems even this is not guaranteed. I personally would be less disturbed to learn that a contradiction had been obtained in standard arithmetic than if I opened my front door one day to be confronted with a formless void in the middle of which a demonic face was grinning at me. The former would provide an opportunity to patch up some technical problems, but the latter would undermine my whole notion of reality.

So why do we believe in the consistency of mathematics? The answer is simply intuition. Over two thousand years of formal mathematics have revealed some important misconceptions, but these have been rectified and we feel confident that we can patch up any further problems that we might encounter in the future. There is no way of *proving* that this confidence is justified, but we have no choice but to rely provisionally on hard-won insights in every other sphere of investigation, and mathematics is no different.

Adopting a pluralistic attitude towards the philosophy of mathematics does not imply that all descriptions of it have equal value. The merit of each depends on the context, and we will argue that Platonism has few real merits, apart from providing a sense of security for those who adopt it. Most philosophers of mathematics agree that it should be deleted from the list of worthwhile theories in the same way as phlogiston and astrology have been.

3.5 The Infinite

Human beings have been interested in the infinite for over two thousand years, in spite of the fact that we cannot apprehend it directly and have no material evidence that infinite entities exist. Only two groups of people claim to have any real knowledge of it, religious mystics and mathematicians. The former claim to have experiences of something that is beyond the normal world and that is essentially incapable of being communicated.

There has been an association between mathematics and religious mysticism since the time of Pythagoras, and most mathematicians believe that they can perceive infinite entities of certain limited types; they can describe them to each other and discuss their properties in some detail. Examples are the infinite set of all even natural numbers and the set of all primes. It is worth noting that St Thomas Aquinas, writing in the thirteenth century, was a strong critic of Plato's philosophy. Question 7 of his *Summa Theologica*, on 'The Infinity of God', contrasted the absolute and essential infinity of God with the limited infinities of mathematics, which he discussed at some length.

It is sometimes said that, without accepting the notion of infinity, one cannot do mathematics. Like most generalizations this is an exaggeration. Combinatorics and graph theory would hardly be affected by its absence. Moreover, large parts of group theory and Euclidean geometry would survive without it. Nevertheless, mathematicians do make use of infinite entities as and when it is advantageous, and most do not give a second thought to the fact that they are doing so.

The notion of infinity is implicit in the equation

$$\frac{1}{2} + \frac{1}{4} + \frac{1}{8} + \frac{1}{16} + \ldots = 1.$$

At face value it appears to assert that if one adds together an infinite number of fractions the sum is equal to 1. Of course an infinite number of additions cannot actually be performed, and a second interpretation is that if one adds together a large enough number of terms the answer is very close to 1. The difference between these two statements is close to Zeno's problem about Achilles and the tortoise. Of course Zeno knew that Achilles did pass the tortoise; what he was pointing out was that at his time, the fifth century BC, there was no mathematical way of dealing with such problems. Today we have one, thanks to Cauchy's fundamental insights in the 1820s; the notion of limit no longer depends on any reference to infinity, and brings the subject into the realm of things that can be expressed in finite terms. It transformed mathematics and led to the rigorous definition of the real number system later in the nineteenth century. This type of infinity has now been banished from the mathematical lexicon.

No coherent theory of infinite sets was forthcoming until Georg Cantor produced a general theory of transfinite sets in a series of articles between 1877 and 1897. Independently Gottlob Frege formulated general laws for symbolic logic, the most important contribution to that subject since Aristotle. He was about to publish the second volume of his book *Foundations of Arithmetic* when Bertrand Russell wrote to him, in 1901, pointing out a serious inconsistency in his account of set theory. Frege never recovered from this blow and did not complete Volume 3. Russell, then a young man, took on the task of rewriting Frege's work in collaboration with Alfred North Whitehead. Their monumental 'theory of types' took ten years to develop, but it was not regarded as a satisfactory resolution of the problem that they faced. The three volumes of *Principia Mathematica* that they completed exhausted the authors and were extremely hard to read. Although of enormous importance for the foundations of logic, they were to be overshadowed by Gödel's later proof that their goal was not achievable.

By the 1920s most mathematicians believed that Cantor's theory of sets, as formulated in the system called ZFC – still, in 2009, the accepted theory of sets – provided secure foundations for the mathematics of infinite entities. Gödel's work in the 1930s destroyed this belief. Gödel himself believed that infinite sets of various types did exist, but that his discoveries merely established that it was not possible to establish some facts about them by purely rational means.

The existence of infinite sets is generally accepted by mathematicians, but it is *assumed* in ZFC, which contains an 'Axiom of Infinity'. This is technical in form but, after reducing it to ordinary language, it amounts to the *declaration* that the infinite set of all natural numbers exists. For those who believe this on Platonistic grounds, ZFC is simply a list of some properties that their intuition leads them to believe that sets possess; it then forms the basis for deducing other less obvious properties of sets.

As time passed an increasing proportion of those working in set theory came to doubt the reality of some of the more abstruse aspects of their theories. One such was Paul Cohen, who eventually succeeded in proving the independence of the axiom of choice and the continuum hypothesis, two major questions in set theory that had defeated Gödel. In contrast to Gödel, he saw the higher reaches of set theory as no more than investigations of the formal consequences of ZFC and related axioms. The formalist position is that ZFC specifies the rules that mathematicians choose to follow in set theory, but there is no assumption that the rules actually refer to anything. Cohen described the position as follows:

> *I think that for most mathematicians set theory is attractive, but lacking the basic impact of arithmetic. There is almost a continuum of beliefs about the extended world of set theory…Through the years I have sided more firmly with the formalist position. This view is tempered with a sense of reverence for all mathematics which has used set theory as a basis, and in no way do I attack the work which has been done in set theory. However, when axiom systems involving large cardinals or determinacy are used, I feel a loss of reality, even though the research is ingenious and coherent. In particular, a strong defect of the [realist] view, for me, is the idea that if mathematics refers to a reality then human thought should resolve all mathematical questions.*[20]

Developments over the last century have cast serious doubt on the proposition that mathematicians have reliable access to the properties of infinite entities. All the efforts to settle this issue in the first decades of the twentieth century eventually fell apart, and we are left wiser but humbler. If the infinite does indeed exist as more than a form of words or an act of imagination, only religious mystics seem to have access to it.

3.6 The Mathematical Brain

In this section we will argue that Kant's theory of innate capacities, described in Section 2.6, is relevant to mathematical skills. Mathematics has strong historical and cultural aspects, but also depends on particular biological characteristics of our brains. Human beings share with many animals the ability to recognize numbers up to about four instantly. (This is called subitizing in the scientific literature.) This is the result of the existence of specific structures in our brains, among which the left inferior parietal lobe is particularly important. We, uniquely, learn to recognize and manipulate numbers much larger than four.

Babies are so helpless at birth that it is not easy to assess their mental capacities. However, it is possible to measure how long they look at a new picture, and, via carefully designed experiments, to draw conclusions from this. By such means it has been shown that babies only a day old can distinguish between the numbers two and three as abstract concepts, and not just on the basis that a picture with three objects in it is more crowded than one with two. This is difficult work, but the obvious objections have all been considered and ruled out as explanations of the results obtained.

Those who would like to know more about this fascinating subject are encouraged to read *The Mathematical Brain* by Brian Butterworth. He describes unfortunate individuals who are able to converse intelligently on a wide variety of subjects, even though they may have enormous difficulties adding three to five, or judging whether six or nine is larger. Even if they manage to develop strategies for coping with their problems, these are often painfully slow and exhibit their failure to fully grasp the concepts involved. Such disabilities are generically called dyscalculia; they may exist from birth but can also be caused by strokes. The reverse possibility also occurs. It might seem bizarre that some people might not be able to tell the difference between 'Mary hit John' and 'John hit Mary' although they can tell the difference between $11-52$ and $52-11$, but it happens. Rosemary Varley, one of the people who reported this observation, regards it as proving that understanding syntax is not essential for processing statements in mathematics.[21]

This research field has developed rapidly since 1990. A major factor has been the use of scanning machines that can show which parts of the brain are particularly active when a mental task is being solved. As a result of this exciting work we now know that there are many different systems in the brain, one of which makes syntactical distinctions, a different one making arithmetic distinctions – and a third capable of being surprised that the two tasks are so different. The first two systems appear to be localized in particular parts of the brain, but the third, our higher level consciousness, is very poorly understood, even with the help of current scanners. The task of understanding the brain as a whole is made far more daunting by the fact that the functioning of specialized modules may be modified when attention is directed to some aspect of the sensory input. Introspection would never have yielded these insights, and there are surely many others to come.

However, mathematics is not just arithmetic writ large. There are many examples of lightning calculators with no knowledge of higher level mathematics. Mathematical ability is uncommon and has to be acquired over a period of years. No doubt the general lack of mathematical competence among the public is partly the result of poor teaching and/or inappropriate syllabuses, but this cannot be the whole story. There are also bad language teachers, but every normal person can talk comprehensibly by the age of twenty. Mathematical ability is heavily dependent on the motivation to spend a high proportion of one's waking hours practising and developing the skill. In this respect it is like music and chess, in which the most outstanding figures have all devoted themselves to the discipline single-mindedly for years. This applied even to Ramanujan, one of the most incomprehensible mathematical geniuses ever. He was obsessed by mathematics from a very early age and taught himself from the very few books that he possessed.

Mathematical ability is very poorly understood. It might be an 'unintended' consequence of the more general growth in cultural and symbolic activity (the creation of ornaments, paintings, religion, formal social hierarchies, etc.) that started about fifty thousand years ago and has been accelerating ever since. Evolution would not have led us to develop an entirely new capacity that had no outlet until eight thousand years ago, and gives those who possess it little if any reproductive advantage. However, linkages between different modules are known to occur in synaesthesia, a rare syndrome in which some people *literally* see letters and numbers as having particular colours, which can be stable over years. It is obvious that geometrical intuition utilizes the visual circuits in our brains, and it is also plausible that algebra involves the parts of our brains that deal with language. If so, the rare people with strong mathematical skills may be those born with synaesthetic linkages between their arithmetic, language, and visual systems.

In an interview in 2004, when he was awarded the Abel Prize, the mathematician Michael Atiyah made the following comment, which is entirely in line with the above ideas about the nature of mathematics:

> Mathematics is an evolution from the human brain, which is responding to outside influences, creating the machinery with which it then attacks the outside world. It is our way of trying to reduce complexity into simplicity, beauty and elegance. It is really very fundamental, simplicity is in the nature of scientific inquiry – we do not look for complicated things. I tend to think that science and mathematics are ways the human mind looks and experiences – you cannot divorce the human mind from it. Mathematics is part of the human mind.[22]

A number of other eminent mathematicians disagree with him, but as an ex-President of the Royal Society his understanding of science is much more rounded than that of most mathematicians.

The psychologist Michael Fitzgerald and the Oxford mathematician Ioan James have recently completed a study of the dynamics of mathematical creation, with descriptions of the lives and personalities of twenty famous mathematicians, almost all from the last two centuries. Their view of mathematics is remarkably like that of Atiyah:

> *Mathematics is no longer seen as transcendental, abstract, disembodied, unique and independent of anything physical. On the contrary, it forms part of human culture, a product of the human body, brain and mind and of our experience of the physical world.*[23]

Throughout their book they refer not to mathematicians 'seeing' something of a Platonic world, but to their ability to transfer problems to their unconscious minds, which later deliver intuitions about where the solutions lie; these intuitions have to be checked and are not always right.

The mathematical physicist David Ruelle has recently compared the capacities of the human mathematical brain with those of computers.[24] Here are some of his conclusions. The architecture of the brain is highly parallel; some computers have a degree of parallelism, but not nearly so much. Our brains are extremely slow. Our memories are very poor; indeed we cannot keep more than about seven items in our short-term memory at a time, and compensate by memorizing, i.e. putting facts in long-term memory. We use a variety of different physical systems, vision, language etc. to help us think. We like short formulations; this is not surprising in view of our limited memory and attention span. We are not good at formal logical manipulations; attempts to check proofs for 'technical' errors frequently fail to do so. We are good at finding regularities, or 'meaning'. Ruelle concludes that, although we do not understand how we do mathematics, the subject itself has a form dictated by the nature of our minds.

Our ability to recognize incomplete visual patterns is easy to explain in evolutionary terms. The avoidance of predators demands the ability to spot an animal that is trying to conceal its presence from its prey for as long as possible. We also need to recognize edible plants that may be hidden under other foliage. Our ability to reconstruct incomplete images operates at several different levels in the brain. Some mental processes are unconscious, in the sense that it is very difficult to look at images without interpretation; for example, Figure 3.3 appears to show a rectangle partly obscured by a circular disc that is in front of it, even when one is told that it was created by putting three flat, shaded regions side by side. In other cases interpretation involves a conscious effort. Fr xmpl, hmn bngs cn rd sntncs tht hv thr vwls mssng, but t rqrs sgnfcnt thght. Interpretations can be long lasting even when they are totally wrong. In particular, we are predisposed to making connections between eating unusual foods and feeling ill several hours later. The fact that these can lead to habits of avoidance that have no basis in reality is readily explained – avoiding an unusual item of food may be less costly on average than taking the risk of dying. Mathematics builds on our inherited tendency to seek patterns, which are much more highly developed than those of other animals. It is reasonable to draw the conclusion from the above that we do not understand mathematics because of a mysterious capacity that allows us to look at a Platonic world outside space and time, nor because we lived in that world before birth and have distant memories of it. We understand it to the extent that we do because of the existence of structures in our brains that evolved by Darwinian selection. We do not understand the nature of these structures at all well, but can reasonably hope that this will be remedied during the course of the present century. Other animals do not understand mathematics because their brains do not contain these structures. Mathematics is no more (or less) mysterious than language. Both exist in very rudimentary forms in some animals, and both are vastly better developed in human beings.

Fig. 3.3 A Partly Obscured Rectangle

3.7 The Mandelbrot Set

The family tree of Roger Penrose is far from ordinary. Among the many people in it are Oliver Penrose, another distinguished mathematical physicist, Roland Penrose, the surrealist artist, and Jonathan Penrose, British chess champion between 1958 and 1969. His family tree has links with the Penrose brothers who founded Waterford Glass in 1783 and with the Wedgewood and Darwin families. Roger Penrose himself has several claims to fame. From 1965 onwards Stephen Hawking and he made major contributions to the theory of black holes. In mathematics his simple and beautiful construction of aperiodic tilings attracted great attention; the existence of such tilings had already been proved by Robert Berger, disproving a conjecture of Hao Wang. The discovery by Peter Lu in 2007 that such tilings appear in certain medieval mosques in the Middle East came as a complete surprise. Yet another idea of Penrose, called twistor theory, has had a major influence on a variety of geometric problems as well as on string theory in physics.

Penrose acquired guru status among the general public as a result of his many articles and lectures on the nature of consciousness. In his two books, *The Emperor's New Mind* and *Shadows of the Mind*, he claimed to use Gödel's theory to prove that the human mind cannot be a mere computer. The philosopher John Searle reached the same conclusion, but by a very different route. Both were reacting to wildly over-optimistic claims by people in the Artificial Intelligence community during the 1960s and 1970s that they were on the verge of reproducing conscious thought in computers. This has turned out to be a vastly harder problem than previously thought. It has to be said that Penrose's applications of Gödel's ideas were criticized by several experts in the field, and that his two books were much better received by the general public than by the academic community. I cannot begin to discuss the many criticisms, because so many of them have been rejected by Penrose, whose refutations have in turn been criticized.

In *The Emperor's New Mind* Penrose uses the Mandelbrot set to argue in favour of mathematical Platonism. I will not give the definition of the set, illustrated in Figure 3.4, beyond saying that a point is put into the set (coloured black) if it passes a simple test, which may have to be repeated *an indefinite number of times*. His argument is based on the fact that the extremely complicated structure of the set was not anticipated when it was defined, and was truly surprising in view of its very simple definition. Figure 3.4 only scratches the surface of the complexities of the Mandelbrot set – as one zooms in on any part of the boundary new repeating fern-like structures appear, only to be replaced by something else at an even finer scale. Penrose considers that this implies that the set must have been discovered rather than invented. This is a stronger argument than for the existence of Platonic triangles or circles, for which one can see that their form was designed into them by us. However, it is not decisive if one believes that invented objects can have properties not anticipated by the inventor.

Pluralists can make a deliberate context-dependent choice about whether to adopt the classical (i.e. Platonistic) description of the Mandelbrot set. Classical set theory is undoubtedly simpler than constructive set theory, because the latter makes distinctions invisible to the former. The classical theory provides simpler mental images and for many purposes is completely adequate. The assumption in this world-view is that it makes sense to ask about the eventual outcome of carrying out a procedure an indefinite number of times, but this is a normal convention for pure mathematicians. Nevertheless deliberately adopting a convention is quite different from asserting that something simply 'is the case'. Platonism, if accepted, guarantees the existence of the Mandelbrot set, but it is significant that comments about its beauty only started after it became possible to produce computer-generated pictures of it. These can be seen with one's eyes, as opposed to the unspecified organ that is supposed to enable one to see the Platonic Mandelbrot set. One has to wonder about the value and even existence of an organ that only allows one to appreciate the beauty of

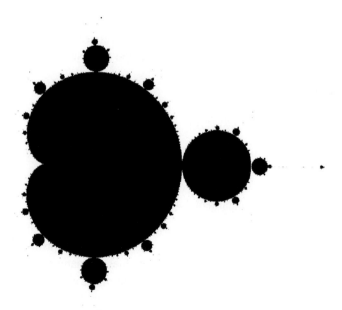

Fig. 3.4 The Mandelbrot Set

a picture after this has become apparent by more mundane means. If one wishes to produce an image of the Mandelbrot set, one immediately confronts issues that the pure mathematician does not worry about. The first is that one can only repeat the relevant procedure a finite number of times on a computer. In the real world one can therefore only produce pictures of something that the Platonist would regard as a good approximation to the set. From a constructive point of view the Mandelbrot set is an idealization of a series of pictures that can be refined more and more as one devotes steadily more computing resources into producing them. Each of the achievable pictures exists, but one need not be committed in the same way to the existence of the infinite abstraction. The constructive point of view is better adapted to such computational problems, because it recognizes that there may not always be an effective way of determining whether or not a point lies in the set.

The beauty of the Mandelbrot set is not intrinsic to it, but lies in the response of our very complex visual systems to it. It is difficult to imagine that one could communicate much about the set to a person who was congenitally blind. If one does not refer to its visual impact, its interest resides in a fairly limited number of theorems that one can prove about it. Without our aesthetic appreciation of it, the set is just another set, considerably less important than the set of all prime numbers.

Pure mathematics is not unique in allowing one to produce objects of great complexity by the repeated application of simple rules. Here are a few other situations in which the same phenomenon occurs:

- The Japanese art of origami;
- The variety of different snowflakes;
- The number of games that can be played following the rules of Chess or of Go.
- The range of organic compounds based on carbon, hydrogen, oxygen, and nitrogen;
- The evolutionary consequences of the huge variety of DNA molecules, all having the same fundamental structure.

Of course all of these have their own distinctive features, and none is exactly analogous to the Mandelbrot set or the set of prime numbers. Nevertheless all demonstrate the open-endedness of nature – the fact that simple rules (or laws) can produce a never-ending variety of complex outcomes. Why are mathematicians the only people who claim that this possibility implies that they have access to entities that exist independently of human society outside space and time?

3.8 The Mathematical Consensus

While agreement about the nature of mathematics is remarkable it is not universal, and there are communities who do not share in it – finitists, formalists, constructivists, pluralists, and some of those who regard computability as their core interest. The people who pursue these interests are certainly mathematicians, and some are aware of a settled indifference that sometimes edges towards hostility.

Among these is Edward Nelson, a highly respected mathematician at Princeton University. In the 1960s he made a crucial contribution to the foundations of quantum field theory, but since about 1980 he has focussed his attention on the mathematical topics that are directly relevant to the foundations of the subject. In a recent article he wrote:

> *My claim is that there is no Platonic reality underlying mathematics; mathematicians prove theorems, but the theorems are not about anything. This is how mathematics differs profoundly from science.*
>
> *Mathematicians no more discover theorems than the sculptor discovers the sculpture inside the stone. (Surely you are joking, Mr. Buonarroti!) But, unlike sculpting, our work is highly constrained, both by the rigorous demands of syntax and by the collegial nature of the enterprise. This is how mathematics differs profoundly from art.*
>
> *To deny the cogency of the Platonic notion of truth in mathematics in no way deprives mathematics of meaning. In mathematics, meaning is found not in a cold, abstract, static world of Platonic ideas but in the human, historical, collegial world of mathematicians and their work.*[25]

In his claim that 'theorems are not about anything', Nelson is adopting a formalist position. His further statement that this does not deprive mathematics of meaning seems to contradict this, but I take him to mean that the ideas behind our theorems are our own creations, individually and collectively. They can be clarifications of initially rather vague intuitions, whose meanings evolve as we work out their consequences.

Nelson dates his rejection of Platonism to a religious experience in 1976, but other perspectives on mathematics have an intrinsic interest even to those who are not religious. It is commonly said that Euclid proved that there are an infinite number of prime numbers, but this is a Platonic gloss on his actual result, to be found in Proposition 20, Book 9 of Euclid's *Elements*. It states that 'prime numbers are more than any assigned multitude of prime numbers', or, in contemporary language, 'given any finite list of prime numbers, there is another prime number not in that list'. Euclid's proof was finitistic and constructive, although hopelessly impractical: he described (rather sketchily) how to produce the new prime number from the given list. He did not use the law of induction, which was not known to the classical Greeks.

The commonest misrepresentation of Euclid's proof starts from the assumption that there are a finite number of primes and obtains a contradiction, leading to the conclusion that the number of primes must be infinite. Proof by contradiction is now a very popular method, but it does not provide as much information as a constructive proof. Sometimes it is said that a willingness to use proof by contradiction is what distinguishes mathematicians from computer scientists, but this is an over-simplification. Mathematicians differ in how much effort they are prepared to put into finding constructive proofs, but few have no interest at all in such matters. One of the jobs of computer scientists is to find algorithms that can be implemented on computers, so their interest in constructive methods is understandable.

Nowadays, most mathematicians are happy to refer in a Platonist fashion to the completed and infinite set of all prime numbers, even though the largest explicitly known prime, namely $2^{43112609} - 1$, has only thirteen million digits. They would therefore be happy to assert that there exists a smallest prime with a trillion trillion digits, in spite of the fact that there is no practical way of saying anything significant about it. A strict finitist might argue that one should not claim that the final digit of this prime has a determinate value unless a feasible algorithm for determining it is available. We have been conditioned to regard such reservations as rather eccentric in mathematics, but in other contexts we would accept them more readily. For example the first girl to be born in the year 3001 will have a name, but most people would regard it as strange to assert that her name already exists in the space-time continuum of general relativity. Apparently Einstein did believe something quite close to this. In 1955 he wrote to the son and sister of his closest friend Michele Besso as follows:

> *Now he has departed from this strange world a little ahead of me. That means nothing. People like us, who believe in physics, know that the distinction between past, present and future is only a stubbornly persistent illusion.*

One should not conclude that Einstein was a committed Platonist. In an article about Bertrand Russell's philosophy written in 1944, he wrote that 'the series of integers is obviously a creation of the human mind, a self-created tool which simplifies the ordering of certain sensory experiences'.

Platonism has other consequences, one of which is invisible to the majority who support it. It diminishes the status of numerical analysis and has delayed the development of topics that focus on quantitative results rather than mere existence. Producing efficient algorithms to locate entities that were known to exist a century ago is not as glamorous as proving the existence of solutions of new problems, but it is arguably just as important and certainly just as hard.

Platonism depersonalizes mathematics and diminishes the respect that we should have for the astonishing creativity of the most able mathematicians. Focussing one's mind on an issue for long enough to be able to 'see' the Platonic world would be far less worthy of admiration than creating something entirely new, just as a photograph is far less impressive than the genius of Monet or Picasso. Some of the most creative mathematicians claim that their work is of the former type, but the rest of us may choose to admire their creativity in spite of that. Nelson expressed this idea in the following poetic/religious language:

> *I rejoice that my chosen line of work, mathematics, has enabled me to bring into being new things that did not exist before, and to greet with wonder and awe many amazing inventions of my fellow workers. I rejoice that daily we live immersed in infinity, that we have the freedom not only to make choices but at times to be the agent, by will or by grace, to sing to the Lord a new song.*[26]

It has been argued that, for those interested in computation, Bishop's constructive mathematics is already out of date, and that the real issue is not the existence of an algorithm but the production of *efficient* algorithms. One of the most important applications of mathematics to medicine involves the Fourier transform. This is a mathematical technique which can be used to convert the information produced by a body scanner into pictures that can be used to diagnose illness. Scanners are not simply large and expensive cameras: they produce quantities of data whose relationship to the final pictures depends upon a very large amount of processing. The theoretical possibility of producing such pictures was never in question, but its realization depended on an idea that made the computations feasible. Even with computers this would not have been possible without the clever idea involved in the fast Fourier transform, a technique that makes the calculation millions of times faster.

The mathematical consensus about what constitutes 'proper' mathematics is a social phenomenon. Calculus was invented more than two hundred years before the rigorous definition of real numbers. The proofs of its validity are now much more rigorous, but nobody had previously thought that integration and differentiation might one day have to be abandoned. The tools that mathematicians have produced work as advertised and have contributed enormously to our current civilization. However, tools can become obsolete, and the rapid advances in computers may render some of our current skills redundant. Mathematics must be viewed on a time scale of centuries, even if the rate of change is accelerating. Our mathematics would have been unrecognizable seven centuries ago, and may be unrecognizable to our descendants in seven centuries time.

In this respect mathematics is similar to the political institutions which govern our everyday lives and relationships. Medieval life is almost unimaginable to us, and our own willingness to fight and even die to preserve our 'nations' may be difficult to explain one day – we may feel a strong sense of belonging to some social unit, but its size has increased enormously, if erratically, over the centuries. Changes in attitudes may seem insignificant over a lifetime, but that is simply because societies alter on a slower time scale.

Bayesian statistics provides a good example of changes in attitudes within the mathematical sciences. It is a field that has attracted its fair share of controversy. It was invented by Thomas Bayes in the eighteenth century, but fell into disrepute during the first half of the twentieth century. The method is difficult to explain in non-technical language, but the source of the controversy was its use of expert judgement in setting up the basic parameters of the model. This was deemed non-scientific and subjective.

Fifty years ago Bayesian methods were usually compared unfavourably with the better established frequentist model of statistics, which conforms much more closely to the Baconian model of science. The difference between the two methods is not purely philosophical – they can give different answers when applied to complex problems. In the frequentist method one collects a mass of statistical data about some subject and then subjects the data to one of many statistical tests and obtains, not only a trend, but also a measure of its statistical significance. Saying that a positive response to a drug is significant at the 95% level means that if one repeats enough similar trials one would expect to get a similar result purely by chance on one in every twenty occasions. This is by no means enough to be certain that the result is a true indication that the drug works, but it is enough to be encouraging.

By comparison with the apparently objective character of frequentist statistics, the Bayesian theory was often derided for depending on subjective judgements, as well as being contrary to the Popperian requirement of falsifiability. It was described as an illegitimate attempt to get around the tedious process of collecting the necessary data, and was therefore not to be trusted, or even admitted into the scientific arena. This was the attitude of the majority of statisticians in the 1960s. Even in the 1990 edition of the *Encyclopedia Britannica*, only half a page out of the nine devoted to statistics dealt with the Bayesian version, and part of that was an account of its subjective character.

A recent study shows that the proportion of Bayesian articles in statistics journals has increased from just over 10% to 35%, in the period since 1970. Adrian Smith was one of the pioneers responsible for demonstrating the advantages of Bayesian methods in many complex situations that could only be analyzed with the aid of computers, not a standard tool of scientists in the 1970s. In 1996 Bill Gates stated 'Microsoft's competitive advantage is its expertise in Bayesian networks', but this advantage was soon eroded as many other organizations, including major international banks, adopted the ideas. The Baconian idea that objective evidence should precede the drawing of conclusions has been found not to work as well as a combination of data and expert judgement, modified by later experience. Indeed it is now being suggested that this might be how the human brain works, and might be the reason that we are able to cope in ill-defined situations that current computers cannot handle.

The Bayesian approach has now been so well integrated into statistics that it takes a little effort to find references to the earlier period. By a sleight of hand the once fatally subjective element of Bayesian theory has become a merit – its ability to make use of expert judgement *as well as* objective evidence when judging the likelihood of various outcomes.

3.9   The Argument from Physics

Eugene Wigner was one of the pioneers in the development of quantum theory. One of his most important contributions was to realize the value of using symmetry (called group theory in the language of mathematicians) to simplify and bring order into the calculations. Group theory was invented (or discovered, as you will) by Galois in 1831, who used it to study the solutions of polynomial equations, a branch of algebra. Gradually it permeated geometry and then fundamental physics, and it is now one of the central tools in both subjects.

In 1960 Wigner published an article whose title, 'The Unreasonable Effectiveness of Mathematics', has become famous. It draws attention to the fact that mathematics provides a description of the natural world that works incredibly well in situations far beyond those for which it was originally devised. Wigner gives several examples, one of which concerns the spectra of the heavier atoms:

> *I wish to recall a conversation with Jordan, who…felt that we would have been, at least temporarily, helpless had an unexpected disagreement occurred in the theory of the helium atom. This was, at that time, [the late 1920s] developed by Kellner and by Hilleraas. The mathematical formalism was too dear and unchangeable so that, had the miracle of helium which was mentioned before not occurred, a true crisis would have arisen. Surely, physics would have overcome that crisis in one way or another. It is true, on the other hand, that physics as we know it today would not be possible without a constant recurrence of miracles similar to the one of the helium atom.*

Wigner unwittingly undermined his own argument by his reference to a possible crisis. It effectively concedes that physicists have an amazing amount of ingenuity, and regularly succeed in inventing new formalisms which get around problems when they arise. In the context of the helium atom one of these involved adding the notion of Fermi–Dirac statistics to quantum theory. There is no reason why discovering that a theory works in a wide range of situations should be described as needing a constant recurrence of miracles.

A number of answers to Wigner's question have been given, but it is not clear that it is the right question. The real issue is not mathematics but reality – why the universe is simple and stable enough for us to have a chance of understanding it. Einstein got it right when he wrote:

> *The most incomprehensible thing about the universe is that it is comprehensible.*

Ancient Chinese records of eclipses demonstrate that the planets obeyed Newton's laws of motion before the laws were discovered, even though the status of the word 'obeyed' is not at all clear. One could alternatively say that the Chinese records show only that the regularities of the planetary motions are not of recent origin, and that Newton's laws describe that regularity (rather than causing it). However, using different types of sentence to express the close relationship between Newton's laws and planetary motions cannot possibly settle which has the prior status. For that one needs a deeper analysis.

The regularity of nature is not exclusively mathematical, and perhaps our concentration on that aspect is a result of our cultural outlook. Here are a few of many non-mathematical regularities of the world that we exploit.

- Hunter-gatherers learn to recognize thousands of plants and fruits and to know which parts of each can be eaten and which are poisonous; this knowledge is stable and can be passed on from one generation to the next.
- The fact that we can memorize many complex routes between places is another comment on the stability of the world as well as on our ability to take advantage of it.
- As we pass through childhood, we gradually learn that certain events can cause others and that this relationship only holds if yet other events do not intervene; a completely chaotic world is imaginable, although human beings could not survive in it.
- A wide range of hard objects do not change in size relative to each other over long periods of time. We learned to exploit this fact thousands of years ago by creating graduated scales (rulers) and using them to convert sizes into numbers.

The development of physics has depended on a further regularity, which is highly surprising. Newtonian mechanics, devised to understand the motion of the planets and medium sized bodies on earth, turned out to be applicable on scales between about one-millionth of a metre, below which quantum theory becomes increasingly important, and many multiples of the size of our galaxy. It seems to have been applicable without modification for several billion years. The fact that the universe is extremely homogeneous over a huge range of scales of space and time explains why rules discovered in one context have also turned out to be valid in very different areas. One can easily imagine living in a world whose laws changed radically at scales below a millimetre and above a kilometre, but our world happens not to be like that. This homogeneity is expressed mathematically by reference to the invariance of the laws of physics under Euclidean or Lorentz symmetries, but it is a physical fact. In a few situations, for example when adjusting the clocks on the GPS satellite network, Newtonian mechanics is seen *not* to provide an appropriate description of the world, and general relativity becomes important.

At the atomic scale the world is fundamentally different from what we experience, but we have been able to gain a partial understanding of it by means of quantum theory. Creating this theory was one of the triumphs of the human spirit, but its success has only been partial. Certain facts, such as the energy levels of atoms, can be predicted with great accuracy, and are known to have been stable over billions of years. On the other hand, understanding particle–wave duality seems to be beyond us, even though we can formulate and often solve the relevant equations. The fact that the quantum theory of measurement only deals with probabilities is believed by most scientists to correspond to a deeply mysterious character of the world itself. Very few physicists still believe that its probabilistic character demonstrates that quantum theory is not the correct description of atomic level phenomena, because of the fact that it has passed so many tests designed to probe its peculiarities. Here are three out of many quotations by world famous physicists:

> *It is safe to say that nobody understands quantum mechanics. (Richard Feynman)*

> *Quantum mechanics makes absolutely no sense. (Roger Penrose)*

> *I do not like [quantum mechanics], and I am sorry I ever had anything to do with it. (Erwin Schrödinger)*

The peculiarities of quantum theory are real and cannot be resolved by mathematical trickery – all of the above physicists knew the mathematics well enough and two of them were involved in developing it. Some physicists would prefer to live in a world in which the fundamental particles behaved in a fully comprehensible manner, but the peculiarities seem to be intrinsic, and not just the result of an incomplete theory.

Quantum theory provides a good counterexample to the suggestion that nature is simple. The subject is conceptually deep and many of its applications involve extensive computer calculations. Some aspects of Newtonian mechanics can be taught at high school, but quantum theory is normally an advanced undergraduate topic in universities. Even after taking the relevant courses university students would have little hope of calculating the first few energy levels of the second simplest atom, helium. Although procedures for calculating relativistic corrections to the energy levels exist, there is no completely consistent framework for doing this. The theory works, but one needs several years of training before one can use it to describe any but the simplest examples. Computations in quantum chromodynamics are even more notorious for their difficulty and are only now becoming possible.

At the quantum level the world has many features that are absent at our scale. We believe that electrons are all *exactly* the same; if they were not they could not obey Fermi–Dirac statistics. They are not like ball bearings, that merely look the same, but which can be distinguished over a period of time simply by watching where each one moves. Electrons can merge and then separate in a manner that makes a similar procedure impossible, even in principle. We incorporate this into our mathematical description of electrons, but it is a physical fact, not a mathematical one. If it turns out to be wrong, our physical picture of the atomic world must be radically incorrect.

The great logical richness and very narrow scope of mathematics admirably suit the treatment of certain rather special aspects of the world (but not the weather a month hence). Fundamental physics is among those aspects, but it is hardly typical of science as a whole, let alone of other aspects of our lives. Should we really be surprised that the use of an extremely specialized form of language is appropriate when describing an extremely special aspect of reality? Ordinary language allows us to discuss topics that mathematics is completely unsuited to deal with, such as our hopes for the future and the motives of other people. We try to teach our children the difference between right and wrong, even though we do not fully understand these concepts ourselves. We teach them how to read and write by example, rather than by a theoretical analysis of grammar. Our socialization is *the* dominant influence on our behaviour and cannot be mathematized. We even explain to our students why the theorems in our mathematics lectures are important, and how they relate to each other, by using ordinary language.

As the philosopher of science, Sundar Sarukkai, has said, the puzzling question is why we somehow seem to take it for granted that there is nothing mysterious about the capacity of natural languages to describe the world. We do not think that languages are 'unreasonably effective' just as mathematics is. What could possibly be the reason for this lack of surprise at the expressive capacities of language? Sarukkai points out that, although languages contain many words that refer directly to the physical world, their power depends upon the fact that they also have a wealth of abstract words; these include 'wealth', 'abstract' and 'word'.

The following quotation of Einstein is famous, but it contains two assumptions:

> *How can it be that mathematics, being after all a product of human thought which is independent of experience, is so admirably appropriate to the objects of reality?*

The 'independence' claim might describe the final form of much of modern pure mathematics, but it has little relationship with the development of the subject, now or in the past. Its historical development can be examined in detail, and large parts, for example Euclid's geometry, were evidently influenced by the desire to explain aspects of the physical world. Arithmetic is a development of our ability to count, and counting is only worthwhile because a substantial number of entities do not change rapidly over moderate periods of time. We learn *by experience* that counting is more useful when discussing cows and stones than clouds. The systematization of geometry and arithmetic is an extreme version of our general ability to understand logical relationships. The progress of string theory shows that very large numbers of mathematical models may have to be generated and then rejected in the process of searching for one that has some value. Even the assumption that space is continuous rather than discrete might well be a result of our need to produce simple mathematical models – nobody knows how to describe space at scales below the Planck length.

Einstein's second assumption – I would even call it an error – is to identify the 'objects of reality' with those that can be described using mathematics and physics. There are many other objects of reality, particularly those relating to the contents of our conversations and the products of our culture, in which mathematics is completely useless. Denying the reality of those things that mathematics cannot describe makes the statement true, of course, but it will only convince those who cannot see beyond their own discipline.

The fact that our most successful description of the natural world is mathematical in character does not imply that mathematics 'controls' the world, in spite of statements by some physicists. One such is Max Tegmark, a very reputable 'precision cosmologist' whose mainstream research uses astronomical data to place sharp constraints on cosmological models. He also courts the popular press by writing semi-philosophical articles (which he himself describes as 'wacky' on his home page), in which he argues 'our external physical reality is a mathematical structure' and 'the interpretative baggage' that we use to understand the world is our own creation. According to him, the most fundamental equations should be the purest and should involve no such baggage at all. He recognizes, as a Platonist, or perhaps a Pythagorean, that the most important problem with this idea is the need to explain how we can recognize the physical relevance of mathematical equations that are entirely free of baggage. It is not surprising that his attempts to address this problem do not get anywhere.

Tegmark is following a similar line to Peter Atkins, an Oxford physical chemist with a string of extremely successful chemistry text-books and popular works on science to his name. One of these is *Creation Revisited*, a strange mixture of orthodox science and spiritual yearning in which he attempts to describe an atheistic and scientifically based faith. The following quotation gives some flavour of the book, and is difficult to make any sense of, even after reading it in context:

> *The biggest hint [that the physical world is mathematics] is that we seem to exist, and therefore the mathematical description of the origin of the world must accommodate the emergence of the apparently something*

from the certainly nothing. We have seen that the seemingly something is actually elegantly reorganized nothing, and that the net content of the universe is now the same as it has always been, and always will be, world with or without end; namely nothing. What mathematics can emulate the emergence of something from nothing? Why, nothing other than the pure numbers! . . . It may be that the logical structures of mathematics and the universe emerged simultaneously and are identical. The deep structure of the universe may be a globally self-consistent assemblage of the empty set. We, like mathematics, and like it or not, are elegant, self-consistent, reorganizations of nothing. . . . It may be that the comprehensible is comprehensible because of the deep structural resemblance, and perhaps even the identity, of mathematics and reality.[27]

There are many examples of physicists who adopt what the philosopher Bas van Fraassen calls the lazy option of 'reifying' theoretical models, that is declaring that the entities in those models actually exist. Although I disagree with much that he has written, the following seems a better account of their status than that of Atkins is.

There are just two realms of scientific investigation, [pursued] hand in hand by experimentalists and theorists. On the one hand there are the phenomena which are investigated. On the other hand there are the models, abstract structures studied in mathematics, which the theory advances as representations of those phenomena. The representation is always partial and selective. You and I are mechanical systems, that is, we are correctly represented by certain mechanical models. But however good those models are, they omit quite a lot about us (and have elements that may not correspond to anything in us at all, as well).[28]

The scientific use of models has several aspects. Models themselves are theoretical (and therefore cultural) constructs, and in that sense fictional, but the procedures for creating them are constrained by the theory that is being investigated. They idealize the situation of interest by pretending that it is simpler than it actually is (for example replacing the Earth by a sphere and reducing the number of gravitating bodies in the Solar System from hundreds to just two or three) and by changing the equations that govern the behaviour of the system (for example ignoring gravity in a problem about semiconductors, or setting the viscosity to zero in a problem about fluids). The supposed relationship between the model and the physical world is governed by the conventions of the theory, but it is inevitably approximate because of the simplifications involved. One may use different models of the same physical system depending on the context and the accuracy required.

Scientists accept a model as a part of their world-view when the correspondence between its properties and those of the physical world is considered to be sufficiently close in a wide range of situations. This often involves reifying its fundamental concepts. Today it would be absurd to refuse to acknowledge the physical existence of atoms, because of the diversity of the evidence in support of this, although it was reasonable to regard them as no more than theoretical constructs throughout the nineteenth century. It is worth noting, however, that our atoms have substantially different properties from the atoms of Dalton and Avogadro. But this success does not give one carte blanche to reify every new concept in physics.

To sum up, the universe as a whole is comprehensible to us because some phenomena have a high degree of regularity over a huge range of scales of time and space. That being the case, we can hope to find a way of describing the regularity, and the specialized language that we have developed to do this is called mathematics. The astonishing things are the physical regularity and our ability to recognize it, not the language that we use to express it. Given the first two, we were bound to start developing the third eventually.

3.10 Mathematical Truth

There are many objective facts in mathematics, but it is not easy to describe their precise status. One is the statement that if one accepts the standard rules of arithmetic then $4 \times 7 = 28$. One of the issues a mathematician or logician would want to clarify about the equation is the precise definition of 4 and the other numbers in the equation. Clearly 4 is not the number itself; it is one of many names for the number, just as 'four' and *IV* are. Early in the twentieth century Alfred North Whitehead and Bertrand Russell put an enormous amount of effort into making such issues precise, but the result was almost unreadable. References to counting the number of elements in the rectangular array

$$\begin{array}{ccccccc}
1 & 1 & 1 & 1 & 1 & 1 & 1 \\
1 & 1 & 1 & 1 & 1 & 1 & 1 \\
1 & 1 & 1 & 1 & 1 & 1 & 1 \\
1 & 1 & 1 & 1 & 1 & 1 & 1
\end{array}$$

cannot amount to a proof, because this would be reducing a truth of *pure mathematics* to a property of *physical* marks on paper. While it might be argued that the physical marks are simply an imperfect version of ideal marks in a Platonic world, nobody is going to be able to determine the product of two hundred-digit numbers by such methods. Most mathematicians have little interest in such questions, since it is clear that the validity of the equation is one of many tests that an adequate theory of numbers will have to satisfy. In some sense the identity is more fundamental than any axiom system in which the meaning of the terms is made precise enough for it to be provable.

Almost every mathematician, including myself, would also say that there are true theorems, not just theorems that current mathematicians agree to accept because we share a common culture, but theorems about whose truth there cannot be any serious argument. As an example one might take the statement that the sum of the interior angles of a (Euclidean) triangle is 180°, irrespective of the shape of the triangle.

Fermat's last theorem is somewhat less secure than the above theorem. It is the statement that there do not exist positive numbers a, b, c and a number $n \geq 3$ for which

$$a^n + b^n = c^n.$$

Before 1993 no mathematician would have claimed that Fermat's last theorem was true. Following the heroic efforts of Andrew Wiles (aided by Richard Taylor in the last stages), the theorem is now regarded as proven. Several mathematicians have read the entire proof in detail, a number of others have mastered large parts of it, and some major advances have been made in areas that were developed by Wiles for the proof.

Wiles' proof is undoubtedly rigorous, but the meaning of the word 'rigorous' should be spelt out. It does not mean that every step in the proof has been proved directly from the axioms using only the laws of logic. It is intended only to imply that a sufficiently detailed, ordered list of steps has been produced for experts in the field to agree that such a formal proof could be produced if it were desired. In particular, the referee of a mathematical paper might question various steps and insist that more detail should be supplied, but published papers take up no more than a fraction of the space that a complete logical deduction would need. Because of these facts rigorous proofs are occasionally wrong, and sometimes it has taken decades for the error to come to light. A complete, formal proof was until recently regarded as beyond the power of mathematicians to provide except in trivial cases. One of the reasons for this was the enormous and eventually self-defeating length of the only serious attempt to provide such proofs in the field of logic by Russell and Whitehead at the start of the twentieth century.

Many mathematicians, whether or not they identify themselves as Platonists, would assert that Fermat's last theorem was already true before Wiles proved it. They would say that either there is a counterexample or there is not. If there is, then it would involve four particular numbers a, b, c, and n that could, in principle, be written down explicitly. If there is no counterexample then the theorem is true, whether or not it can be proved.

The occurrence of the weasel words 'in principle' indicates that all of these statements are contentious. If attempts to find a counterexample with the fastest existing computer fail over a long period of time, this proves nothing. Asserting the existence of a counterexample that is far beyond the scope of a computer as large as the visible universe and running for billions of years assumes the validity of the Platonic position. One might prove the non-existence of such a counterexample by deriving a contradiction from its existence. Until one has a counterexample or a proof that there exists one, or a proof of inconsistency one cannot draw any conclusions about the theorem and should remain silent.

The proof of the four colour theorem by Appel and Haken in 1976 started a new era in which the proofs of some theorems depended on a combination of human insight and laborious computer-based calculations. Some mathematicians found this upsetting, but the next generation have learned to accept it. As computers have grown more powerful, further examples of a similar type have appeared, and there are now fields in which some of the key results depend on the use of computers. Our own human efforts are by no means error free, and it is fortunate that the kind of mathematical thinking that we are particularly good at complements the kind that computers are good at.

The recent development of formal proofs of correctness takes the influence of computers one step further.[29] These can provide extremely strong evidence that mathematical theorems are correct, by expanding arguments that owed their origins to human insight to the point at which every step follows a few logical rules that every mathematician would consent to. The effort involved in producing a formal proof is very substantial, but a number of very difficult theorems, including the four colour theorem, have now been formalized. It is possible that computers will be able to create proofs of major theorems without any help from us one day, but this is not imminent and I personally do not expect to have to adapt to this situation.

The number of professional mathematicians increased dramatically during the twentieth century, and eventually the sheer quantity of mathematics that they had produced made it harder and harder for individual mathematicians to understand more than a tiny fraction of the subject in detail. Then came the classification of finite simple groups, the most ambitious collaborative effort in pure mathematics by an order of magnitude. I am not an expert in group theory, but I wrote a brief account of the history of the Classification theorem in 2005. This turned out to be a far more sensitive issue than I had realized, and I stepped on several sore toes. The current account is not very different from my previous one, but I hope that it is expressed more precisely and tactfully.

The Classification project started early in the 1970s, under the leadership of Daniel Gorenstein, and was intended to lead to a complete list of all the finite simple groups. (It is unnecessary for our purposes to know what these are.) At the peak of the activity over a hundred group theorists were assigned particular parts of the work, and by about 1980 it was believed that the task was essentially finished and that the complete list was known. Since then no new groups have been discovered and there is no reason to believe that the Classification is incomplete.

Unfortunately the proof of the theorem is massive; there were originally over five hundred papers and some parts of the proof were not published in refereed journals. One apparently small gap in the proof turned out to require a further major effort by Aschbacher and Smith, resulting in the production of two substantial books in 2004. A project to present the entire proof in a connected series of about eleven volumes totalling 5000 pages is approaching completion; six of the volumes were published as of November 2007.

This is where we switch from fact to interpretation and commentary. It is doubtful that any single human being could master the details of the entire work to the extent of being sure that there is no error in the proof of the theorem. This is an unprecedented situation in pure mathematics and is a result of the length and lack of global transparency of the proof. In 2005 Michael Aschbacher, one of the leaders in the classification project, wrote the following:

> *If we've made mistakes, so that the [Classification] theorem is false and there is some [extra group not in the known list], then it might be possible to repair the theorem by adding [the extra group to the list] and making minor modifications to the inductive 'proof'. This would be true if the structure of [the extra group] is much like that of the members of [the known list]. But if [the extra group] has a very different structure, one could imagine that such a modification might not be possible.*[30]

Aschbacher is by no means alone in his caution, and the Classification is sometimes said to be a theorem 'by the consensus of the community'. Even if the eleven volumes are completed, as now seems increasingly likely, the number of people capable of understanding them is dropping, as those involved in the original work retire and die. Future generations may be forced to use the results, even though nobody alive may have a proper grasp of the proof.

However much one admires the huge achievement of those involved, it appears that mathematics may have reached a watershed. Some of those who have been involved in the project are not optimistic that a radically shorter and more comprehensible proof will be found. If they are right, then we are finally being forced to move away from the long standing tradition handed down to our students for generations: that they should never accept any theorem on authority, but should read its proof critically and decide for themselves whether they believe it. Mathematics may finally have been forced to join the rest of our intellectual pursuits, in which the honest efforts of a community of experts over a long period of time will have to be accepted, subject to each part being tested as and when necessary.

3.11 Is Our Mathematics Inevitable?

Is it possible to show that, although we might have got to our present state of civilization by a different route, mathematics as we know it was bound to emerge eventually?

Let us marshal some of the arguments in favour of this proposition. Counting is such a basic part of our lives that it is difficult to imagine life without it. Just glance at a quality newspaper today and you will find dozens of numbers on most pages, the majority of which involve counting, from the score in a sports event to the cost of something in the local currency. Addition is not the same as counting, but seems to be inevitable if one needs to keep track of the total number when one combines two largish groups of objects. Multiplication is another matter. It is not used nearly as frequently as addition, but was already well-established early in the third millennium BC; the Babylonians created systematic multiplication tables for all numbers up to 59×59. Their preference for basing their counting system on 60, rather than the 10 that we currently use, presumably arose from the fact that 60 can be divided by all numbers up to 6 exactly. They did not content themselves with this, but developed methods for solving a wide range of quantitative problems in geometry. These were not written down in a general context, and we have to infer their methods from many clay tablets that contain numerical examples, probably intended for teaching purposes.

It is tempting to argue that addition and multiplication are so basic that any intelligent aliens would have been forced to re-invent them is the same form as we did. From a purely logical point of view, this argument is absurd, because there is no evidence that aliens exist. If they do, they might be familiar with counting but simply shrug their alien shoulders when introduced to the notion of multiplication, and tell us that they find our literature far more interesting than our obsession with rearranging abstract pebbles into rectangular arrays. They might have developed space-travel by an evolutionary process without any scientific laws or bureaucratic infrastructure, just as birds fly and animals manage to avoid falling off cliffs.[31] All we *know* is that no other species in our own world, even the great apes, have developed mathematics, and that we will never be able to communicate with some of the most successful – the social insects.

David Ruelle expresses similar sentiments in his recent book *The Mathematician's Brain*.

> *Let me state a conclusion that I find hard to escape: the structure of human science is largely dependent on the special nature and organization of the human brain. I am not at all suggesting here that an alien intelligent species might develop science with conclusions opposite to ours. Rather, I shall later argue that what our supposed alien intelligent species would understand (and be interested in) might be hard to translate into something that we would understand (and be interested in).*

Leaving this aside, it is quite plausible that our ability to count, not just up to four but much further, is quite close to our genetic inheritance, even though some tribes have not developed it. According to the Bible, shepherds did not need to count their sheep: they recognized each one by name. Arithmetic might not have developed as it did if we could distinguish between numbers up to a thousand at a glance in the same way as we can actually distinguish between numbers up to four. This is not an idle fancy. The neurologist Oliver Sacks has described twins who were unable to add and subtract accurately and could not comprehend what multiplication and division meant. He wrote:

> *A box of matches on their table fell, and discharged its contents on the floor: '111' they both cried simultaneously; and then, in a murmur, John said '37'. Michael repeated this, John said it a third time and stopped. I counted the matches – it took me some time – and there were 111. 'How could you count the matches so quickly?' I asked. 'We didn't count,' they said. 'We saw the 111.'* [32]

We know a lot about the historical development of more advanced aspects of mathematics. I have already written about the law of mathematical induction in *Science in the Looking Glass*, so here I will concentrate on negative numbers. The history of this subject is typical for a culturally transmitted concept. In the third century Diophantus referred to the equation $4x + 20 = 0$ as absurd. Negative numbers were used to represent debts in India and the Islamic world before 1000, for example by Brahmagupta in the 7th century, but they were avoided in Europe for much longer. If one looks at seventeenth century mechanics in Europe, one regularly sees what we would regard as the same mathematical calculation being written down twice, or even more times, to take account of whether each of the bodies concerned is moving to the left or the right. This is even visible in *Principia*, where Newton felt the need to do this in his law of conservation of momentum. Nowadays we would simply declare the convention that bodies moving to the right (or left) should be assigned positive (or negative) speeds, and forget the issue. European resistance to the use of negative numbers continued well into the eighteenth century. For example, Clairaut, already mentioned in Chapter 1 for his crucial resolution of the anomalies in the Moon's orbit in 1752, still worried about the meaning of such expressions as $(-400) \div (-10)$.

The rule for multiplying negative numbers is not obvious. While one can eventually convince oneself that $(-2) \times 3 = -6$ is a natural result, it is not so clear why $(-2) \times (-3) = 6$. Adding two negative numbers leads to a negative result, so why should multiplying them lead to a positive result? Perhaps the best answer is that one must adopt this convention if one wants the 'distributive law'

$$a \times (b + c) = a \times b + a \times c$$

and other rules of arithmetic to apply to any combination of positive and negative numbers. The distributive rule is so useful that it is now taken for granted, with the effect that the choice seems to be *almost forced* on you, but outstanding mathematicians felt uneasy about the concepts involved for hundreds of years.

The fact that society has now converged on agreed rules for manipulating negative numbers does not imply that these rules were somewhere out there waiting to be discovered. Indeed, the long period during which people knew about negative numbers but preferred to avoid them is difficult to reconcile with the discovery of a new aspect of the Platonic realm. A large number of societies have also converged on common designs for suitcases and bicycles. The next addition may be wheely bins. In each case there are good reasons, based on physics and physiology, for the type of design that has emerged, but this does not imply that the concepts pre-existed their historical appearance. Traditions and skills relating to the production of stone-age axes lasted *much* longer than any of these, but they eventually died. Cultural transmission is an extremely powerful force, and can explain most of what we now see as the common core of mathematics.

If human beings had not possessed eyes, we might well have developed a sophisticated counting system and even arithmetic, but it is difficult to believe that the efflorescence of research into different arrangements of lines and circles that started with Euclid would ever have emerged. Solid (i.e. three-dimensional) geometry has many applications to the design of structures, but the theorem about the nine-point circle, proved independently by several mathematicians early in the nineteenth century, was pure 'blue-skies' research. The theorem, illustrated in Figure 3.5, states that there is a circle passing through nine points associated with any triangle; three of them are the mid-points of its sides and another three are the bases of the perpendiculars from a vertex to the opposite side. The beauty of this theorem would be entirely lost to a blind mathematician. Projective geometry, which arose from the use of perspective in art, is even less likely to come to the attention of a sightless alien. Without the spur provided by visual experiences, the study of patterns, and then of group theory, might not have occupied the central place in mathematics that it now does. An intelligent species without eyes, but with a more highly developed sense of smell might have developed chemistry far more deeply and accorded it the central place in our understanding of the world, rather than mathematics. The conclusion that I draw from such considerations is that our science and mathematics are much more dependent on our sense organs than we usually admit.

Of course we do have eyes, and we all think in roughly the same way because we belong to the same species and our various civilizations have influenced each other throughout our history. Moreover we have little choice but to accept the world view of the civilization in which we were born. For both these reasons the contents of Euclid's *Elements* have an immediate conceptual content for us, and provide a source of theorems whose truth is as clear today as it was over two thousand years ago.

I have not answered the question posed in the title of the section, nor do I think that it is possible to do so. Twenty thousand years ago our distant ancestors lived in a world in which there were no mathematical theorems, no money and no mechanical means of transport. Their world was very different from the one we live in today, but whether one could have what we like to call civilization without all three of these is a moot point. Of the three one might guess that theorems are the most dispensable. I cannot imagine space probes, computers, the electricity industry, or telecommunications developing without a very substantial amount of computational

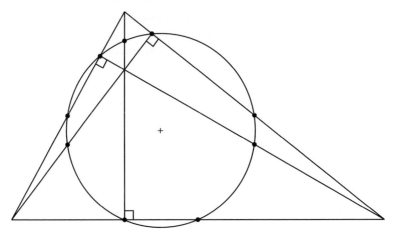

Fig. 3.5 The Nine-Point Circle

underpinning, but, like the philosopher Hilary Putnam, I can imagine an advanced society without theorems. I can also imagine one without art, music, novels, and poetry, but am glad that our culture contains all four.

3.12 The Irrelevance of Platonism

The final criticism of Platonism is based on its irrelevance. Research papers are not accepted on the basis of the assurances of the authors that they have seen the truth of their assertions in the Platonic world. They are required to produce detailed arguments that can be checked line by line. The proofs may be logically incomplete, but the task of referees is to decide whether they feel convinced that the details could be filled in. They carry out this task by reading the papers, carefully, comparing the theorems with others that they have met in the past, trying to find contradictions with other knowledge that they have, and in the last resort, asking the authors to expand certain arguments that are too sketchy to be comprehensible. In the end, the referee has to be convinced that the individual parts of the article could in principle be written out in a completely formal manner that anyone could check. Because the author and referee rely on experience and analogy, they may both falsely judge a proof to be correct.

It could be argued that the final stage of writing up a paper in the form required by journals is the least important, and that Platonic insight is needed during the earlier and more creative part of the research. If this is the case, one has to explain the fact that papers are regularly found to contain fatal errors, not just in the details of the proofs, but even in the insights behind the main results. This was the fate of Frege's set theory and of Hilbert's program for formalizing mathematics, and well as of the work of many other mathematicians. It appears that the 'direct perception' of the Platonic world is much less reliable than careful checking of the results by more conventional methods.

Since Frege's set theory is not internally consistent it cannot exist within the Platonic realm. However, Alain Connes, one of the most committed Platonists among Fields medallists, also excludes the theory of Jordan algebras – a subject to which many able mainstream mathematicians have devoted their lives.[33] Perhaps this is simply Connes' way of saying that he does not like the subject, but where is one to put Bishop's constructive mathematics? A committed Platonist who recognizes that it is mathematics can hardly assign it to the Platonic realm, when its basis is the rejection of Platonism. Does there exist a Platonic hell to which one can send it, or is it a perversion of mathematics that does not even deserve such recognition?

Platonism is attractive to many pure mathematicians, but unsupported intuition is a bad basis for deciding about truth. The historical evidence shows that mathematics is learned and culturally transmitted, just like natural languages. On close inspection Platonism just replaces one mystery by another. Instead of wondering about how we are able to understand mathematics, one has to wonder how the Platonic realm can exert any influence on the physical world. Plato dismissed this problem by declaring that the physical world was not worthy of the attention of serious seekers after truth, but this option is not open to us. Asserting that the world is mathematics, as Tegmark, Atkins, and some others do, is no more than an empty form of words until its content is explained.

The key to mathematical progress has been the possibility of recording our successes so that they may be transmitted to our descendants. After walking for over two thousand years down this one-way road, we have progressed a considerable distance. Every generation starts further down the road, and builds a new section using tools that are themselves becoming more efficient. We do not know where it will lead, but it is clear that we are not yet near the end.

Notes and References

[1] Wells, David (1997). *Mathematics and Abstract Games, An Intimate Connection*. Rain Press, London.

[2] This idea was developed by a group of philosophers including Carnap, Reichenbach, and Wittgenstein in the middle of the twentieth century.

[3] For similar views see van Benthem, Bridges, Hellman, and other articles in Vincent F. Hendricks and Hannes Leitgeb, eds. (2008), *Philosophy of Mathematics, Five Questions*, Automatic Press, VIP.

[4] Feferman, S. (1999). Relationships between constructive, predicative and classical systems of analysis. In Vincent F. Hendricks, Stig Andur Pedersen, and Klaus Frovin Jørgensen, eds., *Proof Theory: History and Philosophical Significance*. Synthese Library Series, Univ. of Roskilde, Denmark.

[5] Maddy, P. (1997). *Naturalism in Mathematics*, pp.102–7. Clarendon Press, Oxford.

[6] Lax, P. D. (2008). Mathematics and Physics. *Bull. Amer. Math. Soc.* **45**, 135–52.

[7] Dummett, M. (1978). *Truth and Other Enigmas*, p.202. Duckworth, London.

[8] Schwartz, J. T. (2006). Do the Integers Exist? The Unknowability of Arithmetic Consistency. *Comm. Pure Appl. Math.* **58**, 1280–6.

[9] Penrose, R. (1989). *The Emperor's New Mind*, p.428. Oxford Univ. Press.

[10] Connes, A. *et al.* (2001). *Triangle of Thoughts*, pp.26, 27. Amer. Math. Soc. (The word in parenthesis is included on several earlier occasions, and I have inserted it here for clarity.)

[11] Balaguer, Mark (1998). *Platonism and anti-Platonism in Mathematics*. Oxford Univ. Press, Oxford.

[12] See Hendricks, Vincent F., and Leitgeb, Hannes eds. (2008). *Philosophy of Mathematics, Five Questions*. Automatic Press, VIP.

[13] Hendricks *et al.* eds. (2008), p.128.

[14] Davis, Philip J., and Hersh, Reuben (1981). *The Mathematical Experience*. Birkhäuser, Boston.

[15] This is adapted from Hersh and Reuben (1997), *What is Mathematics, Really?*, Oxford Univ. Press, USA.

[16] Mazur, B. (June 2008). Mathematical Platonism and its Opposites *European Math. Soc. Newsletter* 19–21.

[17] Dummett, M. (1978). *Truth and Other Enigmas*, p.xxv. Duckworth, London.

[18] Dummett (1978), p.216. The articles in this book were written over a period of more than twenty years, during which time Dummett's views developed and sometimes changed.

[19] Deutsch, D. (1997). *The Fabric of Reality*, p.251. Penguin Books, London.

[20] Cohen, P. A. (2005). The Nature of Mathematical Proof. *Phil. Trans. Royal Soc.* **363**, 2416.

[21] Varley, R. A. *et al.* (2005). Agrammatic but numerate. *Proc. Nat. Acad. Sci.* **102**, 3519–24.

[22] See http://www.abelprisen.no/en/prisvinnere/2004/

[23] Fitzgerald, M. and James, I. (2007). *The Mind of the Mathematician*, p.5. Johns Hopkins Univ. Press, Baltimore.

[24] Ruelle, David (2007). *The Mathematician's Brain*. Princeton Univ. Press, Princeton, NJ.

[25] Nelson, E. (2008). *Mathematics and Faith*. http://www.math.princeton.edu/~nelson/papers/faith.pdf

[26] Nelson, E. (2006). Warning signs of a possible collapse in contemporary mathematics. *Conference on New Frontiers in Research on Infinity, San Marino.*

[27] Atkins, Peter (1994). *Creation Revisited*, pp.113–25. Penguin Books, London.

[28] van Fraassen, Bas C. (2006). Structure, its shadow and substance. *British J. Phil. Sci.* **57**, 275–307.

[29] The December 2008 issue of the *Notices of the American Mathematical Society* has several articles about this.

[30] Aschbacher, M. (2005). The nature of mathematical proof. *Phil. Trans. Royal Soc.* **363**, p. 2402. I have replaced some symbols by words to make the text easier to understand.

[31] For further arguments of this type see Kukla, A. (2008), The one world, one science argument, *Brit. J. Phil. Sci.* **59**, 73–88.

[32] Sacks, Oliver (1986). *The Man Who Mistook His Wife for a Hat*, Chapter 13. Picador, London.

[33] Connes, A., Lichnerowicz, A., and Schützenberger, M.P. (2001). *Triangle of Thoughts*. Amer. Math. Soc.

4
Sense and Nonsense

Nature provides plenty of real problems.
One does not need to invent them.

4.1 Fundamental Constants

This chapter describes theories that range from the most profound that we have yet discovered, to others that strike me as completely wacky. Although it seems clear to me which is which, there is a problem. Some very eminent scientists disagree with me. On the other hand they also disagree with each other, so it is worth considering how one should make such judgements. This is not as easy as it sounds, because of the existence of quantum theory, as bizarre a theory as could be imagined. If it had not been found again and again to predict what actually happens in experiments, it would not have been entertained for a moment. It is a philosopher's dream – or possibly nightmare – because of the absence of any plausible *physical* explanation of many observed phenomena. Some crucial 'double-slit' experiments are sometimes even described as involving a single particle interacting with itself in a non-trivial manner. The mathematics is unambiguous, but most physicists do not feel that it provides anything like a full understanding.

The first part of this chapter is descriptive and is common ground for all those involved in particle physics. When one comes to discussions of the multiverse one starts to find major differences of opinion. These depend on people's religious and philosophical world-views, even though many of those involved appear not to recognize this. More specifically, a willingness to take the multiverse seriously depends on the prior belief that every part of a mathematical theory must correspond to something real. The multiverse is at, or possibly just beyond, the boundaries of what can sensibly be discussed, but we also mention some much more exotic theories that have led to serious 'scientific' discussion, in spite of the fact that they are fairly obviously science fiction. We set the scene by discussing the planetary orbits, and then pass to similar problems confronting physicists at the present time.

Chapter 1 described Kepler's wish to explain the motion of the planets by means of the laws of physics. His three famous rules, only much later called laws, were eventually incorporated into Newton's theory of gravitation. Kepler also believed that he had obtained a rule for calculating the sizes of the planetary orbits by nesting the regular polyhedra inside each other. The rule worked moderately well, but we now consider that it had no physical basis.

The Titius–Bode law of the late eighteenth century provided another rule for calculating the distances of the planets from the Sun. The formula and its fit with the data are shown in the following table.

Planet	Formula	Distance
Mercury	4	3.9
Venus	$4 + 3 = 7$	7.2
Earth	$4 + 3 \times 2 = 10$	10.0
Mars	$4 + 3 \times 2^2 = 16$	15.2
(asteroids)	$4 + 3 \times 2^3 = 28$	~ 27
Jupiter	$4 + 3 \times 2^4 = 52$	52.0
Saturn	$4 + 3 \times 2^5 = 100$	95.4
(Uranus)	$4 + 3 \times 2^6 = 196$	191.8
(Neptune)	$4 + 3 \times 2^7 = 388$	300.6
(Pluto)	$4 + 3 \times 2^8 = 772$	395.3

The unit of distance in the table was chosen so that the Earth is at a distance 10 from the Sun; the planets in brackets were not known when the Titius–Bode 'law' was invented. The asteroids and Uranus were only discovered after the 'discovery' of the law, so it had significant predictive success. However, it was not trusted: by the nineteenth century explanation was considered to be an essential feature of a good theory, and it provided none. As a result it died unlamented when it failed to fit the data for Neptune, discovered in 1846. The further discovery of Pluto in 1930 was not needed – and in any case Pluto is not considered to be a planet at the present time.

Physics involves trying to separate phenomena into those that need to be explained by means of laws and those that cannot be, which are then called data. Explanations may be mathematical, but are not now considered to include isolated formulae such as the Titius–Bode law. The laws are then declared to be the essence of the field, while the data are assigned a lower status. In the year 1500 the key astronomical data were the numbers needed to specify the epicycles. By 1700 they were the five parameters needed to fix the elliptical orbits of each of the planets. These parameters are still needed today. We believe that they were determined by the history of the Solar System, and it is highly implausible that anyone will ever compute them from first principles.

The distinction between theory and data is not as simple as it seems. Data are often highly theoretical constructs, and the theory involved in evaluating them might even be the same as the one being tested. At any time one does the best one can, and declares facts that one cannot explain to be data. Unexplained constants are said to be fundamental if they occur in fundamental theories and nobody has any idea about how they could be calculated.

4.2 Panspermia

It is hard to believe that the values of certain fundamental constants could lead to serious discussions about the existence of God, but they did. The story starts with Fred Hoyle. Born in Yorkshire in 1915, he won a place at Cambridge University to read mathematics. A few years after starting to do research in astronomy his career was interrupted by the Second World War, when he worked on developing radar. After the war he returned to astronomy and started a series of papers on the synthesis of the elements by nuclear fusion processes in the stars. Developments of these ideas by many people were eventually to explain the distribution of the chemical elements in the universe. These discoveries led to a Nobel Prize for his collaborator William Fowler in 1983, but, scandalously, not for Hoyle as well. In the course of this research, he revealed the necessary existence (soon confirmed) of a resonance in the spectrum of carbon, which depended on a certain fundamental constant having a value which lay in a fairly narrow range. The possibility of life as we know it depends entirely on this fact: if the constant had been significantly different stellar fusion would not have led to the production of large quantities of carbon, which eventually became the key ingredient in the organic molecules essential to life. Hoyle's atheism was shaken by this discovery and in 1959 he concluded:

> *I do not believe that any scientist who examined the evidence would fail to draw the inference that the laws of nuclear physics have been deliberately designed with regard to the consequences they produce inside the stars.*

In spite of many awards recognizing his extraordinary contributions to astronomy, Hoyle resigned from his position as Director of the Institute of Theoretical Astronomy at Cambridge 1972 in protest at what he regarded as politically motivated interference and even conspiracy against him. He left Cambridge and soon afterwards started a collaboration with Chandra Wickramasinghe in which they proposed, with Hoyle's characteristic disregard for the conventional wisdom, that biological molecules, or conceivably life itself, originated in dust clouds in deep space and spread over the whole universe, eventually raining down on the Earth and, presumably, all other planets. This theory was explained in his popular book *The Intelligent Universe*, published in 1983. Their notion of 'panspermia' was ridiculed for many years. It is rejected with less confidence today because of the continuing discovery of molecules in interstellar clouds. Over a hundred, such as water, ammonia, methane, formic acid, and acetaldehyde, have been identified by means of their spectral characteristics; a few contain eight or more atoms, mostly carbon, hydrogen, and oxygen. A number of amino acids, the building blocks of proteins, have been found in the type of meteorites called carbonaceous chondrites, and there is fairly convincing evidence that they are not the result of recent contamination. There is no evidence of extraterrestrial life, let alone intelligent aliens. We are, however, aware of extremophile microbes that can survive extremely hostile conditions for long periods of time, and that might conceivably be transferred from one planet to another inside meteorites.

Hoyle's 'deliberate design' argument disturbed many cosmologists and continues to provoke serious discussion. The popular term 'fine tuning' is presumably intended to conjure up an image of a being who designs the universe using a machine with dials for tuning the fundamental constants, and then adjusts these very carefully to ensure that carbon-based life can come into existence. The most puzzling instance of fine tuning involves the 'cosmological constant', which controls the expansion of the universe. Its value is so much smaller than what might be expected that some cosmologists conjectured that it might be exactly zero, for a reason that had not yet been discovered. However, the most recent observations of distant galaxies suggest that it is non-zero. Why it has its actual value is a mystery, but we would not exist if it were very different from zero.

The deliberate design argument is often associated with the anthropic principle. This has several formulations, but one is the assertion that it is very significant that the fine tuning is just right to favour the development of carbon-based life. The physical and religious aspects of this debate are discussed on pages 163 and 211 respectively. Many scientists do not find either particularly appealing, but others do.

4.3   The Standard Model

If one were to list the buzz-words in popular articles on physics today, one would probably include quantum mechanics, general relativity, black holes, and string theory. It is less likely that the standard model would appear in the list, in spite of the fact that its creation has been one of the greatest triumphs of modern physics. It brought order to the menagerie of elementary particles that have been discovered since 1932, when there were only three – the electron, proton, and neutron. In subsequent years many more were discovered, including mesons, neutrinos, and quarks; moreover each had its own antiparticle. All of these particles are important at high energies, and they play a vital role in describing the early moments of the universe after the Big Bang. Finding out why they exist has been one of the greatest theoretical challenges of modern physics.

The level of detail in this section is quite high, and the reader can skim rapidly through it if so desired. It is included to give an impression of the vast amount of knowledge that has been gathered as the result of the collaboration of many physicists over several decades. The final picture is far from simple and is still being revealed. The next section discusses whether the realist presentation given here is to be trusted.

Everything in our bodies is composed of tiny atoms, each of which is composed of a cloud of electrons orbiting a much smaller but relatively heavy nucleus. Different nuclei correspond to different chemical elements, each atomic nucleus being composed of a certain number of protons and neutrons. For example, a hydrogen nucleus consists of a single proton, a helium nucleus contains two protons and two neutrons and a carbon nucleus contains six protons and six neutrons. The synthesis of carbon in stars depends on the fact that a carbon nucleus can be built by combining three helium nuclei. If one is only interested in chemistry then one does not need to know any more than this.

Most of the elementary particles were discovered in high energy accelerators, with a variety of exotic names such as synchotron and bevatron. These accelerators are used to force particles to collide with each other at extremely high speeds, and then photograph the tracks of the resulting fragments. It is amazing that such a procedure yields worthwhile information – imagine trying to understand how a car works by repeatedly crashing vehicles into each other at a very high speed and then measuring the directions in which the wreckage emerges – but that is all that is available. Figure 4.1 shows a simplified generic collision event, which might be only one of hundreds of different collisions in the same picture. In the early days

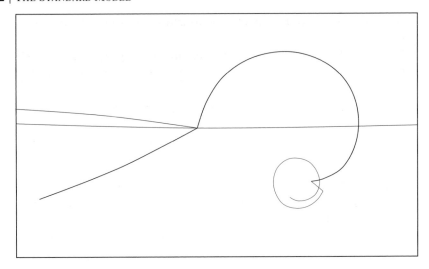

Fig. 4.1 A Simplified Particle Collision

these were measured by hand, but now the volume of data generated is so vast that a computer has to analyze the pictures as they are produced and reject most as being of no interest.

One of the particles discovered in this way was the neutrino. These interact with normal matter incredibly weakly, with the result that, initially, their properties were inferred rather than observed. Eventually experiments have confirmed their existence, but the detectors concerned have to be extraordinarily sensitive. In 1987 a burst of neutrinos associated with a new supernova, rather unimaginatively known as SN 1987A, provided an outstanding confirmation of our understanding of supernova physics. The total of 24 neutrinos observed at three different sites was an unimaginably small fraction of about 10^{58} emitted by the supernova, which is 170 thousand light years away.

The following list summarizes the relationship between a few of the various particles that physicists now deal with.

- All atoms are very roughly the same size, although their masses vary widely from one element to another. If ten million atoms lie next to each other on a straight line, their combined length is about one millimetre.
- A carbon atom consists of six very light electrons orbiting in a cloud with an ill-defined boundary around a dense nucleus that is very roughly twenty thousand times smaller than the atom itself.

- A carbon nucleus consist of six protons and six neutrons packed closely together.
- Protons and neutrons are themselves composed of quarks. There are six types of quark, whimsically labelled up, down, charm, strange, top, bottom.
- A proton is composed of two up quarks and one down quark, while a neutron is composed of two down quarks and one up quark.
- Quarks and electrons are currently believed to be truly elementary (i.e. indivisible) particles.

Figure 4.2 gives an impression of what an atom is like, but the various parts are wildly out of scale. The electrons are incorrectly but conventionally depicted as though they were classical point particles.

There are also four forces in nature, electromagnetic, weak, strong, and gravitational. Chemists only need one, the electromagnetic force, provided that they are prepared to accept the existence of the many different types of atomic nuclei. Traditionally astronomy relies on gravity to explain the motions of the heavenly bodies, and spectroscopy (taken from the chemists) to understand the internal structures of the stars. The weak and strong forces were only discovered during the twentieth century, but they are just as fundamental as the other two. The strong force is what allows protons and neutrons to stick together in atomic nuclei.

The weak force is, as its name suggests, much weaker and its best known effect is to allow an important type of radioactivity, the so-called beta decay of nuclei. In this process a neutron in an atomic nucleus is converted into a proton with the consequent emission of a high energy electron and a more or less invisible neutrino. Beta decay occurs randomly and at very different rates for different elements. It is a quantum mechanical

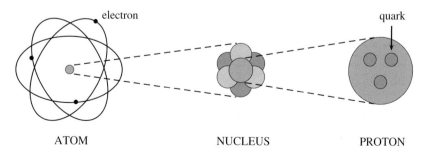

Fig. 4.2 Parts of an Atom

phenomenon, and the randomness is believed to be intrinsic, rather than the result of a lack of enough relevant detailed knowledge.

The probabilistic character of quantum theory is of fundamental importance. It states that however closely one duplicates a situation at the atomic level, the outcome may be different – the theory only predicts the averages over many repetitions. Moreover, this is not a failure of the theory but a consequence of how nature itself is. Enormous efforts have been made to find realistic physical explanations of quantum theory, but in the opinion of most physicists, they involve ideas that are even more bizarre than the problem that they claim to solve.

The attempt to bring order to the growing and chaotic list of elementary particles started in the 1950s and was to be completed in the 1970s. It is a complicated tale, in which the key participants often did not know that they were developing similar ideas. The following account is written with the benefit of hindsight; it only refers to ideas that contributed to the final solution and completely ignores the technical details. It must be borne in mind that the final breakthroughs were not immediately accepted by everyone, and that much painstaking experimental evidence confirming their correctness was produced in subsequent years.

One strand in the new research was the attempt to unify the weak force with the electromagnetic force. Key breakthroughs were made in 1967–8 and led to Nobel prizes for Glashow, Salam, and Weinberg. By 1973 there was a unified theory accounting for the interactions of the four leptons then known – the electron, muon, and their two associated neutrinos. A little later the tau lepton and its associated neutrino were discovered and incorporated into the theory. All six of these particles are point-like – they have no internal structure.

In 1964 Murray Gell-Mann and George Zweig independently proposed that protons and neutrons were not elementary, each of them being composed of three quarks carrying fractional electric charges. They were initially called 'mathematical' by Gell-Mann, and their physical existence was not generally accepted for about ten years. One of the problems was the failure of several attempts to observe fractionally charged particles, now explained by a concept called confinement. In 1967–8 Taylor, Kendall, and Freidman carried out very high energy electron–proton scattering experiments without any commitment to a particular theoretical model. These suggested that protons had some internal structure, and soon afterwards Feynman wrote a paper that described hadrons as being composed of partons, less specific subparticles than quarks. A few years later Fritzsch and Gell-Mann unveiled quantum chromodynamics, a quantum field theory of quarks and gluons that described how quarks interacted; although it had a cool reception initially, by the middle of the 1970s their theory had moved right to the centre of the experimental and theoretical stages.

Subsequently these results were incorporated into the standard model, which unified the electromagnetic, weak, and strong interactions into a single theory that incorporates almost all of our current understanding of particle physics. The only thing missing from the standard model is gravity. A large number of further experiments at CERN and elsewhere have shown that the accuracy of the model goes far beyond what could have been expected when it was first written down. It has survived tests at higher and higher energies and under steadily more extreme conditions. All currently known particles fit into the model, and, conversely, all except one of the basic particles predicted by the model have been observed. Most calculations in quantum chromodynamics are incredibly difficult to perform by traditional methods, but over the last few years direct numerical simulations using the most powerful available computers have started to confirm the main predictions of the theory. The main outstanding problem at currently accessible energies is that the theory requires the existence of a so-called Higgs boson, which has not yet been observed.

The construction of the standard model was driven by the wish to simplify and unify a vast amount of data produced by a range of particle accelerators over several decades. Many different teams and theorists made contributions to the final result, but it was far from being the result of routine data analysis. The whole process was heavily led by theoretical intuitions, a key ingredient in the solution being the use of symmetry. Almost every technical paper in fundamental physics now refers to symmetry groups called $SU(2)$, $SU(3)$, or, recently, more exotic groups such as E_8. Nobody knows why symmetry is so important, but we might never have been able to unify the three forces without using it.

The achievements described above are amazing by any standards. The physicists involved have succeeded in providing a successful description of a whole range of events that occur at scales down to considerably less than one million millionth of those that we can observe directly. It may not be the final description, but that does not detract from its magnitude. There is no a-priori reason why it should have been possible, and a hundred years ago it would have been inconceivable. We may legitimately be astonished that our animal brains, which evolved for quite different reasons, are capable of such a feat. Those of a religious persuasion are left to consider why God has chosen to give us brains that can understand the behaviour of elementary particles, but not that of the weather in a month's time, when both must be equally transparent to him. Those who are not religious face much the same question, but without references to God. Perhaps it is simply extraordinary luck that our brains are configured in a way that made our discoveries possible. Or perhaps the behaviour of elementary particles is in truth fairly simple, but we inevitably consider anything we can only understand after an enormous collective effort as astonishing. We are contingent beings, and trying to explain everything is sometimes futile.

These developments involved close collaborations between theorists and experimentalists. After 1980 a rift between theoreticians and experimentalists slowly developed. (The reader will appreciate that when talking about entire communities, one must necessarily paint with a broad brush.) Many theoreticians started to take the experimental progress for granted, and gradually lost interest in it. Their goal during this second period, which has now lasted for thirty years, has been the unification of the standard model with gravity. This has proceeded very slowly because it is almost impossible to conduct experiments in this field – gravity is so weak that it has no direct influence on what is seen in particle accelerators. Particle physics and gravity were both important in the first few moments after the Big Bang, so it is not surprising that theoreticians and cosmologists are now highly interested in each other's ideas. The best idea of the theoreticians, superstring theory, shot to prominence in 1984 as a result of papers by Michael Green and John Schwarz. It is still far too immature to be called the definitive solution, but the fact that it operates in ten-dimensional space-time, rather than the four dimensions that Einstein taught us about, gives some impression of how exotic this subject is.

String theory is necessarily presented to the general public in a highly impressionistic way, with the result that its real content is invisible. The mathematics involved is extremely challenging, whether one approaches it rigorously or not. Terms such as non-commutative geometry and duality mean as little to many mathematicians as they do to the general public. Nevertheless, theoretical physicists have found totally unexpected ways of carrying out explicit calculations in certain special situations, and the results convince them that they are progressing towards the resolution of problems that have plagued other theories for many decades.

Not everyone is enthusiastic about the prospects of string theory. It needs fundamental new ideas before it can be called a proper part of physics, and there are eminent critics who think that it has failed. Sheldon Glashow, one of those responsible for the standard model, considers that it is not healthy for so many of the brightest theoretical physicists to be committed to the subject to such an extent that they have no real contact with anyone else in the physics community. It is also worrying that some young theorists are doing research in superstring theory because they know that they have few prospects of a permanent position otherwise. There are alternatives, for example quantum loop gravity. It is much less well developed, and far fewer people are working on it, but which is the cause and which the effect is not clear.

4.4   A Philosophical Digression

The last section described the standard model in a completely realist mode, as though there could be no question about the reality of the elementary particles that it describes. If one is a true sceptic about invisibly small entities, then they must be regarded as theoretical constructs. However, there is a huge variety of evidence for the existence of atoms and molecules, and no alternative explanation for 'atomic level' phenomena has emerged over the last century. For almost all scientific purposes it is clear that atoms are here to stay; indeed there is little point in looking beyond them for those interested in biology, chemistry, or solid-state physics. That is not to say that atomic level physics, namely quantum theory, is fully understood. High temperature superconductivity remains an enigma twenty years after its discovery, in spite of its enormous technological potential. The atomic world is astonishingly complex, and is continuing to provide new challenges that may well have profound effects on the course of civilization.

One needs to be more cautious at the next level down, which includes some very elusive entities, such as neutrinos and quarks. We do not have a final theory of everything, and present attempts to create one suggest that reality may be very different from anything that ordinary mortals can visualize. To say that neutrinos and quarks exist in the same straightforward sense as ordinary, visible objects do may be trapping ourselves in a particular type of language simply because we feel comfortable with it. Indeed the mathematics used to study elementary particles already involves terms such as 'resonance' and 'virtual particle', which acknowledge the dramatic difference between quantum theory and our usual ideas about reality. The quantum vacuum is supposed to be full of virtual particles continually appearing and disappearing; its resemblance to the traditional notion of the vacuum as empty space is rather tenuous.

That is not to say that these notions are mere fictions. The twenty four neutrino observation events that accompanied the supernova SN 1987A conformed closely with theory, and there must be a deep reason why the events, at three well separated experimental facilities, coincided with each other and with the explosion of a star that was an almost unimaginable distance away. Similarly the standard model, with its quarks, has successfully explained a huge number of experimental observations in particle accelerators in the thirty years since its formulation. It is also an important ingredient in understanding what happened in the earliest moments of the universe. Its success cannot be mere chance.

As this book is going to press, the Large Hadron Collider (LHC) is being brought into operation in CERN. This monumental machine has taken fifteen years to design and then build and has cost billions of dollars. The thousands of physicists who have devoted large parts of their careers to the task are optimistic that it will lead to a revolution in our understanding of the fundamental constituents of matter, as well as of the earliest moments in the history of the universe. They also hope to find evidence that the known particles have supersymmetric partners, because this would indicate that superstring theory might be proceeding along the right lines. Assuming that the Higgs boson is indeed observed – in the same sense as anything of that tiny size and strangeness can be said to have been observed – the next level of theory, whenever it appears, will need to explain *why* the standard model works so well.

We have already seen this happen with Newtonian mechanics, which can be derived from general relativity under certain special conditions. These relate to medium sized, slowly moving bodies, in other words the everyday world that we are familiar with. The Newtonian model is wrong, particularly in its reliance on action at a distance and its complete separation of space from time, but it nevertheless emerges from more fundamental theories in a manner that explains why it works. It remains a valuable, if partial, picture of the world, alongside other pictures that are more accurate in particular respects at the cost of being considerably more complex. The Newtonian world-view is retained as a part of physics because it works extraordinarily well in a huge variety of important applications. It would be impossible in practice to design a paper clip using general relativity, let alone a steam locomotive. It may be a deeper theory but it is computationally impotent in almost all of the applications that technologists have needed to manage since the nineteenth century. This is unlikely to change.

One concludes that it may be perfectly possible to say that neutrinos and Higgs bosons exist, within the theoretical framework provided by the standard model. That framework is not the last word on the nature of reality any more than Newtonian mechanics was. Nevertheless it will have to be incorporated into any further fundamental theory. As far as most physicists are concerned, saying that quarks are real means only that calculations based on their existence capture observed phenomena so well, that one can be confident that future theories will have to incorporate the standard model *in some manner*. In order to be accepted, they will need to explain why it works, probably by deriving its basic equations as limits of, or approximations to, some more fundamental equations. Many physicists believe that string theory will provide the framework for the next advance, but that still remains to be proved.

Recent scare stories about the possibility that the LHC might produce mini black holes which will devour the Earth provide insight into the mentality of some physicists, as well as of the general public. The reassurance that even if mini black holes are produced they will immediately evaporate because of Hawking radiation is no doubt well meant, but it is also misguided. Hawking radiation is a nice theory and many physicists believe that it is correct, but there is no experimental evidence for it, and relying on it to protect us from such an extreme danger is absurd. Moreover there is a far better argument. The LHC will produce protons with energies of about 10TeV. The Earth is regularly bombarded by cosmic rays, mostly protons, whose energies go up to and occasionally beyond 10 million TeV. In other words we have been hit by particles millions of times more energetic than those produced by the LHC for several billion years, and nothing has happened. Nothing more need be said.

Probing the limits of fundamental physics turns out to be probing the ultimate power of mathematics to explain the world. One does not need to believe as a matter of faith that there are no limits to our intellectual abilities in order to find the enterprise fascinating. Our ignorance of the eventual outcome, indeed of whether there will be one, is a part of what makes the subject so interesting.

4.5 The Multiverse

Until Copernicus introduced his heliocentric theory, it was taken for granted that the Earth was the centre of the universe and that human beings were the most important entities in it. Gradually discoveries have pushed scientists towards the opposite point of view: that the Earth, our solar system and even our galaxy are in no way special, that the universe is more or less homogeneous and that the same laws apply everywhere in it. This is sometimes called the mediocrity principle.

In 1948 Hermann Bondi, Thomas Gold, and Fred Hoyle proposed that the universe is also homogeneous in time, in other words that it is in a steady state, has existed for ever, and has always looked more or less the same as it does now. This was difficult to reconcile with the observed steady expansion of the universe and they had to assume that this was compensated for by the very slow continuous creation of matter in the empty space left by the gradually separating galaxies. Although the (atheistic) authors regarded their theory as metaphysically, and probably also aesthetically, attractive, they realized that it would stand or fall on the basis of its predictions:

> *It is not a point in support of this theory that it contains conclusions for which we might happen to have an emotional preference. Herbert Dingle has quite correctly warned us recently against promoting a theory simply because we happen to like it. The grounds for the acceptance of a theory are its agreement with observation. The grounds for a serious discussion of a theory lie in the possibility of subjecting it to observational test.*[1]

Unfortunately for its authors the discovery of cosmic microwave background radiation in the 1960s provided some of the key evidence that led to the rejection of their steady state model. It is now widely agreed that the universe came into existence about 14 billion years ago in a Big Bang – a term introduced as an insult by Hoyle. However, the growth of the universe in its first fractions of a second is not well understood. The leading explanation, the so-called inflation model, was proposed by Alan Guth in 1981 and has substantial observational support, even though one cannot observe the universe directly until 300,000 years after the Big Bang. The theoretical mechanism behind inflation is still far from well understood, partly because particle physics at such energies is in a very unsatisfactory state.

The progress of astronomy from the time of Copernicus steadily diminished the plausibility of religions based on a God who was particularly interested in the fate of human beings. For some religiously inclined people, the Big Bang theory reverses this trend, by proving scientifically that something analogous to the creation myth in Genesis did indeed happen. However, the connection between a God who created the universe 14 billion years ago and a God who is personally concerned with the lives of individual human beings today is a huge one. If one believes in the latter type of God, it is natural to conclude that he is the same as the former type, but an argument in the reverse direction is hard to construct. Debates about this matter have been intense and wide ranging, even involving appeals to Thomas Aquinas, and it seems safe to say that they are not close to resolution.

The universe is only visible up to a distance of about 14 billion light years, but there is currently no reason to believe that it stops there. Bigger and better telescopes will not help us to see much beyond the current limits, but that does not imply that there is nothing there. On the other hand, it has recently been suggested that if one looks in opposite directions in the sky, there are correlations between the distant fields of galaxies that suggest that the universe is closed, in the same sense as the surface of the Earth is. In other words, the universe has no boundaries but if you travel far enough in the same direction you might eventually arrive back at your starting point from the opposite direction in which you started. This may well be settled within the next ten years or so (but not by making the journey!) but it would be very hard to distinguish between a universe that stretches to infinity in all directions and one that is a hundred times bigger than what we can see with our telescopes.

Before speculating about parts of the universe that we will never observe, it would be nice to understand the part that we can. In 1933 Fritz Zwicky observed anomalies in the motions of galaxies in the Coma Cluster and proposed that they were caused by unseen, or dark, matter. Galactic dynamics is a much more complex field than the motion of the planets in the Solar System, because it involves so many different processes, whose importance may vary from one galaxy to another. Explaining the structure of barred spiral galaxies such as that in Figure 4.3 is a research field in its own right, in which progress has depended on the possibility of large-scale computer simulations.

Zwicky's proposal was initially dismissed, but it provided the possibility of understanding the way in which stars orbit within galaxies,

Fig. 4.3 The Barred Spiral Galaxy NGC 1300 © NASA, ESA, and The Hubble Heritage Team (STScI/AURA), Hubble Space Telescope ACS, STScI-PRC05-01

including the Milky Way. Their speeds do not depend on their distance from the centre in the way that Newtonian mechanics would predict; the discrepancy is large and cannot be explained by known mechanisms. Today, most cosmologists believe that 'normal' matter comprises only five percent or so of 'what is out there', and that dark matter really exists. Its nature is unknown but the particles involved must interact very weakly with normal matter. It has been suggested that neutralinos or axions are involved, but the existence and properties of these particles is conjectural. It is likely that dark matter does indeed exist, but other explanations of the anomalies have also been proposed, such as a modification to Newton's law of gravitation. This is an extreme solution; the law can be deduced using general relativity, and one cannot abandon that theory lightly. It would be foolhardy to say more because the field is developing so rapidly.

The difficulty of explaining galactic dynamics provides another reason for doubting the usefulness of Popper's notion of refutation as the sole arbiter of scientific progress. Something is clearly wrong, but seventy years after Zwicky's discoveries we still do not know whether Newton's law of universal gravitation applies to the movement of stars in galaxies. It may have been refuted, but equally it may be perfectly okay, the problem being the existence of dark matter. As Popper's student Imre Lakatos recognized, scientific theories have to be considered in a much broader context than the simplistic notion of refutation imagines.

If this seems problematical, the nature of dark energy, supposed to comprise three quarters of 'what is out there', is much worse. Its existence is conjectured on the basis of recently discovered anomalies in the rate of expansion of the universe as a whole. Its nature is understood even less than that of dark matter and it may be an inevitable consequence of the final Theory of Everything, if and when that eventually appears.

The existence of dark matter is likely to be resolved within the next decade, but beyond this point the distinction between science, speculation, and even science fiction is harder to determine, and I can only highlight some of the ideas that are being discussed. Readers might wonder why I am putting so much effort into debunking some ideas that are obviously crazy. There are two answers. The first is that it is useful to understand *why* certain proposals that are presented as a part of science actually are not. The second is that some very eminent physicists and cosmologists have made statements which seem to take the ideas seriously.

The difference between those who are willing to indulge in extravagant speculations in public and those who are not might simply be a matter of temperament. Imagination is of vital importance, but Darwin and Newton are not famous because they spread their ideas to all and sundry as soon as they had them. Imagination needs to be tempered by judgement, evidence, and hard toil if it is to be distinguishable from science fiction. Unfortunately, the prospect of becoming famous by publishing a best seller or winning a Nobel Prize puts great pressure on scientists to be the first to air a new idea.

This pressure is very evident in string theory. In its early days (the 1970s), its supporters hoped that they would be able to prove that there was only one viable theory, and that the fundamental constants in that theory would have the values that we observe. This would have provided a complete solution to the fine tuning problem. By 1985 it was generally agreed that there were a few different superstring theories, more than one but still controllable. However, things did not stay that way. Further investigations revealed that the theories were related by what are called dualities, and that they were different aspects of a single higher level theory. However, a vast number of solutions of the string equations, with different fundamental constants, is now believed to exist. The set of all possible solutions is now called the string landscape.

The rest of this section discusses the so-called 'multiverse'. This embodies the tendency of theoretical physicists to endow elements of a mathematical theory with a degree of reality that is even stronger than that envisaged by Plato. The alternative universes considered in the theories are not supposed to exist in a Platonic realm of ideal mathematical forms: they are deemed to exist in as real a sense as our own universe. Max Tegmark, Peter Atkins, and others have taken this idea to its logical conclusion by identifying the physical and mathematical worlds (see page 132). Some others have little sympathy with this attitude, which they regard as pure metaphysics.

The 'multiverse' embraces at least three different scientific theories, all of which need a lot of further development before it will become clear whether they have permanent value. It is also used in a generic way to refer to any theory that assumes that the whole of physical reality is far more extensive than the part we happen to be capable of seeing; the latter is called the (visible) universe. The multiverse has also been used as a vehicle for a metaphysical alternative to religious belief. The various aspects of the subject are regularly mingled with each other in the popular writings of very eminent scientists. The metaphysical side of the debate is an argument against Hoyle's statement that the values of the fundamental constants imply the existence of design in the universe. It is claimed that there exist a large (and possibly infinite) number of entirely different universes, each with its own values of the fundamental constants. Since they have no space-time connections with each other, we cannot observe them directly. The string landscape provides an example of such a multiverse if each solution of the string equations is supposed to correspond to a separate universe. An important issue is whether one should regard the other universes as physically real if it turns out that the multiverse model makes predictions that are confirmed observationally. Steven Weinberg put it this way:

> *The test of a physical theory is not that everything in it should be observable and every prediction that it makes should be testable, but rather that enough is observable and enough predictions are testable to give us confidence that the theory is right.*

He has also pointed out that we believe in quarks on this basis, even though we have never seen one, and never will. He is not sure that the multiverse theory meets this test, but Martin Rees is more confident now than he was in 1979. (It is arguable that his earlier caution was a more appropriate attitude; see page 212.)

> *What we've traditionally called 'our universe' is just a tiny part of something which is infinite, so allows for many replicas of us elsewhere (in our same space-time domain, but far beyond the horizon of our observations), but even that infinite universe is just one element of an ensemble that encompasses an infinity of quite different universes. So that's the pattern adumbrated by cosmology and some versions of string theory. What we have normally called the laws of nature are not universal laws – they're just parochial by-laws in our cosmic patch, no more than that, and a variety of quite different regimes prevail elsewhere in the ensemble.[2]*

Leonard Susskind is strongly committed to the multiverse theory. In 2003 he wrote:

> *What we've discovered in the last several years is that string theory has an incredible diversity – a tremendous number of solutions – and allows different kinds of environments. A lot of the practitioners of this kind of mathematical theory have been in a state of denial about it. They didn't want to recognize it. They want to believe the universe is an elegant universe – and it's not so elegant. It's different over here. It's that over here. It's a Rube Goldberg machine over here. And this has created a sort of sense of denial about the facts about the theory. The theory is going to win, and physicists who are trying to deny what's going on are going to lose. These people are all very serious people. David Gross, for example, is very harshly against this kind of view of diversity. He wants the world to be unique, and he wants string theorists to calculate everything and find out that the world is very special with very unique properties that are all derivable from equations.[3]*

David Gross still hopes (October 2007) that at least some of the fundamental constants might be calculated once we know what string theory actually is, and considers that giving up at this stage is misguided.

The idea that one should ascribe physical reality to all solutions of some equations is not accepted in other branches of physics. If one shakes soap mixture in a bottle one obtains a complex foam composed of bubbles of many different sizes. The variety of possible outcomes is huge, and each outcome has a definite probability, but almost nobody would suggest that when a person shakes such a bottle they thereby turn into many doppelgängers, one for each outcome. Probability theory need not be interpreted this way, and no genuine probabilist does. The standard interpretation is that probability theory is a mathematical model, and that one should start questioning the appropriateness of the model if enough events occur in the real world whose probability is extremely small. If one accepts this way of looking at theories, the quotation from Weinberg might be rewritten as follows:

> *The test of a probabilistic description of the world is not that every element of it should correspond to something that exists physically, but rather that enough of its predictions are confirmed to give us confidence that the description is useful.*

The idea that each of us has many almost identical twins living in parallel worlds originated in the 1950s. It was conceived by Hugh Everett as an alternative to the dominant Copenhagen interpretation of quantum theory, while he was a graduate student at Princeton University. In a nutshell, Everett's many-worlds interpretation of quantum theory is based on the idea that there are many equally real worlds, corresponding to all logically possible sequences of events. As we make observations of the world, we narrow down which one we actually live in, but other versions of ourselves, who observed different things, co-exist in other worlds. Everett's theory is undoubtedly mathematically interesting, but his academic adviser John Wheeler soon came to reject Everett's interpretation, which was removed from the thesis before its acceptance. Most physicists still do not accept the metaphysical aspects of Everett's theory. Murray Gell-Mann, for example, does not believe that there many parallel universes and prefers to refer to 'many alternative histories of the universe...all treated alike by the theory except for their different probabilities'.[4] The distinction between a theory of reality and reality itself is of crucial significance here.

Quantum theory is paradoxical by any standards, but the paradoxes differ from one interpretation to another. Suppose that you open your purse in a shop to pay for a newspaper. According to the standard interpretation of quantum theory there is a *fantastically* small, but nevertheless positive, chance that the coins that you had earlier put into it will have disappeared, jumping by quantum mechanical tunnelling straight into the shopkeeper's till. The probability is so small that you can rest assured that no such event has happened in the history of the universe. On the other hand Everett's theory states that every time you look inside your purse there are two (actually many) equally real copies of you, one of whom finds to your astonishment that your purse is empty. Philosophers, who consider such problems sympathetically, argue that if one believes that both outcomes actually occur one should base one's actions not on probability theory but on what is called rational decision theory.

David Deutsch at Oxford is famous for his work on quantum computation, and considers that most physicists are simply wrong to reject Everett's interpretation.[5] By doing so, he contends, they are abandoning a realistic description of the world and accepting that we should not try to understand what is going on in quantum situations. The problem is that his multiple-worlds explanation seems to most physicists to be even less plausible than others that have been given. Everyone agrees about the observational predictions of quantum theory, and that the quantum world is bizarre, so this is *purely a question of metaphysics*. Deutsch's metaphysics posits shadow photons moving in huge numbers of parallel universes that hardly interact with ours. The conventional alternative is that quantum particles are *radically different* from classical particles: a photon may go through several slits simultaneously, much as a water wave can, and then recombine, provided the experimental set-up does not perturb it during its passage. The interference effects observed when extremely low intensity photon beams pass through double or multiple slits do not involve interference between different photons, but between the phases of different fractions of each photon. If one puts detectors at each of the slits then one does not see fractions of a photon hitting each detector, because photons are not entirely like water waves – they are what are called probability waves, about which one has to develop a new intuition. Yet another explanation of what happens in such experiments was given by David Bohm, but once again it leads to exactly the same predictions – indeed one does *exactly the same mathematical calculations* in all three cases.

One of the best known examples in quantum computation is Shor's algorithm which, *in principle*, allows one to factorize huge numbers far more rapidly than can be done using standard, classical computers. This is an exciting field, but at present nobody has yet managed to produce a quantum computer that can solve any practical problem. Deutsch has laid down the challenge of explaining how Shor's algorithm works within a single-universe world-view.[6] No doubt people have not taken up the challenge because, as he says himself, predicting how the algorithm works is merely a matter of solving a few uncontroversial equations. It is not clear that replacing a routine and elementary mathematical explanation by a very extravagant physical explanation constitutes progress.

If one adopts a pluralistic stance, which Deutsch does not, then one can be fairly relaxed about these different explanations of quantum theory – and others that have been devised. Each of them obviously helps some people while being disliked by others, and all lead to the same predictions. There is simply no need to make a choice between them until some scientific advantage for doing so emerges. Most physicists do not believe that this has happened yet. If the fundamental difficulty is the fact that our brains evolved to deal with events at our own scale, we may never find an intuitive explanation of quantum phenomena.

The dangers of trying to infer the nature of the world from a mathematical theory of it are illustrated by considering the world of finance. One of the great advances in the subject was the development of the Black–Scholes equation, which models prices by using random variables in certain stochastic processes. This theory has been quite successful and important, even though it does not explain the frequency of large deviations from the typical behaviour of the market. The hedge fund LTCM founded by Scholes caused a major financial storm when it collapsed as a result of one such event – the Russian Government's default on their bonds in 1998.

It is clear that no amount of analysis of the Black–Scholes equation could lead anyone to the insight that the world is round, that the market is driven by the activities of human beings, and that it is influenced by factors such as weather and politics. One would rightly not be taken seriously if one claimed that all possible realizations of the financial markets actually exist in different parallel universes. Even stranger would be the suggestion that most of them provide little support for the development of a vibrant civilization, so we should not be surprised that we live in one of the most 'financially interesting' ones.

One is similarly under no compulsion to believe that every string theory solution is physically instantiated – this is an extreme example of the constant temptation to indulge in reification, mentioned on page 133. It was plausible when it was hoped that the theory might have a very small number of solutions. However, the subject now seems analogous to the theory of partial differential equations: it is a new field of mathematical physics that has led to a large number of extremely interesting new conjectures, some of which have been proved by traditional methods. Gross calls it a framework rather than a physical theory. It has the potential to transform physics, but only when used in conjunction with appropriate physical inputs. Which, if any, of the string theory solutions are relevant to physics remains to be determined, but there is no need to suppose that they all are. Nobody supposes that every partial differential equation has physical significance, and there is currently no compelling reason to take a different attitude towards string theory.

Two eminent cosmologists, Paul Steinhardt and Neil Turok, have recently constructed a model in which our universe collides every trillion years or so with another universe.[7] In this model there is no Big Bang, and inflation is replaced by a mechanism which ensures that the cosmological constant and certain other phenomena are as we see them today. This is exciting but controversial research whose fate remains open. The new theory lacks experimental support, but it has the advantage of avoiding appeals to the anthropic principle to explain the astonishingly small value of the cosmological constant. Whatever its fate, it demonstrates that cosmologists are not totally convinced that the current inflationary scenario is correct.

The word 'multiverse' has been used with several other meanings. Instead of many completely separate universes, one might imagine that our own universe is vastly bigger and more diverse than the rather flat and homogeneous part that we can see. It is possible that if one could travel far enough in our universe, one might find regions with quite different values of the fundamental constants. If this is the case, we are bound to find ourselves in the part of the one universe in which the fundamental constants have the value that they do. The problem, as before, is finding any reason to believe that the universe is like this.

We have already considered the possibility that the universe stretches to infinity in all directions. Suppose, in addition, that it is roughly flat and that its basic properties do not change however far away one goes. Under certain assumptions one can prove that at truly unbelievable distances you will have an almost perfect copy, or twin (indeed you will have an infinite number of almost identical twins), doing almost exactly what you are now doing. Nobody pretends that these twins will ever be able to signal their presence – the distances involved are not just much larger than the diameter of the visible universe, but unimaginably larger. The fact that this is a mathematical theorem does not in any way prove that it has any relevance, because the assumptions need not be valid. There can be no scientific justification for extrapolating known laws a hundred or more orders of magnitude beyond what can be observed. For two thousand years everyone wrongly extrapolated from our approximately flat local environment to the belief that the universe was necessarily governed by Euclidean geometry. Descartes 'knew' that atoms could not exist on the basis of general arguments about the nature of space at smaller and smaller scales.

Bondi, Gold, and Hoyle turned out to be wrong when they proposed their steady state universe, conceived on the basis of its metaphysical attractions; a merit of their theory was that it was testable and could be abandoned within twenty years because it failed those tests. On the other hand, current discussions about the various types of multiverse are speculations even when they contain real mathematical calculations. There are few facts to support them – references to what might, *or equally might not*, happen billions or even trillions of years in the future are metaphysics, not physics. The existence of vast numbers of solutions to the string equations is not a rigorously proven fact. Nobody knows what string theory actually is or whether a fundamental new insight will lead to a successor with radically fewer solutions. David Gross hopes so and encourages people to continue looking for it, but others believe, with various degrees of conviction, that we have to accept that this is not likely. When string theory matures or a different successor emerges we may well have to throw most of our current ideas about the world out of the window, as happened with general relativity and quantum mechanics. Of course new and presently unsuspected ideas will replace them, but that is part of the joy of science.

4.6   In Praise of Observation

Astronomy and cosmology involve a mix of theory and observation. In this section we argue that throughout the last century observation was the more important. Theoreticians are extremely clever, and once they have been given some new facts (or inconsistencies between existing theories) they can often find ways to explain (or resolve) them. These can be of great value as a source of new experiments or observations. The weakness of theoreticians is that they can get carried away by their theories and persuade themselves that their theoretical analyses *must* correspond to something in the real world.

The existence of supernovas, the red shift of galaxies, the discovery of pulsars, the existence of gamma ray bursts, and the accelerating expansion of the universe all came out of the blue, before any theoretical prediction. The following examples need more detailed discussion.

Relativity

At first sight Einstein's relativity theory seems to demonstrate the primacy of pure theory. In fact both special and general relativity were created to unify two theories each of which was separately confirmed to high accuracy. In the case of special relativity the problem was the incompatibility of electrodynamics and Newtonian mechanics. General relativity was constructed to unify special relativity and Newtonian gravity. So in both cases the theory was created in response to real problems that demanded some form of resolution. The same applies to current attempts to unify general relativity and quantum theory.

CMBR

The existence of cosmic microwave background radiation was first predicted by Ralph Alpher and Robert Herman in 1948. Several groups rediscovered the idea in the early 1960s, but the CMBR was first observed, inadvertently as background noise, in a very sensitive microwave receiver built in 1965 by Arno Penzias and Robert Wilson at the Bell Telephone Laboratories. No doubt the discovery would eventually have led to the theory if it had not already existed, but conversely, observational tests of the theory were already being planned by Robert Dicke when the discovery by Penzias and Wilson was announced. This seems to be a dead heat between theory and observation. The observations were among those that settled the conflict between the steady state and big bang theories of the universe in favour of the latter.

Black Holes

Black holes provide a striking example of cosmic objects that were predicted long before they were discovered. They correspond to certain solutions of Einstein's equations discovered by Schwarzschild in 1916; Einstein himself always regarded the solutions as being of no interest. The status of black holes changed sharply when Penrose and Hawking started investigating them in the 1960s. It turned out that under certain quite plausible conditions on a region of space-time, either something like a black hole must exist in the region or Einstein's theory must be wrong. This provided a definite reason for taking the black hole solutions seriously, and also suggested that they might be found in regions where the mass density was particularly high, such as the centres of galaxies. Cosmologists now believe that there are black holes at the centres of most, and possibly all, galaxies. The black hole at the centre of the Milky Way has been identified as Sagittarius A*. It is about the same size as our Solar System in spite of being over a million times more massive than our Sun. In spite of convincing evidence for their existence, the physics of black holes is still not well understood, because of the need to take account of quantum effects.

Time Travel (Anyone who is doing research on wormholes is advised to skip this section.)

Since Einstein invented general relativity (GR) many particular solutions of his equations have been investigated in great detail by Schwarzschild, Kerr, Gödel, and others. Some have such bizarre properties that one is tempted to reject them out of hand, but this would lead to a disbelief in black holes. Nevertheless the fact that a few strange solutions of the GR equations have turned out to be physically important does not imply that they all are. There is no evidence that solutions of the GR equations in which it is possible to follow a path that takes one back to one's own past have any physical significance. Such solutions have been popularized by the use of the epithet 'wormhole'.

Hundreds, possibly thousands, of popular articles and science fiction stories have been written about wormholes. They are supposed to be tubes in space-time that allow you to travel backwards in time to prevent some disaster that has already occurred, or possibly to kill your own grandfather. Theory indicates that standard types of wormhole are unstable, so their construction (or continued existence if they are natural) might require the existence of phantom matter, with negative mass and energy.

One reason for studying wormholes is the belief that *any solution of some important set of equations must correspond to a physical phenomenon.* This led Dirac to predict the existence of the positron, a positively charged version of the electron. In spite of his success in this instance, the idea has few merits as a philosophical or scientific principle. Dirac's equation itself is compatible with the existence of electron-like particles with arbitrary positive masses, but in reality only a few such masses correspond to actual particles.

One does not need to invoke human agencies to demonstrate that wormholes lead to physical paradoxes. In Figure 4.4 a ball travelling in a straight line enters a wormhole and returns to an earlier time. It then continues along a straight line to collide with itself, preventing it entering the wormhole in the first place. Note that the vertical axis is time, so inside the wormhole, represented by a part of a circular tube, the ball is moving backwards in time. The paradox, of course, is that if the ball does not enter the

Time

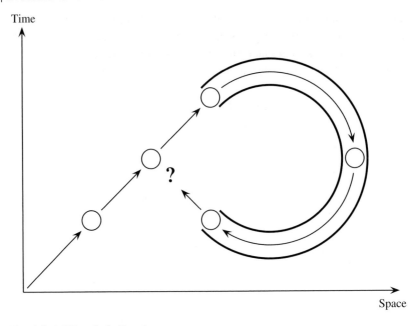

Space

Fig. 4.4 A Wormhole Paradox

wormhole then it could not have gone backwards in time to prevent it doing so. Whether or not one believes in the notion of cause and effect, describing a self-consistent dynamics for the ball seems to be impossible.

Deutsch and others have suggested that one can avoid these paradoxes if the wormhole takes one to a parallel but different universe. This is correct, but it is then not time travel. The person that you might kill is not your grandfather but a different person whose physical similarity to your grandfather depends on the particular parallel universe to which you have travelled. A trip 'back in time' in this sense is similar to the journey of the pilgrims to America in the seventeenth century, with the word 'ship' replaced by 'wormhole'. You arrive at a different place, which may or may not be recognizable to some extent. On Deutsch's interpretation one should ask not only whether wormholes can be manufactured (extremely unlikely in itself), but whether one can arrange for the other end to emerge in a universe that is moderately similar to one's own, but at an earlier stage in its development. Even if this is possible it raises no metaphysical or logical paradoxes.

An argument against the possibility of travelling backwards in time is the fact that we have never met any such travellers. Even if the vast majority of them concealed themselves, even *one person* who was able to show us a bit of sufficiently advanced technology (such as a hand-held device that provided perfect high speed translations between a hundred or so languages) would prove the case. This is not to say that wormholes could not exist, but only that they are extremely unlikely to allow people to travel backwards in time. In the meantime, analyses of wormholes do not merit the public attention that they are getting.

4.7 Machine Intelligence

Before starting this section some comments on machine intelligence might be useful. I first describe some possible developments in this field and then discuss whether the scenarios are realistic.

Present computers are not conscious in any reasonable sense. They can certainly carry out numerical calculations far faster than we can, but they have no understanding of what they are doing. If one asked a ten-year old why counting is useful, one might get a variety of answers, but there is no way of asking a normal computer the same question, let alone hoping to get an answer. There are computer-based systems that can respond in an apparently sensible manner to a limited range of questions, but it is easy to detect their lack of real understanding.

Maxwell Bennett and Peter Hacker have argued that considering the possibility of computer consciousness is simply a misuse of language, or at best a potentially confusing figure of speech. They consider that psychological terms such as remember, calculate, think, and believe cannot be applied to parts of the brain, let alone to computers; they can only refer to an entire person.[8] On the other hand Justin Sytsma has recently argued that the primary meanings of words should be decided by evidence rather than conceptual analysis. His surveys show that most people consider that computers can actually carry out calculations, rather than merely produce displays that we interpret as calculations. In the absence of any method of resolving the philosophical disagreements about computer consciousness, he considers that such surveys must have some significance.[9]

One is not compelled to resolve such questions by philosophical arguments or even to agree that there is a logical distinction between literal and figurative language. We designed computers and wrote their programs, which have structures reflecting our own conscious thought processes, so it would be perverse not to acknowledge this when referring to their operation. The issue is not whether it is philosophically or linguistically justified to use such psychologically loaded terms; it is *pragmatically impossible* for us to understand how computers function and why they are useful if we confine ourselves to the language of circuits, transistors, and electric currents.

There is a temptation to use the language of emergent phenomena in this situation, by saying that conscious behaviour emerges from electronic circuitry that is sufficiently complex. However, the word 'emergence' has different implications for different people, and it is safer to say only that it is *convenient for us* to use two types of language, one when discussing the electronic circuitry in computers and the other when describing the uses to which they are put. Making references to computers calculating or remembering data is a strategy that we choose to adopt, because we find it helpful; it does not imply that computers themselves have two natures.

At present we have very little understanding of our own minds. The problem is made much more difficult by the huge diversity of our personalities and abilities. The difference between our capacities and those of chimpanzees is enormous even though our brains are only about three times larger than theirs. The most important difference anatomically is the size of our neocortex, and functionally it is our possession of language. These are obviously related, but almost all the details remain to be revealed. The complexity of the task is staggering – our brains contain approaching a trillion neurons, but the number of interconnections dwarfs that.

The gross anatomy of the brain has been understood for many decades, but at a more detailed level much remains to be revealed. The results do not reveal nearly as much about its functioning as one might have hoped. Real progress on the latter problem is less than twenty years old, and has depended on the development of a variety of brain scanners. Some of these can show which areas of the brain are active when one engages in a particular mental activity. Thousands of research papers in neuroscience are being published every year and activity in the field is still increasing rapidly.

There are also an increasing number of attempts to produce accurate simulations of small parts of the brain using highly parallel computer architectures. The Blue Brain Project, to produce a computer model of ten thousand neurons of a mammalian brain with all their interconnections is testing computer technology to its limits, but this is an insignificant fraction of what is in our brains. Progress in this field will depend on advances in computer technology, and in particular on the continued validity of Moore's law – that computer power doubles about every two years. This has held true for over half a century, but presumably must stop at some stage.

The above developments have turned the study of consciousness from a branch of philosophy into a rapidly growing field of experimental science. In spite of grossly exaggerated claims in the past, one can reasonably expect that machines will exhibit something indistinguishable from true intelligence within fifty years. This might seem a long time, but it is typical for the development of a mature technology from the first breakthroughs. By the end of this century it might be possible to construct something similar to a human brain in silicon – or whatever is used at that time.

It is advisable to use the phrase 'machine intelligence' instead of 'artificial intelligence' because the latter term is usually taken to refer to expert systems, which follow detailed rules of inference that have been devised by human experts. Although the computer Deep Blue beat the world's best human chess player Garry Kasparov, it was an expert system, programmed by human beings and incorporating their understanding in algorithms about whose significance it knew precisely nothing. We do not refer to an autopilot that is capable of landing an airliner as conscious because we know that its capabilities are constrained to some carefully specified situations in which it has precise instructions about how to behave.

For machine intelligences to convince us that they are aware they would have to be able to interact with the world in an open-ended manner, as do animals. We do not doubt that a cat that plays with a mouse or frog is genuinely conscious and should have no more doubts about a machine that exhibits appropriate behaviour. If machine intelligences develop self-awareness, at a pragmatic level there will also be no doubt that this has happened. The machines will be able to defend their own existence as independent intelligences as coherently and convincingly as we can. The legal and moral problems raised by such entities will make debates about human rights, cloning, and abortion seems tame by comparison. The really big questions will arise when they surpass us in intelligence, as will presumably happen – there is no reason why machines should be limited to our own level of intelligence, set by the sizes of our brains.

Here are objections to the above scenario.

- The time scale may be much too optimistic. It may actually take hundreds of years before they can be constructed; however, this makes no difference to the issues raised.
- There may be a world-wide decision to stop the development of superintelligent machines. The problem here is that the benefits of using them and allowing them to communicate with each other will be enormous. Any nation or group that evades such controls as might be set up will

soon dominate the world economically. It is implausible that no such group will ever succeed.

- The cost of producing such machines will be so great that it will not be worthwhile. This seems unlikely: so far, every new development in computer technology has been pursued energetically because its benefits far outweigh its perceived costs.

- Computer viruses may develop even more rapidly than computers, and may limit their possible development. This might be solved by providing each individual machine with a vast amount of read-only software, and adopting a much more rigorous attitude towards their operation. The problem is not that avoiding viruses is impossible, just that it diverts resources from things that seem to be more desirable.

- Alternative technologies involving machine enhancement of human powers may be preferable. This is very plausible, but the end result may not be so different. The biological part of a sufficiently enhanced human being might be so small a fraction of the total system that the rest might decide to replace it by something faster or more reliable.

- There may be an irreducible human spark that will prove to be incapable of being reproduced in silicon. This would be a discovery that would shake Western science to its foundations, and it is not logically impossible. We can face it when we find out how far computer technology can be pushed.

- One could argue that machines that appear to exhibit conscious behaviour are in fact zombies. Logically this position is unassailable, but it is also logically possible (for anyone who is female) to argue that all males are zombies and that genuine self-awareness depends on having two X chromosomes. In the real world we accept that people of both genders are self-aware on the basis of convincing external evidence, namely their behaviour.

- Intelligent machines might not have many of the characteristics that make us human. For example our sense of humour may be a biologically determined way of coping with internal conflicts caused by our limited mental capacities, and our fear of death may be the result of not being able to download our essential characteristics to a safe place on a regular basis. If this is so, machine intelligences might consider us prisoners of our biology, while we might find them emotionally cold.

- The thought processes and motivations of very advanced machines might be incomprehensible to us, just as ours must be to chimpanzees. They might regard most of our problems as irrelevant in the light of considerations that we cannot hope to understand.

This last objection is no joke. One only has to think of our own inability to agree about basic questions such as whether early stage embryos have rights and whether it makes sense to talk about a God who 'is not a member of any class of existent beings' (see page 219). Machine intelligences, like aliens, would differ from ourselves in profound respects related to their own physical natures.

4.8   Simulated Universes

In this section we enter the area of science fiction. The ideas presented here are bizarre, but so are the concepts in quantum theory. The idea that a molecule as large as C_{60}, composed of sixty atoms of carbon in a spherical ball, might be able to move from one place to another by two different routes, simultaneously, would be laughed out of court were it not for the fact that the experiment has been done and the standard explanation of the result involves precisely that. Quantum theory is as weird as any subject on Earth, but it has been retained in spite of that, not because of it. After decades of looking for a theory that would describe the behaviour of atoms, some people were prepared to accept anything that worked. Others, including Einstein, were not, but they were not able to provide an alternative. The ideas below start with plausible conjectures about our future development, but move far beyond the possibility of experimental tests. Their only merit is that they are not intrinsically impossible.

John Barrow

The existence of many universes with different properties is positively tame when compared with theories involving super-civilizations. John Barrow has written:

> It has long been recognized that technical civilizations, only a little more advanced than ourselves, will have the capability to simulate universes in which self-conscious entities can emerge and communicate with one another. They would have computer power that differed from ours by a vast factor.[10]

His paper discusses how we might be able to tell that we exist only as simulations in one of these computers, declaring, 'Firstly, the simulators will have been tempted to avoid the complexity of using a consistent set of laws of Nature in their worlds when they can simply patch in realistic effects.' He concludes:

> *In this kind of situation, logical contradictions will inevitably arise and the laws in the simulations will appear to break down now and again. The inhabitants of the simulation – especially the simulated scientists – will occasionally be puzzled by the experimental results they obtain. The simulated astronomers might, for instance, make observations that show that their so-called constants of Nature are very slowly changing. It's likely there could even be sudden glitches in the laws that govern these simulated realities.*

These passages make far too many assumptions about hypothetical civilizations to be convincing. One must first ask the intention of the super-civilizations in creating the simulated universes. If they are interested in investigating the laws of physics then they will not achieve anything by 'patching in realistic effects'. Glitches (i.e. the need to reset the initial conditions) only become necessary if one needs to adjust a simulation to some external reality or to some desired scenario. If, on the other hand, the simulators are interested in the development of societies, then they could stop the simulation at the level of our Solar System (or galaxy) without any consequences before the start of the seventeenth (or twentieth) century. Why should they bother to include simulations of the rest of the universe?

Barrow does not mention the possibility that a civilization that has such computers will not find it hard to stop the inhabitants of the simulation from noticing its inadequacies. If one accepts his basic premise then, presumably, we have not already noticed or been informed that we are living in a simulation because they do not want us to know this. This being the case, they can simply feed anything they want directly into our (simulated) brains so that evidence of their existence never comes to our attention. Or they can rerun the program whenever one of its 'inhabitants' notices an inconsistency, deleting the 'inappropriate' memories of the person involved.

Another, although much less enjoyable, way of attempting to discover whether one lives in an imperfect simulation would be to walk around a library and randomly pick books off the shelves to find out whether they contain anything within their covers. Or one could walk around inspecting dustbins (trash cans) to discover whether the contents are what would be expected if the people living there were real people. The film *The Truman Show* reveals as much about simulations of reality as the 'scientific' articles do.

A final objection to the suggestion that our world may be a simulation, is its extraordinary similarity to religious descriptions of the world. In the religious case God maintains the rule of physical law in the world that he created; in the other the super-civilization does the same. In the religious case, God occasionally provides evidence of his existence by performing miracles; in the second the same happens inadvertently because of unavoidable glitches. The main difference is that God is supposed to have a moral concern for his creation, but super-civilizations are driven to create their simulated universes by curiosity or some other benefit to themselves. A disturbing aspect of the super-civilization scenario is that one can only be attracted to it if one is willing to believe that we are being deliberately deceived about everything in our perceived reality. Either hypothesis about the nature of our world might be true, but we will only discover this if the relevant creator chooses to reveal himself; in both cases it is argued that he has good reasons for not doing so. If one were forced to make a choice, religion wins, because there are many claims that miracles do sometimes occur and no observations of glitches. It is interesting that one known breakdown of physical law, the singularities in general relativity associated with black holes, is not put forward as evidence that our world has been designed by a super-civilization that is not sufficiently concerned to get the details right; it is correctly considered to indicate that our understanding of nature is not yet sufficiently deep.

Nick Bostrom

The Oxford Concise Dictionary gives five slightly different definitions of the word 'simulation' but most include words such as 'imitate, counterfeit, not genuine'. If we are one day able to construct computers that are as complex as our own brains and use similar processes for coming to decisions, they may be conscious in the same sense as ourselves or they may be zombies, behaving appropriately but lacking genuine consciousness. The fact that we could turn off their power supplies is no more relevant than the fact that we can kill people by shooting them. The possibility of duplicating a computer personality by copying the relevant 'personality files' from one computer to another one has no analogue for people, just as producing a new person by biological methods would not be possible for computers. Such issues do not determine whether something is genuine.

It is impossible to have a serious discussion about the possibility of consciousness in computers without knowing what consciousness is. This problem is made more difficult by the fact that octopuses appear to be conscious even though their brains are organized in a completely different manner from ours and evolved independently. Some people consider that any sufficiently complex object that responds as though conscious, actually is conscious, and that any other attitude is simply obfuscation. Others, such as the philosopher John Searle believe just as firmly that computers cannot possibly be conscious, however well they simulate the true phenomenon. A third position is that consciousness arises in *people* as the result of a particular type of neural structure in their brains that we have not yet identified, but that consciousness is not a property of the *brain* itself.[11] If computers cannot be conscious, then arguments that we may be living in computer simulations do not get off the ground. In order to continue the argument we will temporarily adopt the position that all *appropriately designed* and sufficiently complex computers are genuinely conscious.

In 2003 Nick Bostrom posed the following mutually exclusive and exhaustive possibilities:[12]

- the human species is very likely to go extinct before reaching a 'posthuman' stage;
- any posthuman civilization is extremely unlikely to run a significant number of simulations of their evolutionary history (or variations thereof);
- we are almost certainly living in a computer simulation.

While not choosing between them he argues that one of these must be correct. In a later paper he emphasizes that his 'view is that we do not currently have strong evidence for or against any of the particular disjuncts.' The next few paragraphs describe some plausible arguments in support of the second item in the list. My deeper intention, however, is to suggest that attempts to predict the behaviour of an extremely advanced civilization are futile. How successful would a futurologist living in 1500 have been in describing our society?

Future civilizations may be able to run extremely sophisticated simulations of human society, but they will have to choose between a variety of subjects to which they can devote their resources. Their own societies will be incredibly complex, simply because they possess such sophisticated computer resources, and realistic simulations of their own societies will be extremely hard for them, for the same reason as the construction of economic models of our society is hard for us. Even quantum computers, if they ever materialize, will not easily simulate a society containing many other computers of that type. It is easy to believe that future societies will put most of their effort into improving their own lot, as we do, and not into examining their distant past.

There might well be historians who will want to delve into the past and who will use simulations to do so. It is reasonable to suppose that our descendants will have reached a stable population and that the number of historians at any time will be more or less constant. They will have to decide what period they wish to study. It is not plausible that a significant proportion of them over a long period would be interested mainly in the twenty-first century. Indeed most may well be interested in the century immediately before their own, when events had the most immediate consequences for themselves. If we assume that a half of all historians at a particular time study the previous century, a quarter the century before that, and so on backwards in a geometric progression, then it is quite possible that our own period would never be studied. This depends on the length of time before it becomes possible to make simulations of entire global civilizations, including the thoughts of, and interactions between, all of the individuals in them and the effects of all of their technological innovations.

The final possibility in Bostrom's list is that future civilizations repeatedly simulate the entire evolution of our species from, say, a million years ago. He introduces a formula, one component of which is the 'average number of ancestor-simulations run by a posthuman civilization'. How such simulations are to be produced is not spelled out. Throwing computational resources at the problem is hopeless, unless and until we have far more information about the distant past than we can currently imagine. In particular we would have to know whether there have been any significant changes in the wiring of our brains over the last hundred thousand years. Currently we have next to nothing on which to base realistic simulations, and only an extreme optimist would believe that anything useful could come out of such a programme of research.

Even if we did one day have a detailed knowledge of what the society of our very distant ancestors was like, the simulations might need such frequent corrections to keep them on the desired course, that it is quickly realized that they do not provide any useful information. We know that such chaotic effects exist in many physical situations (e.g. weather forecasting), and it is almost certain that they apply to anything as complex as the development of civilization. One can try to persuade oneself that the limits of chaos will be transcended by future computers, but everything we know about chaotic systems suggests that this cannot happen.

A different objection to repeated large-scale simulations of our evolutionary history may be based on Julia Driver's 'Artificial Ethics', in the 'Matrix' website. If computer mentalities can be genuinely conscious then it would be a moral crime to annihilate them when they have ceased to be of interest to the creators. Those who actually create such entities and have extended interactions with them would presumably come to feel the same much more strongly. By assuming that our descendants will be happy to delete large numbers of genuinely conscious and intelligent computer personalities as soon as they have served their purpose, we are also assuming that our moral senses are much more highly developed than theirs will be.

I am not arguing that any of the above scenarios are correct, only that they are not obviously impossible. With a little imagination one can find alternatives to any scenario about the future. The development of knowledge ultimately depends on facts, and these are noticeably absent when people discuss the future development of civilization.

Barry Dainton

The essay 'Innocence Lost' by Barry Dainton extrapolates from developments in computer technology that are already taking place. Dainton points out that computers comparable in power to the human brain may exist within a few decades. Within a century there could be more machine consciousnesses than human beings. More disturbingly those machines could be led to believe that they were in fact human beings, by being fed data of an appropriate type.

This is only one of several possibilities discussed by Dainton, who presents his arguments with some care. He envisages the possibility that people will take virtual reality holidays to the twenty-first century in which some of their memories will be suppressed in order to render the holidays fully convincing. If this happens then we might be experiencing simulations of the twenty-first century while actually living in the distant future. He raises the possibility that:

> *even if reality is much as it seems, there is a significant likelihood that our current consciousness is simulated. Having to live with this knowledge may well be part of the normal lot of technologically advanced conscious beings the universe over. When this realization fully dawns on our descendants, attempting to recapture their lost innocence by imposing restrictions on simulatory practices will very likely strike them as futile. Since any restrictions on simulation creation can always be lifted subsequently, it will be obvious that their imposition would offer only meagre protection against the menace of simulation.*

It is impossible to prove that this scenario is false. It may be correct – we have no evidence to make a judgement either way. Dainton attempts to quantify the number of future simulations of twenty-first century lives, but his numbers are not convincing: they assume for example that the human race remains interested in this century for ten thousand generations (up to a million years). Perhaps future generations will quickly realize that their own world is much more interesting than ours. If we think about our own past we see that anyone who spent a few weeks living a virtual life as a medieval peasant would not be likely to recommend the experience to their friends. (This may be particularly true for women.) We think that our lives are much richer than those of our remote ancestors, but by comparison with those of our descendants they may seem very unpleasant and dull. Spending a substantial part of one's life in traffic jams or packed trains is not obviously the kind of thing that our descendants will feel they have to experience for themselves. Nor is living for years in a refugee camp in Africa. Or are we to suppose that only the simulations of highly successful individuals will be conscious, while the rest are cardboard characters only included to fill out the picture?

4.9 Discussion

The standard model of the 1970s synthesized and unified a vast amount of experimental data. It has been one of the great successes of modern physics. Attempts to unify it with general relativity have not yet borne fruit, partly because the expected unification would only be relevant at energies far beyond any that one can achieve in a laboratory. Superstring theory is mathematically very appealing, but it has not yet matured and has not proved that it can solve this problem. The main weakness of the standard model, that it does not explain the values of the fundamental constants, led to speculations involving so-called anthropic principles. Some people regard these as pointless while others call them intriguing. One outgrowth of this, the multiverse theory, may turn out to have real scientific merits in spite of the explosion of bizarre speculations that it has spawned.

The idea that our sense impressions might not mirror the nature of the real world is not new. Indeed Descartes recognized that there was no purely logical way out of this dilemma; he resolved the problem by accepting the existence of a transcendent God who, embodying all perfections in himself, would not create deliberate and systematic deceptions. The development of science depends on some such assumption. The scientific outlook may be fundamentally flawed, but it has been extraordinarily successful over the last five centuries, as measured by our ability to control our environment and to explain its detailed behaviour.

Postulating super-civilizations solves none of the problems associated with our existence. It simply transfers the decision to create our universe from a conventional religious deity to a super-civilization. The main difference between these is that a deity is usually supposed to have a particular interest in our moral well-being, and this is not acceptable to some physicists. There is no evidence that we are simulations, and never will be unless those supposedly responsible for the simulations want us to discover this. The fact that some scientists are willing to spend so much time on idle speculations may unwittingly encourage those who think that the pursuit of scientific knowledge is not worthwhile. If scientists talk about their subject in a frivolous manner, the public may come to believe that resources should be transferred to others who will make better use of them.

Notes and References

[1] Hoyle, F. (1955). *Frontiers of Astronomy*, p.353. Heinemann, London.

[2] Rees, M. (May, 2003). In the Matrix. *Edge*, 116.

[3] Susskind, L. (December, 2003). The Landscape. *Edge*, 130.

[4] Gellman, Murray (1994). *The Quark and the Jaguar*, p.138. Little, Brown and Co.

[5] Deutsch, D. (1997). *The Fabric of Reality*, Chapters 2,13. Penguin Books, London.

[6] Deutsch (1997), p.217.

[7] Stenhardt, Paul J. and Turok, Neil (2006). Why the cosmological constant is small and positive, *Science* **312**, 1180–3.

[8] Bennett, M. *et al.* (2007). *Neuroscience and Philosophy*. Columbia Univ. Press, New York.

[9] Sytsma, J. (2009). The Proper Province of Philosophy: Conceptual Analysis and Empirical Investigation. *Review of Philosophy and Psychology*, to appear.

[10] Barrow, J. (2007). Living in a simulated universe. In Bernard Carr, ed. *Universe or Multiverse?*, pp. 481–6. Camb. Univ. Press.

[11] Hacker, P. M. S. and Bennett, M.R. (2008). *History of Cognitive Neuroscience*. Wiley-Blackwell, Oxford and Malden, Mass.

[12] Bostrom, N. (2003). Are you living in a computer simulation? *Phil. Quarterly* **53**, no. 211, 243–55.

5
Science and Religion

⸺◦◦◦⸺

> We must learn to live with the fact that some
> disagreements cannot be resolved.

5.1 Introduction

In the last chapter we have seen that philosophical assumptions have had
a strong influence on physicists' thoughts about the origin and nature of
the universe, particularly with respect to the existence of a multiverse. The
repeated use of the word 'realism' in the popular works of scientists frequently goes along with unstated assumptions about what is or is not a
realistic point of view; it is often taken as axiomatic that the writer is a
realist and that his/her adversary must therefore be misguided. The beliefs
of scientists range from 'mere' Platonism to a wide variety of explicitly
religious (or anti-religious) beliefs. We also saw, on page 75, that one
cannot understand the historical development of Christianity without reference to St. Augustine, and cannot understand St. Augustine without
reference to Plotinus and Plato. The inclusion of a chapter on religious
belief is therefore justified, both by its often uneasy relationship with
science, and by the fact that it is the third refuge of Platonism, a central
theme in this book.

If one walks into Blackwell's bookshop in Oxford, one discovers that it
has on sale several thousands of books on theology and religion. Many of
these contain sections on the supposed conflicts between science and religion. Strict limits therefore have to be imposed before one can attempt to
say anything worthwhile. It is also vital to recognize the fundamental disagreements about the answers to important religious questions, and even
about what the relevant questions are. John Hedley Brooke described the
problem as follows:

There is no such thing as the relationship between science and religion. It is what different individuals and communities have made of it in a plethora of different contexts. Not only has the problematic interface between them shifted over time, but there is also a high degree of artificiality in abstracting the science and the religion of earlier centuries to see how they were related.[1]

Take, for example, Descartes. He regarded his mechanical philosophy as embedded in his general religious beliefs about the relationship between God and man. Unfortunately it proved only too easy for others to break his link between body and soul and to use his mechanical philosophy in support of their own beliefs. His system led eventually to reductionism and materialism. Newton suffered a similar fate. He spent as much of his life pursuing his (heretical) religious beliefs as he did on physics. The General Scholium of *Principia* shows that he regarded the Sun, planets, comets, and stars as having been designed by God, who did not subsequently need to act on them, although he was omnipresent. Within a century some regarded Newton's laws as providing a complete account of the motion of the planets and needing no reference to God. The growth of knowledge during the seventeenth century and later, gradually forced people to specialize in particular fields of science and led to the separation of science from theology. The idea that these deal with different *types* of question is now frequently considered to be self-evident, but it was not always so. Religious fundamentalists still do not accept this, and for that reason are frequently derided by those who consider them not to have absorbed the lessons of the last three centuries of scientific progress.

This chapter does not attempt to chart the changes in beliefs over the ages, but focusses on some present-day attitudes towards science and religion. Even this is a Herculean task, but it should not be assumed that the debate has become more sophisticated as time has passed. The increasingly bitter disputes about Darwin's theory of evolution in the USA often ignore two other major issues that occupied people in the nineteenth century. The first was the systematic study of geological strata and the fossils that they contained, which started late in the eighteenth century. These made the creation story in Genesis wholly implausible if taken literally, particularly after the discovery of radioactivity made it possible to provide absolute, as opposed to relative, dating of the strata. Independently, the growth of Higher Criticism – the detailed analysis of the Bible considered as a series of historical texts – caused immense controversy. It developed rapidly in the nineteenth century in Germany, but had been anticipated by one of the earliest rationalist philosophers, Baruch Spinoza, in his *Tractatus Theologico-Politicus*, published in 1670. Its growth made it increasingly difficult to represent the New Testament as an account of actual events by eye witnesses. During the twentieth century many mainstream theologians reacted to this by focussing increasingly on the ethical and spiritual messages in the Bible, or by emphasizing the value of myth, considered as something beyond rational analysis.

In the physical sciences some of those who profess no religious belief create substitutes that provide them with some type of comfort. We have seen that pure mathematicians may declare themselves to be Platonists, while physicists may prefer to believe in multiple parallel universes than in a creator God. To those who do not share their beliefs, it is apparent that they are of a metaphysical character and that both depend on assigning mathematics a mystical status. Such beliefs cannot be proved wrong, but their nature should be recognized. The same applies to religion. Our task cannot be to prove or disprove the tenets of some or all religions by scientific analysis. One can simply try to understand why people have the beliefs that they do and examine their internal consistency and relevance to the ethical problems that scientific advances are posing.

What people write about religious belief is so heavily influenced by their own background that I should reveal my own. My father was raised in a strict Baptist community in the Welsh valley town of Tredegar, where damnation was preached regularly. He abandoned his faith as an adult, and I was brought up in a non-religious atmosphere. Unsurprisingly I was an atheist as a teenager, although I have moved towards humanism since then. This chapter is the result. It expresses my dissatisfaction with what both scientists and theologians write about religion. Scientists have the responsibility to investigate the vast size, age, and diversity of the universe, and the growing unity of our knowledge about it, just as religious leaders have the duty to acknowledge these. Several of the scientists mentioned below have been awarded the Templeton Prize, given for insights or discoveries about spiritual realities. I am not persuaded that the depth of their insights bear comparison with those of Nobel Prize winners.

Humanists, as exemplified by Confucius and Socrates, have two characteristic beliefs. The first is that they do not accept statements or values based solely upon authority, but seek evidence before coming to judgements. In particular they support the scientific enterprise. The second, perhaps even more important, is that humanists endeavour to improve themselves morally and to have compassion for all other people, not because of an expectation of reward in some future life, but for their own sake. Some humanists share the Confucian optimism that people are essentially virtuous – except to the extent that they have suffered evil influences during their lives. Although they do not accept supernatural views of reality, their beliefs are compatible with those of certain religious sects. The distinction between humanism and atheism may seem small to some people, but it is vital. Humanism makes positive statements about human values, whereas atheism is merely the assertion that there is no God. Whether atheism is a quasi-religious belief or a rejection of religious belief is not an interesting question. More important is that, unless supplemented by some other beliefs, it provides no support for ethical behaviour, leaving those committed to it alone drifting in an ocean in which every action is equal in value to every other action. Humanism is usually regarded as a secular movement, but it shades into religious humanism and then Unitarianism. Many of the criticisms of traditional dogmas presented below would be accepted by many Unitarians.

This chapter considers how to describe the religious world-view and asks whether it is compatible with the scientific world-view that drives Western society at present. The first question is hard enough, because theologians admit that they have not been able to provide a comprehensive definition of religion. This being so, the answer to the second question depends on the particular religion that one is considering.

There is another, easier question. Why do people disagree so vehemently about religious issues? Almost everything written about this subject is an attempt to justify the beliefs of the writer and to point out the errors of others *when viewed from the writer's own point of view.* Maybe this is inevitable: if you truly believe in your own world-view, you cannot easily entertain a radically different one. However, if you genuinely try to find out why another person, of considerable intelligence, holds the beliefs that he (or equally she) does, you might hope to identify issues that they can be persuaded to reconsider – or that you might want to consider. The alternative to patient discussion is confrontation, often by a mixture of tendentious arguments and ridicule. Its goal is not to change the views of the opponent, but to persuade others that your opponent's beliefs do not deserve any sympathy. In some situations it may lead to social or even legal discrimination. It hardly ever leads to the disappearance of the opponent's belief system, least of all in a religious context.

Many of those who criticize religious faith present parodies of what moderate religious people actually believe. In order to avoid this trap, I have based my comments about Christianity on extensive quotations of people who must be regarded as mainstream authorities in their fields. I do not pretend to agree with everything that they have written, but disagreement is quite different from misrepresentation, and there is plenty of the latter on record. I readily admit I have not absorbed the full range of theological literature, but if eminent theologians cannot agree about basic aspects of their belief systems, the onus is on them to do better rather than on me to read everything that they have written. When reading apologetic works, one quickly realizes that they are usually directed at believers who wish to be reassured that their beliefs are reasonable; an outsider may therefore see the flaws in weakly constructed arguments more easily than those who share the beliefs of the writer.

A Definition of Science

Science can be described fairly precisely. Indeed we can enlist the help of the lawyers, because of a trial in the USA about whether creation science is indeed science. The following is taken from the ruling of Judge Jones in the 'Intelligent Design' trial in Dover, Pennsylvania, 2004:

> Since [the seventeenth century], science has been a discipline in which testability, rather than any ecclesiastical authority or philosophical coherence, has been the measure of a scientific idea's worth. In deliberately omitting theological or 'ultimate' explanations for the existence or characteristics of the natural world, science does not consider issues of 'meaning' and 'purpose' in the world. While supernatural explanations may be important and have merit, they are not part of science. This self-imposed convention of science, which limits inquiry to testable, natural explanations about the natural world, is referred to by philosophers as 'methodological naturalism'.[2]

Judge Jones's description of science is very close to the views of the USA National Academy of Sciences, to which he refers several times. Nevertheless, it must be admitted that scientists sometimes make prophetic statements that are far in advance of what is testable. An obvious example, already discussed, was Kepler's declaration that the planets were ordinary material bodies that obeyed the same physical laws as bodies on the Earth. The laws governing the motion of Earthly bodies were largely unknown at the time, and his prophecy was not to be proved correct for almost eighty years, by Newton. Routine science may be systematic, but mould-breaking ideas are often not.

One of the fundamental aspects of scientific thinking is that it does not depend upon the opinions or beliefs even of its greatest heroes – such as Newton and Darwin. Their monumental books are important to historians of science, but not to scientists. Their theories have both developed, indeed have been modified, in ways that they did not anticipate. We admire them for starting entirely new lines of thought that have proved immensely fruitful, but believe what they wrote, to the extent that we do, because we ourselves can independently test their claims. Unfortunately science also has authoritarian aspects, because of the expense and training needed to understand and test its theories. In spite of this, one of the guaranteed ways of obtaining a Nobel Prize is to prove that an established and important theory is wrong – the more established the better. The culture thrives on disagreement, rather than on attempts to suppress it. The few exceptions to this openness are mostly in medicine, where incorrect science has sometimes persuaded the public to refuse treatments that would have saved many lives.

The goal of scientific research is the production of theories that yield successful predictions and understanding of a wide range of phenomena. These are always provisional, in the sense that they may need to be revised at some time in the future, but this does not mean that they are no more than stories that scientists find plausible. Newton's theory of gravitation was revised by Einstein, but it is still used for calculating the orbits of planets, comets, and space probes, and yields extremely accurate results. The myth that it is easy to produce several plausible general theories that explain observations equally well is completely false – it may take decades of intensive effort to produce even one. Philosophers may point out that this statement depends on providing clear criteria for plausibility, but this is rarely a genuine problem in scientific contexts.

The Nature of Religion

Religion is a much harder concept than science. Indeed theologians seem to agree that it is impossible to provide a definition of religion that applies to everything from Scientology and Buddhism to Marxism. We will find it useful to divide religious belief into the following *very tentative* categories. Many of the statements in this section are sweeping generalizations: Christianity, Islam, and Judaism all contain many sects with radically different views about fundamental aspects of their religion and the importance of various rituals. Arguments about these internal differences are often more vehement than are discussions between people with different religions.

Some Categories of Religious Belief

- Beliefs that are of a religious character but lack specific ritual or other content, for example some forms of pantheism. These are more common than one might expect among scientists.
- The belief that there is no conflict between science and religion because the two involve unrelated spheres of discourse – facts and ethics. Gould calls them non-overlapping magisteria (NOMA).

- The belief that science and religion overlap substantially, and that the two will eventually be reconciled and support each other without compromising either.
- Fundamentalism. This claims that some particular religious tradition contains the full truth. When other beliefs conflict with it, they are simply wrong and vigorous objections to them are justified.

People usually belong to a religion because of the community and social environment in which they were raised. As a result, some defences of particular religions and sects are undoubtedly based on familiarity more than on rational considerations. There are those who believe that all religions are different routes to the same God, but others equally sincerely claim that their own religion has an exclusive access to the truth. In the next few paragraphs I list a few of the differences between some of the major world religions, without making any attempt to be comprehensive. Some might regard these as evidence of the richness of human culture, but they also provide evidence of fundamental disagreements. Unfortunately there is little evidence that these are being resolved with the passage of time; indeed some would say that the tensions between the major religions are worse than they were some decades ago. This is partly due to the news media, which spread bad news around the world very rapidly and unwittingly encourage people in different cultures to take sides against each other. Of course there are people who exploit this new form of propaganda.

The following may seem obvious to many, but it needs to be said.

Religion is much more than a matter of commitment to a particular set of theological propositions.

A result of this is that what might seem to a non-believer as questioning a specific belief, for example whether the Bible is literally the direct word of God, is interpreted by believers as an attack on their sense of identity and on the community to which they belong. Indeed they might be right: giving up or even questioning such a belief might result in their being ejected from their community. It is very difficult to overcome this problem. Perhaps the belief that a solution must exist is itself the feature of Western rationalism.

If we restrict attention to the major world religions, we find that, although they vary widely, they all include three components: ritual practices, beliefs, and ethics. These are not of equal importance in all cases, and they are not always easy to distinguish. The following examples of differences between religions are illustrative only, and we do not claim that they form the core beliefs of the religions. Orthodox Jews put less stress on beliefs and more on observance of the Jewish law, or Halakhah; this is based upon interpretations of the Torah by generations of scholars. Christianity does not have such strict rules, but it is strong on doctrines and beliefs; these include the resurrection of Christ and the continuation of the soul after death. Most religions have some form of God, but Hinduism has many, while Buddhists do not believe in a supreme creator.

Many Catholics venerate the Virgin Mary almost as though she were a divine figure – a substantial part of Pope Benedict's second encyclical in November 2007 is a declaration of her fundamental role in the Catholic faith. It has an active programme of declaring people to have been saints, and its current list of over ten thousand saints may soon include Mother Theresa of Calcutta. In order to be declared a saint at least two miracles must be attested. The Protestant churches do not currently make people saints, and are suspicious of sainthood to varying extents.

The attitude of Judaism and Islam towards idolatry, the worship of graven images, is simple: it is forbidden and the rule is taken very seriously. Catholics and Orthodox Christians venerate (but do not worship) a huge variety of icons of the saints, the Virgin Mary, and Christ; fierce objections to this over several decades by the Iconoclasts were eventually brought to an end when they were excommunicated at a synod in Constantinople in 842. Protestants have varying practices, but many limit their use of icons to worshipping in front of Christ on the cross. The distinction between icons as symbols and icons as idols involves tortuous theological arguments. To an outsider it seems evident that these are designed to justify the practice of the sect in question. These differences still provoke passions, and have resulted in tendentious variations in translations of the Second Commandment. Hinduism has a much more relaxed attitude towards the use of religious images.

In Islam, the natures of men and women are supposed to be different, and this is incorporated into Islamic law. Catholics agree about this with respect to their roles in the Church hierarchy, while the Anglican community is deeply divided on the issue. Many Protestant sects allow women essentially the same status as men, as does the law in most Western countries. Judaism accords men and women different religious roles, and passes the religion on from one generation to the next through the female line.

Readers will notice that I devote a substantial number of pages in this chapter commenting on various books by Keith Ward, until recently the Regius Professor of Divinity at the University of Oxford. I do so because of his interest in the relationship between science and religion and because I regard him as coherent and rational – in spite of my lack of agreement with his religious position. No doubt I could have chosen someone else, but Rowan Williams, the current Archbishop of Canterbury, would have been a poor choice, because I am among the many people who cannot make any sense of much of what he has written.

Ward agrees with much of what is written above. Here is a quotation from his book 'God, Faith and the New Millennium':

> *Different religions have different beliefs, and even different Christians have different beliefs from one another. I am not, in this book, trying to find a way in which such seemingly irreconcilable beliefs can be somehow harmonized. In fact, I think that such programmes will never succeed in producing some sort of universal agreement in religion, since orthodox believers in each religious tradition will reject them.*[3]

Such statements make the task of a non-believer trying to understand religious belief almost impossible. If one asks a theologian how to reconcile two apparently mutually inconsistent beliefs, one is liable to be told that one or other is no longer a part of mainstream religious belief, or that most religiously informed people now agree that they must be interpreted metaphorically. The problem is that ordinary worshippers appear to be unaware of this. Theologians of various sects and religions discuss such matters in a reasoned way, but they are frequently unable to come to agreements on doctrinal matters. The result is that in the end many people who are not religiously committed give up listening.

Fundamentalism

Each of the three Abrahamic religions has experienced a variety of fundamentalist movements over the last few centuries; sometimes these have been less active, but in recent decades they have posed a significant threat to the dominant secular rationalism of Western societies, particularly in the USA. We will concentrate on Protestant fundamentalism as it is at the present time and, even then, only provide a generalized snapshot.[4]

Protestant fundamentalists place the Bible at the centre of the faith, and reject liberal revisionist interpretations, as exemplified by the Anglican Church. They maintain that the Bible is strictly without error because it is the direct word of God, and regard it as a reliable account of events that actually happened as described. They emphatically reject the concept of Higher Criticism.

One will never understand fundamentalism if one regards it as an intellectual position. It is based on a social/political rejection of the dominant secularism of Western society, which is considered to have abandoned conventional moral values, replacing them by a glorification of material consumption that is becoming ever more degenerate. Science is not seen (by fundamentalists) as a liberating force when it is used ruthlessly to enforce the political and material interests of the dominant groups, whether at home or abroad. Many scientists share this dismay, but their scruples have little effect. The increasing Western tolerance of a variety of sexual and other lifestyles is seen as further evidence of moral corruption and as a threat to family values. The theory of evolution is interpreted as an attack on the literal truth of the Genesis story. A serious failing of some groups of fundamentalists is their lack of compassion for those who do not belong to their own sect; outsiders are consigned to Hell and sometimes killed without apparent regret. (I do not claim that religious fundamentalists are unique in this respect, but it does come oddly from people who claim to worship a God of love.)

Many recent debates about the relationship between science and religion have focussed on the agenda of the American creationists. The standard of the exchanges has been very low, for various reasons, including the low level of scientific understanding of much of the population, and the tendency of the press to report disagreements in lurid terms in order to boost sales. According to a series of Gallup polls about 40% of the United States population believe that God created human beings pretty much in their present form some time within the last 10,000 years or so. Creationists have repeatedly tried to get some type of 'creation science' into the high school syllabuses, but have been thwarted every time by the guardians of the American Constitution.

Science and creationism are so strongly opposed that it is difficult to have a rational discussion about their relative merits. Unfortunately some people on both sides of the debate use rhetorical tricks to defeat their opponents – serious misrepresentations and even outright misquotation, combined with statements that the *other* side needs to adopt higher standards when they write. Misquotation is only successful if readers do not check the references, and most do not. The more one reads about this topic the lower one's spirits are liable to sink.

Sensible discussions of these issues, as opposed to the passionate but unproductive debates that draw audiences, should be informed by, but not necessarily limited to, as wide a variety of evidence as possible. Historians, archeologists, physicists, geologists, geneticists, and theologians understand that knowledge needs constant reconsideration and revision. They all consider that the mere reiteration of traditional beliefs is not a viable option if careful investigations undermine them. There is no simple key to all of life's problems, and if there seems to be, it may well turn out not to fit the next lock.

The Catholic Church, particularly Pope John Paul II, seems to have accepted this lesson and is now firm in its commitment to the theory of evolution.[5] The Anglican Church has accepted the theory much longer, and has a web site devoted to promoting it; the contents of the site are closely in line with current scientific opinion. Unfortunately theologians often dismiss Christian fundamentalism as an unrepresentative fringe movement, whose religious views are not worth discussing. This is a serious mistake.

Christian theologians ignore the fundamentalist challenge at their own peril. It is the greatest threat to rational thought and toleration at the present time.

Conservative evangelical Christianity is not just an American phenomenon. In a speech given in October 2006 the Principal, Richard Turnbull, of Wycliffe Hall, Oxford said that 'ninety five percent of the people in [England are] facing hell unless the message of the gospel is brought to bear'. He went on to say, 'If the liberals seek to capture the theological colleges in order to exercise strategic influence, the first step will be to encourage liberal evangelicals to capture the evangelical colleges. And I just want to draw that challenge to your attention and not overlook it and not to think all is well.'[6] This cannot be dismissed as an isolated statement by someone of no significance. Turnbull had been appointed to an influential position in a theological college of the University of Oxford by people who must have known what his beliefs were. In spite of widespread protests about his attitudes, he is still the Principal.

There is another explanation of the widespread American rejection of the theory of evolution that de-emphasizes the religious aspect. There are many groups in the United States and elsewhere willing to invent bizarre explanations of unwelcome facts. One of the most recent is the attempt to argue that Barack Obama became President fraudulently, on the grounds that he was not born in the USA. The fact that his birth certificate and much other evidence demonstrate that he was born in Honolulu does not deflect such implausible claims, because they are based on a deep rooted need to reject his election rather than on rational arguments. Theories that the events of 9/11 were organized by the CIA, other Government agencies, or even Mossad can only be described as paranoid, but were invented by European journalists before being taken up in the USA. Evidence that our supposed rationality is only a thin veneer on top of other ways of thinking is by no means confined to the USA. A more benign example is the persistence of astrology and the publication of horoscopes by many magazines long after any possibility of justifying them has disappeared. None of these excuse irrationality, but they do provide warnings that a rational approach to life's problems is not bound to triumph.

Ethics

Although everyone agrees that ethical behaviour is of the greatest importance, there are profound disagreements about what this means in practice. Arguments about whether abortion and euthanasia, to cite just two examples, might be ethical in any conceivable circumstances provoke fierce disagreements that have led to major legal battles. One may approach the subject from a number of quite different perspectives.

Let us start by discussing the fundamental standards by which one decides whether actions are right or wrong. Most religious authorities consider it obvious that ethical standards must be grounded in religious belief. Their God is by definition good, and anyone who truly believes in him must inevitably try to behave as they believe he would want. Conversely, it is argued that without God there can be no absolute ethical standards and humanity would be lost in a sea of relativism.

The abolition of slavery provides very mixed support for this proposition. In support, one should mention that the Quakers were amongst the earliest communities to oppose slavery in England and Pennsylvania, and that a substantial part in the abolition of slavery in Britain was taken by Christians such as William Wilberforce and Thomas Buxton. However, it would be absurd to characterize the abolition of slavery in America during the nineteenth century as being a movement of Christians against the rest, because the rest were also Christians, who considered slavery and white supremacy to be sanctioned by God, at least in the southern part of the USA. Thomas Jefferson, who tried (unsuccessfully) to abolish slavery in his first draft of the American Declaration of Independence, in 1776, was not a Christian in any conventional sense. Although a deist and deeply interested in spiritual matters, he regarded much of the New Testament, in particular the virgin birth, the resurrection, and all aspects that had any miraculous component, as completely false. In essence, he placed great weight on the ethical aspects of Jesus's teachings and rejected the remainder. George Washington was equally opposed to slavery. He clearly recognized the importance of religion to others, but it is very hard to find evidence of personal religious belief on his part. John Quincy Adams, the sixth

President of the USA, another committed opponent of slavery, was a Unitarian.

Lest it be thought that the above comments are selective and tendentious, let me mention that the Anglican Dean of King's College London, Richard Burridge, said much the same in a lecture that he gave in Westminster Abbey in May 2007. He stated that in the eighteenth and nineteenth century slavery was viewed as a 'biblical' doctrine, supported by the laws of God and human law, while the abolitionists were seen as dangerous liberals, preaching sedition and revolution.

Whatever the above example might or might not prove, Confucius, Socrates, Aristotle, and others regarded ethics as a subject of great importance long before the Christian era. In the more recent past some of the major ethical debates have been driven by social rather than religious forces. Indeed the progress of women's rights has been actively impeded by many major religions, and still is in Islamic law. The ethical basis for women's rights was provided by utilitarianism, a philosophical theory developed by Jeremy Bentham and later by John Stuart Mill, an early humanist. In Mill's remarkable essay 'The Subjection of Women', written in 1869, the case for their emancipation is presented in terms of natural justice and human dignity, with hardly any references to religion. The provision of university education to women was led by University College, London in 1878; it is not a coincidence that it was also the first English university to admit students without regard to their religious affiliation, when it was founded in 1826. The movement to allow women equal educational rights only came to a successful conclusion in the 1970s and early 80s, when the last bastions of male supremacy, including the Universities of Oxford and Cambridge, capitulated. The debate was not phrased in religious terms, but focussed on the disruptive effect that the admission of large numbers of women might have (on male students), and even whether it would be a waste of resources to educate women at that level, particularly in medicine.

Women's rights have progressed enormously over the last forty years in Western countries, but discrimination is still commonplace. Article 16 of the Universal Declaration of Human Rights, about marriage and families, is far from being accepted by everyone. Arranged marriages may be acceptable if the couple involved consent to them, but there are still cases in which women are forced into marriages against their will. The Forced Marriage Act in the UK is there for a reason: every year about two hundred people are repatriated to the UK after they have been taken abroad against their will to marry, and, occasionally, women are killed for refusing to accept their families' decisions.

The development of equal rights for gay and lesbian people is even less complete and is anathema to many religions and sects. Nor is this attitude confined to religious circles. The English courts allowed employers to discriminate against and even dismiss homosexual staff until 2003. Many societies are even less tolerant of their human rights and some politicians even deny the existence of homosexuality within their countries. Those lacking sympathy for the rights of gay people might ponder the fate of the English mathematician and logician Alan Turing. He was a leading light at Bletchley Park during the Second World War, where crucial contributions to the defeat of the German forces resulted from methods devised by him to break the German codes. After the war he played a major part in the development of computers until he admitted to being homosexual and was convicted and subjected to chemical castration. This was one of the things that eventually drove him to commit suicide in 1954.

Another possibility is to try to ground ethical standards in biology. The attempt to subordinate ethics to science led to one of the most disastrous episodes in the history of science. The eugenics movement cited Darwin's theory in its support, even though Darwin himself would have been horrified at this. In 1893 Thomas Huxley, 'Darwin's Bulldog', wrote:

> There is another fallacy which appears to me to pervade the so-called 'ethics of evolution'. It is the notion that because, on the whole, animals and plants have advanced in perfection of organization by means of the struggle for existence and the consequent 'survival of the fittest'; therefore men in society, men as ethical beings, must look to the same process to help them towards perfection. I suspect that this fallacy has arisen out of the unfortunate ambiguity of the phrase 'survival of the fittest'. 'Fittest' has a connotation of 'best'; and about 'best' there hangs a moral flavour. In cosmic nature, however, what is 'fittest' depends upon the conditions…As I have already urged, the practice of that which is ethically best – what we call goodness or virtue – involves a course of conduct which, in all respects, is opposed to that which leads to success in the cosmic struggle for existence…Let us understand, once for all, that the ethical progress of society depends, not upon imitating the cosmic process, still less running away from it, but in combating it.

In spite of this a movement, often called social Darwinism, led, particularly in Germany, to the idea of racial purification, a means of 'improving' the human species by eliminating unfit individuals and even inferior races. Eventually this led to the horrors of Nazi Germany. People of many different nationalities, including Thomas Robert Malthus and Francis Galton in England, Nietzsche in Germany and Charles Davenport in the USA, share the responsibility for the evils perpetrated in the name of eugenics, but associating it with Darwin does a great injustice to a person who could never have drawn such conclusions from his scientific theories. When he died in 1882, many public figures honoured his 'noble character'. The Church of England was happy to hold his funeral and bury him in Westminster Abbey, in spite of knowing about his agnostic views.

Almost everyone now agrees that one cannot argue from Darwin's theory to how we ought to behave. Ethics should be informed by science, but it cannot be deduced from it. Richard Dawkins, regarded by many as the ultimate atheist, wrote the following in his most important book, *The Selfish Gene*:

> *Let us try to teach generosity and altruism, because we are born selfish. Let us understand what our own selfish genes are up to, because we may then at least have a chance to upset their designs, something that no other species has ever aspired to do.*

Edward Wilson has argued that our willingness to help people, even complete strangers, may be explained in terms of tribal instincts. He claims that ethical precepts do not come from divine revelation; they are reached by consensus under the guidance of the innate rules of mental development.[7] He also believes that some of our fundamental moral instincts are ill-adapted and persistently dangerous in modern societies.[8] A number of scientists are involved in a research programme that is trying to flesh these ideas out in specific cases, the best known of which is the avoidance of incest. The research should be pursued, but it is in its infancy, and much more work is needed before anyone can be confident about how far it will get. Understanding the biological origins of our social behaviour may one day be of great value in explaining our ethical predispositions, but ultimately it cannot tell us what choices to make.

In recent years there have been some attempts to provide biological explanations for religious belief. These purport to identify innate mechanisms in the brain that predispose people to accept religious or supernatural explanations of phenomena in certain circumstances. Apologists are clearly logically right to point out that such investigations are unrelated to the *truth* of the religious beliefs that most people have. However, matters are not so simple. Suppose that someone were to produce a pill that affected some subtle aspect of the development of children's brains, rendering them deeply religious (or irreligious) in later life without altering their other faculties. This would not have any logical implications concerning the existence of God, but it would certainly provoke deep unease.

Humanists base their ethical standards on personal fulfilment and a respect for human dignity. They may refer to whether a particular action is likely to promote happiness or to a principle of reciprocity: one should behave towards others as you would like them to behave towards you. This was advocated by Jesus, but it is an important concept in a variety of earlier Eastern religions. The principle of reciprocity has merits, but it is not readily applicable if two people are in sufficiently different circumstances. In particular, it is not at all clear that men should be able to determine the laws related to abortion, although, in practice, they do so in almost every country.

In applied ethics, one avoids general principles and tries to base particular ethical decisions on rational analysis moderated by the perceived attitudes of the community, which may well develop over a period of time. This works well in countries where expert panels can command respect and the population is relatively homogeneous culturally. It has not been so successful in the USA, where the population is extremely diverse and disagreements tend to lead to litigation.

Cardinal Cormac Murphy-O'Connor and others have contrasted religious views about marriage and the family with a lack of values in liberal, secular societies.[9] Identifying secularism with 'liberalism' (his inverted commas) is a mistake. Humanist organizations value marriage and provide their own ceremonies for births, marriages, and funerals as alternatives to the usual religious ceremonies. The prevalence of divorce and single parenthood are certainly legitimate matters for concern, but it is simplistic to take it for granted that they are caused by the collapse of religious belief. If this were the main cause, the divorce rate in the UK would be many times higher than that in the USA, but actually statistics show the UK as having a somewhat lower rate. The problem is much more complicated than he suggests.

The God-centred view of ethics also has problems, because those who follow this line of justification do not agree about how God wants us to behave. Although (almost) everyone agrees that good and evil exist, there are major differences about whether particular activities are evil. Here is the Archbishop of Canterbury, Rowan Williams, trying (unsuccessfully) to defuse the debate about the religious status of gay people within the Anglican community in June 2006, by arguing that the unity of the Church is more important than modern views about human rights:

> *Thus if other churches have said, in the wake of the events of 2003, that they cannot remain fully in communion with the American Church, this should not be automatically seen as some kind of blind bigotry against*

*gay people. Where such bigotry does show itself it needs to be made clear
that it is unacceptable; and if this is not clear, it is not at all surprising if
the whole question is reduced in the eyes of many to a struggle between
justice and violent prejudice. It is saying that, whatever the presenting
issue, no member Church can make significant decisions unilaterally and
still expect this to make no difference to how it is regarded in the
fellowship.*

By June 2008 it appeared that the Anglican communion was heading
towards an outright schism between conservatives for whom the authority
of the Bible and the sanctity of the family were at stake and liberals in the
Episcopal Church who regarded freedom of conscience as the more fundamental issue within the Anglican tradition; the final outcome of this dispute
may take many years to determine.

In 2006 Williams also wrote about some major ethical differences
between Christianity and Islam in the following terms:

*So one of the questions which Christians will want to pursue in their
continuing dialogue with Islam is whether the idea of a secular level of
citizenship – with all that this implies about liberties of conscience – is
indeed compatible with a basically Islamic commitment in the shape of
society at large; whether the Muslim state will distinguish between what
is religiously forbidden and what is legally punishable as a violation of
the state's order – so that adultery or apostasy, to take the obvious examples, do not have to be regarded as statutory crimes (let alone capital
ones). Muslim jurists in several Muslim societies are raising these questions already, with much sophistication and sensitivity, and the dialogue
between our communities needs to attend carefully to this debate.*

I tried without success to find any comment of his about the sentencing of
a woman to 200 lashes and six months in prison after being a victim of a
multiple rape in Saudi Arabia in November 2007. (The offence was being
alone with an unrelated man before the rape took place.) The sentence and
subsequent pardon by King Abdullah were a comment on the Saudi legal
system rather than on Islam – what religions themselves stand for is often
hard to tell, because they have such varied manifestations.

Williams has defended his unwillingness to criticize particular events
in public as follows:

*What I'm deeply uncomfortable with, I think, is saying things that really
don't change anything, that don't move things on. So much of the language that we use about scapegoats – whether it's the couple in Kilburn
or whatever – doesn't change anything...Now I realize that's not very
popular in all quarters. People feel, you know, 'Why don't you give a*

clear defence of Christian moral standards?' There are contexts in which you can do that – and I am actually rather old-fashioned about some of these issues – but saying it loudly and aggressively in public doesn't change it.[10]

Unfortunately, Pope Benedict is more willing to commit himself and has failed to anticipate the likely reactions to what he says on several important occasions. His harsh statements about Islam in a speech in the University of Regensburg, Germany in September 2006 drew a very unfavourable reaction. He later tried, unconvincingly, to extricate himself by pointing out that he was merely quoting an 'erudite Byzantine emperor' circa 1400, but he had given no hint of any disagreement with that emperor in his original speech. Nevertheless in October 2007 one hundred and thirty eight Muslim scholars came together to issue an unprecedented open letter calling for better relations between the two faiths. Entitled 'A Common Word Between Us and You', this has been warmly received throughout the world, and may have a long lasting effect.[11]

5.2   Varieties of Belief

In this section I describe the religious beliefs of a number of famous, or at least eminent, scientists. We will see that these have no more in common than those of other people. This conclusion may disappoint some, but it demonstrates that scientists have no special access to fundamental religious truths.

Galileo and Newton

In Chapter 1 we saw that Galileo was a committed and faithful Catholic, whose views only conflicted with those of the Church because he claimed the right to apply doctrines advocated a thousand years earlier by Augustine. Even the Vatican now accepts that 'Galileo's writings offered a path to explore how faith and reason were not incompatible'.

Newton, on the other hand, was a Puritan with strong but heretical religious beliefs. He went to great lengths to keep them to himself because they would have cost him his position in society and his Lucasian Professorship in Cambridge. He spent years of his life studying the Bible in great detail and his private notebooks show that he came to reject the doctrine of the Trinity, which he considered to have no Biblical basis and to have been a later perversion of Christianity. In religious terms he was committed to Arianism, which made Christ subordinate to God and had been declared a heresy in the First Council of Nicaea in 325. *Principia* carefully avoids references to religion except in the General Scholium, added to the second edition in 1713. Even then he avoided any mention of Arianism or anything even slightly heterodox. Indeed he concealed his beliefs so well that they only came to light in the twentieth century, when his notebooks became generally available.

Michael Faraday

It is no exaggeration to say that our present civilization depends on machines driven by or using electricity. These machines became possible because of the discovery of a connection between electricity and magnetism made by the Danish scientist Hans Christian Ørsted in 1820. His breakthrough was followed up rapidly, in particular by Michael Faraday.

Faraday was born to a family of very modest means, in London in 1791, and was largely self-educated. His ability came to the attention of Sir Humphry Davy, for whom he worked as a scientific assistant. Eventually he became a Professor of Chemistry at the Royal Institution in London, where he was to stay for the rest of his life. His greatest discoveries were made in the 1830s, when he elucidated in some detail the relationship between electricity and magnetism; he also constructed one of the first electric dynamos, the key to the generation of electrical power. He also made other important contributions, for example to chemistry, but rejected a knighthood offered in recognition of his services.

One would not guess from the above that Faraday was a lifelong member of a Protestant sect called the Sandemanians, numbering less than a thousand members in total.[12] The sect formed a closed and tightly knit community who observed the lack of any Biblical authority for the existence of the Anglican Church. They had no ministry and were governed by a group of elders who could exclude anyone from the sect for not obeying its strict rules. Faraday did not regard membership of the sect as a mere formality; he was fully committed to it and regarded it as one of the central features of his life. His integration of his religious and scientific attitudes runs contrary to the often expressed claim that these two world-views are necessarily in conflict.

The next three people in our selection also regard(ed) their spiritual beliefs as important parts of their lives. Their beliefs are peculiar in that they make almost no contact with the major world religions. Indeed they do not relate to anything that would generally be dignified with the name of God.

Albert Einstein

Albert Einstein is one of the three most famous scientists of all time, and wrote on a wide range of topics, including his religious beliefs. I could, therefore, hardly omit him from the list of those discussed here. He was born to non-observant Jewish parents in Ulm in 1879 and spent much of his childhood in Munich. He had a deeply spiritual attitude towards the world and science in particular, and wrote about a wide variety of matters in later life, but his beliefs did not fit into conventional religious categories. On one occasion, irked by false statements about this, he wrote:

> *It was, of course, a lie what you read about my religious convictions, a lie which is being systematically repeated. I do not believe in a personal God and I have never denied this but have expressed it clearly. If something is in me which can be called religious then it is the unbounded admiration for the structure of the world so far as our science can reveal it.*

On other occasions he wrote:

> *My position concerning God is that of an agnostic. I am convinced that a vivid consciousness of the primary importance of moral principles for the betterment and ennoblement of life does not need the idea of a law-giver, especially a law-giver who works on the basis of reward and punishment.*

and:

> *It seems to me that the idea of a personal God is an anthropological concept which I cannot take seriously. I feel also not able to imagine some will or goal outside the human sphere. My views are near those of Spinoza: admiration for the beauty of and belief in the logical simplicity of the order which we can grasp humbly and only imperfectly. I believe that we have to content ourselves with our imperfect knowledge and understanding and treat values and moral obligations as a purely human problem – the most important of all human problems.*

One should not infer that the beliefs of Spinoza and Einstein lay at the same point on the spectrum between mystical pantheism and atheistic rationalism. Although both were non-practising Jews, they lived in very different societies and were separated by two and a half centuries in time.

Einstein did not believe in immortality of the individual, and considered ethics to be an exclusively human concern with no superhuman authority behind it. His views about the role of religion in human life were based upon divesting it of its myths and focussing on its ethical aspects. We will see a remarkable parallel between his beliefs and those of Gould, below; no doubt their common Jewish background has something to do with this.

Stephen Gould

Stephen J. Gould, who died in 2002, was an agnostic whose grandfather had been a New York Jewish immigrant. He was famous as an evolutionary biologist, an essayist, and the author of many extremely successful popular science books. It should also be mentioned that he was criticized for exaggerating the importance of 'punctuated equilibrium', a facet of the theory of evolution which was not as radical as he maintained. Richard Dawkins and he engaged in a long standing and ferocious debate about the details of Darwinian theory, to the great delight of creationists. In one of his last books, *Rocks of Ages*, he argued that science and religion could co-exist peacefully as non-overlapping magisteria. They were supposed to deal with two unrelated issues, the form of the natural world and our ethical standards, neither of which had anything to say about the other. Gould's willingness to equate religion and ethics attracted considerable comment, mostly unfavourable. He devoted a chapter of *Rocks of Ages* to the struggle against creationism in America, in which he played a substantial part. He claimed that the creationist movement was not primarily religious, but had its roots in *cultural* divisions in America. These divisions included north versus south, urban versus rural and rich versus poor. In his opinion religion provided the label by which the minority group identified their separateness, and the more they felt overwhelmed, the more they were bound to fight back. According to Gould:

> *the great majority of professional clergy and religious scholars stand on the same side with the great majority of scientists – as defenders of NOMA and the First Amendment, and against the imposition of any specific theological doctrine, especially such a partisan and minority view, upon the science curricula of public schools. For example, the long list of official plaintiffs who successfully challenged the Arkansas creationism statute in 1981 included some scientists and educators, but even more ordained clergy of all major faiths, and scholars of religion.*[13]

Gould made many references to Judaism and Christianity in *Rocks of Ages* but none to the various branches of Islam. This seems incomprehensible today, but *Rocks of Ages* was published in 1999, before the destruction of the World Trade Center in 2001 and the Iraq War. Since then attitudes have changed dramatically, and not for the better.

Another feature of *Rocks of Ages* was Gould's attitude towards the Catholic Church, probably explained by the fact that most of the non-Jews that he met in his childhood were Catholics. The intolerance of the Church towards Galileo cannot be excused as easily as Gould did. He was perfectly right to say that Galileo provoked, even ridiculed, senior figures in the Church, and in that sense deserved what he got. Gould suggested that we cannot understand 'a world so profoundly different from our own that modern categories and definitions can only plunge us into incomprehension'.[14] This has some basis but it avoids facing some rather inconvenient facts. Jews had been persecuted by the Inquisition in Spain and Portugal for a considerable time, but during Galileo's lifetime many were being permitted to settle as refugees in the much more liberal Netherlands, particularly Amsterdam. The only Italian city which admitted large numbers of Jewish refugees was Venice, which had a long tradition of political independence from Rome. The Roman Church was repressive even by the standards of the time, and this deterred many people, including Descartes, from expressing ideas about which they had thought long and hard.

Before science and religion can live amicably together, the different sects and religions have to agree that their common ground is more important than their differences. Reconciliations between different sects within the major religions are, unfortunately, only a hope in the minds of a few; those between different religions are even further off. Ritual practices might have seemed as unimportant to Gould as they do to other agnostics, but to the religious they are central components of their faiths. The fact that religious and cultural divisions often coincide, as in Northern Ireland and Iraq, is the source of much of the intolerance between the many sects and religions that exist today. Hope may be what keeps us going but Gould was excessively optimistic about human nature.

Gould was strongly opposed to the belief that science and religion might support each other: he really did regard them as logically unrelated. He had no sympathy with the idea that the Big Bang theory is in some sense consistent with a sufficiently broad interpretation of Genesis. He agreed with the general view of both scientists and theologians that the Big Bang was a scientific theory, while the creation story in Genesis was a myth.[15] He was probably right to claim that no recent scientific discoveries have interesting religious implications, but that does not imply that they could not have, unless one defines religion very narrowly. If, for example, archeologists were to discover an extensive *contemporary* manuscript chronicling the life of Jesus by an otherwise reliable historian in Palestine, it would surely have a substantial effect on the Christian religion, in spite of the fact that it would not resolve any ethical questions. It was possible that the Dead Sea Scrolls would have done this, but it turned out that they made no mention of Jesus or any of his followers. (I am accepting the consensus that the synoptic gospels were all written more than thirty years after the death of Jesus; the significance of the brief references to Jesus by Josephus will probably never be resolved.)

Freeman Dyson

As a third example of highly personal religiosity I choose Freeman Dyson. He has unusual religious beliefs by any standards, but one must include him in the list of scientists who view the world with a strong sense of awe and wonder. Born in England in 1923, his education at Trinity College, Cambridge was interrupted by the Second World War. He emigrated to the United States in 1953 and spent most of his life in the Institute for Advanced Study at Princeton. After very distinguished early work in pure mathematics, quantum electrodynamics, and other areas of theoretical physics, he turned to a range of engineering and space projects. He promoted the merits of obtaining results cheaply and quickly, but many of his ideas were ahead of their time. In later life he wrote a number of popular science books, and was awarded the Templeton Prize in 2000. In his acceptance speech he described himself as a Christian who did not care much about the doctrine of the Trinity or the historical truth of the gospels (elsewhere he said that for him religion was a way of life and not a belief). Viewed in isolation, this might be regarded as a form of Unitarianism, but his statements below place him among those who have created highly personal *substitutes* for traditional religious belief.

> *I do not make any clear distinction between mind and God. God is what mind becomes when it has passed beyond the scale of our comprehension. God may be either a world-soul or a collection of world-souls. So I am thinking that atoms and humans and God may have minds that differ in degree but not in kind. We stand, in a manner of speaking, midway between the unpredictability of atoms and the unpredictability of God. Atoms are small pieces of our mental apparatus, and we are small pieces of God's mental apparatus. Our minds may receive inputs equally from atoms and from God. This view of our place in the cosmos may not be true, but it is compatible with the active nature of atoms as revealed in the experiments of modern physics.*

Dyson's reference to 'the active nature of atoms' is difficult to interpret without further explanation – their behaviour is described by well-established quantum-mechanical equations whose correctness have been confirmed by many detailed calculations. The passage as a whole provides evidence of his spirituality, but it describes pantheism (actually panpsychism) rather than Christianity. This has a long history, but there is little evidence elsewhere that Dyson has grappled with it. Perhaps he was simply allowing himself to indulge in speculations; later in the lecture he quoted Francis Bacon as having said 'God forbid that we should give out a dream of our own imagination for a pattern of the world'.

In 1988 Dyson wrote an inspirational book called *Infinite in All Directions*, in which he pursued Desmond Bernal's hope that the human species would live for ever, gradually transforming itself into a non-material form in accordance with the laws of information theory. A more technical version of the idea, which demonstrated that it did not contradict any laws of physics, had already been published by him in a physics journal. Dyson's view of the ultimate destiny of the human race is shared by some other mathematical physicists, particularly Frank Tipler, described by the Anglican physicist John Polkinghorne as a 'kind of Southern Baptist atheist'.[16] Indeed there was a conference in Rome on this subject and its religious implications recently.[17] It has a rather odd fascination, but I would prefer to know whether our civilization will survive the present century.

Why Dyson feels so passionately about the desirability of such a future is unclear, but it has nothing to do with Christianity. It makes no contact with the crucifixion of Christ, the conflict between good and evil, or redemption through the grace of God. It involves *replacing* God by a self-sufficient and eventually omnipotent post-human race. In spite of Dyson's optimistic and inspirational style, this aspect of his book is too close to science fiction for my taste, and he himself admits the similarity. Nevertheless, it is obviously very important to him.

Richard Dawkins

My personal background makes it very easy to sympathize with the views of Richard Dawkins, but even if I did not, I would have to mention his involvement in the current debates between science and the creationist movement. He was born in Nairobi, but has spent most of his life in England. He obtained a degree in zoology at Oxford University and subsequently studied evolutionary biology and made a particular contribution by arguing that the unit of evolution was the gene rather than the whole organism. He held the Simonyi Chair in the Public Understanding of Science at Oxford between 1995 and 2008. In later life he has written many popular science books and obviously enjoys the controversies that some of them have generated. They are extremely well written as well as entertaining, provided you are not the butt of his attacks. *The God Delusion* is one of his most controversial and has enjoyed great popular success. Nevertheless, the following dictum of Bertrand Russell prevents me giving a positive assessment of it:

> Be scrupulously truthful, even if the truth is inconvenient, for it is more inconvenient when you try to conceal it.

The worst feature of Dawkins' book is its failure to get to grips with the variety of religious belief. Dawkins' real enemy is fundamentalism, but he attacks religion indiscriminately. In his eyes 'Gould carried out the art of bending over backwards to positively supine lengths' to avoid giving offence to the religiously inclined. He does not believe that Gould could possibly have meant much of what he wrote in *Rock of Ages*. Similarly he puts Michael Ruse into the 'Neville Chamberlain school of evolutionists' for not taking his (Dawkins') line, in spite of 'claiming' to be an atheist. He is unable to grasp that many moderate believers dislike fundamentalists of all religions as much as he does.

Dawkins would have done better if he had focussed on the anti-scientific attitudes of the creationist movement. Michael Ruse, a non-believing philosopher of science, thinks that Dawkins has been an absolute disaster in the fight against intelligent design, because he is not willing to study Christianity seriously and to engage with the ideas. I am afraid that *The God Delusion* is a deeply flawed book that does not approach Dawkins' usual standards, and suspect that he got carried away by the sheer enjoyment of writing it.

Several books criticizing *The God Delusion* have been written. One of the best is *The Dawkins Delusion* by Alister McGrath, a one-time atheistic scientist who is now Professor of Theology, Ministry, and Education at King's College London. If one has to point to a weakness in *The Dawkins Delusion*, it is that McGrath concentrates heavily on the Christian Anglican tradition. He rarely mentions Catholicism, dismisses creationism summarily, and only refers to Islam in the context of jihadist fundamentalism.[18] These are issues that McGrath should have discussed in much more detail, because extreme fundamentalism provides the strongest support for Dawkins' case.

If one strips the diatribe out of *The God Delusion*, admittedly a major task, one finds pockets of good sense there. Dawkins and Rowan Williams will no doubt be surprised to hear that I consider they have a lot in common. Both are opposed to the teaching of creationism in schools, and both reject as absurd the idea of a supernatural being who might have created the universe in the same sense as human beings created New York. Both consider that Darwin's theory is extraordinarily comprehensive and successful in dealing with biology. They also agree that much evil that has been done in the name of religion, even in the recent past. Their differences stem from their beliefs about human nature. Dawkins hopes to persuade people to abandon religion, and believes that intolerance would thereby decrease, even though there are few grounds for optimism. Williams has set himself the task of trying to persuade the leaders of other sects and religions to open a dialogue by emphasizing what they have in common. Conciliation is a more positive strategy than confrontation, so I support Rowan Williams' activities, even though I do not understand many of his beliefs.

John Polkinghorne

John Polkinghorne was an eminent theoretical physicist at the University of Cambridge for much of his career. He resigned his chair in 1979 and was ordained into the Anglican church in 1982. He returned to Cambridge, became the President of Queen's College, and has won many honours, including a knighthood in 1997 and the Templeton Prize in 2002.

Polkinghorne has written extensively on science and religion, and his conclusions are thoughtful and well worth reading because he has a deep understanding of both fields. His comments about the philosophical assumptions of other scientists are particularly interesting. However, he exhibits a common failing of believers – he writes about his own brand of religion, liberal Anglican Christianity, without considering the vast variety of other faiths. This is particularly true of his recent book *Questions of Truth*, supposedly about God, Science, and Truth, but actually of little interest except to those who are a part of his own community. It contains hardly any references to other sects of Christianity, let alone to other religions.

It is hardly surprising that Polkinghorne has little good to say about Dawkins, whom he considers to be religiously illiterate. He would do far better, both for science and moderate religion, if he were to concentrate his attention, not on Dawkins, but on the fundamentalists in various religions, and even in other branches of his own Anglican faith. Dawkins is an easy target, but not ultimately as important as the tens of millions of young earth creationists. Dismissing their beliefs as unworthy of serious attention will not stop their attempts to undermine the whole concept of rational discussion.

Atkins and Coulson

I finally mention two professors of chemistry in the University of Oxford.

The religious beliefs of Peter Atkins have already been described briefly on page 132. He is uncompromising about the adequacy of the scientific world-view, and has described religion as being a fantasy without any explanatory content. Here is another typically outspoken quote:

> There is of course one big, cosmically big, seemingly real question: Where did it all come from? Here we see most sharply the distinction between the methods. Religion adopts the adipose answer: God made it – for reasons that will forever remain inscrutable until, perhaps, we become one with Him (that is, until we are dead). Such an answer, while intrinsically absurd and evil in its implications, appears to satisfy those for whom God is a significant part of their existence. Science, in contrast, is steadily and strenuously working toward a comprehensible explanation.[19]

Charles Coulson was much older than Atkins and died in 1974 at the end of a distinguished career. During his lifetime he was awarded many prizes and honorary degrees for his insights into molecular chemistry. He was raised as a Methodist and was a committed Christian as an adult. He was an energetic lay preacher and wrote a number of popular books relating his religious and scientific beliefs. He became Vice-President of the British Methodist Conference in 1959 and a member of the Central Committee of the World Council of Churches in 1962. A greater contrast between two chemists in the same university could hardly be imagined.

The short biographies above show that scientists occupy a wide range of beliefs in the religious spectrum. There are also innumerable scientists, including Stephen Hawking, Francis Crick, Harold Kroto, and Stephen Weinberg, who have no religious belief or are active atheists. If the examples that I have chosen demonstrate anything, it is that there is no 'scientific consensus' about the status of religion. Neither religious belief nor atheism are consequences of scientific expertise. If one wishes to assess religious belief in greater depth, counting heads, even the most distinguished heads, is not a valid way of proceeding. One needs to discuss its underlying assumptions in some detail.

5.3   The Anthropic Principle

One is by no means forced to accept arguments about the metaphysical or even religious significance of the fine tuning of the fundamental constants. All sorts of conclusions have been drawn from it, but in most cases they depend rather obviously on the prior beliefs of the person involved. The weak anthropic principle is no more than the observation that the universe must be such as to allow us to exist, because we do. This is pretty unexciting, but some people feel the need to elaborate on this explanation by dragging a vast number of other equally real universes into the picture. Considering the amount of effort still needed to understand our own universe, this seems a distraction, to say the least – our own universe is rich enough and contains enough mysteries to keep everyone occupied for many more decades.

In 1979, Bernard Carr and Martin Rees published a much quoted paper arguing that the structure of the physical world was determined to an order of magnitude by just four constants. They noted some unexplained coincidences between the magnitudes of certain combinations of these four constants, without which life as we know it would not be possible. In their conclusion they stated that:

> *[the Everett picture of quantum theory and the Wheeler description of the universe] go a little way towards giving the anthropic principle the status of a physical theory but only a little: it may never aspire to being much more than a philosophical curiosity.*[20]

In 1999 Rees developed the same ideas in his popular book *Just Six Numbers* in which he referred again to the carbon resonance. In this book he was more enthusiastic about the anthropic principle than he had been in 1979:

> *If one doesn't accept the 'providence' argument [for fine tuning], there is another perspective, which – though still conjectural – I find compellingly attractive. It is that our Big Bang may not have been the only one. Separate universes may have cooled down differently, ending up governed by different laws and defined by different numbers.*

Steven Weinberg, who knows as much about the physics as anyone, is one of many physicists who regard use of the anthropic principle as a confession of failure. In an article written in 2005 he argued that Hoyle's carbon resonance did not seem to him to provide any evidence of fine tuning.[21] Later in the same article, in which he himself used anthropic arguments to estimate the vacuum energy, he concluded as follows:

> *Some physicists have expressed a strong distaste for anthropic arguments. (I have heard David Gross say 'I hate it.') This is understandable. Theories based on anthropic calculation certainly represent a retreat from what we had hoped for: the calculation of all fundamental parameters from first principles. It is too soon to give up on this hope, but without loving it we may just have to resign ourselves to a retreat, just as Newton had to give up Kepler's hope of a calculation of the relative sizes of planetary orbits from first principles.*

Weinberg is not the only person willing to question the existence of fine tuning. In a recent research paper Fred Adams has run numerical simulations that demonstrate that stellar structures operating through sustained nuclear fusion can exist for a wide range of the three relevant fundamental constants.[22] He does not discuss the conditions relevant to the existence of life, but his paper is a significant addition to discussions of the anthropic principle. Whatever the outcome, it is somewhat disturbing that the very existence of a phenomenon that has been the basis of so much philosophical discussion is still open to question.

The following quotations illustrate four attitudes that one might adopt towards the values of the fundamental constants.

- Their values have no fundamental explanation, just as there is no such explanation of the size of the Earth's orbit. If it had been substantially smaller or larger, life would not have developed here.
- They may be calculated from some as yet unknown theory.
- They were chosen by God during the act of creation to ensure a universe of the greatest possible richness.
- They may be explained by invoking the multiverse theory and the anthropic principle.

The last two explanations discourage one from pursuing the second possibility, which would be far more desirable an outcome if it were possible. There may be no explanation, but we are much less likely to find it if we stop looking. The small number of such constants suggests one might have some weak optimism in this respect, *if it suggests anything*. Or to put it the other way around, the existence of a much larger number of fundamental constants would discourage hopes that their values could be explained.

From this point onwards we will assume, purely for the sake of pursuing the argument, that there does not exist a theory that enables one to compute the values of the fundamental constants – if there does then there is one less mystery to explain. If there are many physical universes with different values of the fundamental constants, then, being what we are, we are bound to find ourselves in one in which there is abundant hydrogen, carbon, nitrogen, and oxygen, and this seems to require the existence of stars. This issue was discussed by Polkinghorne in his book *Beyond Science*. He asks whether the multiverse explanation of the universe is offered to us as physics or as metaphysics, and eventually concludes that it is a metaphysical guess. In his mind it is on a par with his own metaphysical guess that there might be a God, whose will and purpose is expressed in a single universe.

The final item in the above list proposes that extreme coincidences might be explained by the existence of multiple realities. Following John Leslie, suppose that you are facing a firing squad and fifty marksmen all fire at you and miss. Let us suppose that each of the marksmen has a 50% chance of missing, so that the chance that all of them will independently miss is about one in about a thousand trillion. The multiverse explanation for your survival asks you to believe that there are a thousand trillion different worlds, each of which contains a version of you facing a different firing squad. In all of these except one 'you' die, with a variable number of bullets in you. The anthropic principle amounts to the statement that since you are still alive, you are bound to have been in the world in which all of the marksmen missed – purely by chance. It is not at all clear that this argument should reduce your amazement about still being alive, but perhaps this is a psychological issue rather than a rational one.

Weinberg has noted that the multiverse theory had also been contrasted with religious belief, by the Cardinal Archbishop of Vienna in 2005; as a committed atheist he was obviously amused that the two of them agreed about this. Belief in the multiverse may or may not be compatible with Christianity, but it does depend upon a willingness to embrace a form of Platonism, which is also a metaphysical belief. Many theoretical physicists do not notice that they are moving into the area of metaphysics, when they fail to distinguish between mathematical models of physical reality and physical reality itself.

If one wants to engage in metaphysics, discussion about the values of the fundamental constants is not the most interesting choice of topic. Surely one should focus on the basic laws of physics – string theory, quantum theory, general relativity, etc. I would be quite willing to live in a world without general relativity, because it has little apparent influence on our everyday lives, even if it was vital just after the Big Bang. On the other hand, our type of life could not exist without quantum theory, because it controls the *present day* behaviour of the atoms and molecules that comprise all of the objects around us. We have no idea why the universe can be described by laws that are formulated using quantum theory. String theory has nothing to say about this because it uses the standard rules of quantum theory. The metaphysics of multiple universes that only differ in the values of their fundamental constants is much less significant than such questions.

Although the anthropic principle refers to the existence of carbon-based life, most people are more interested in the existence of self-conscious intelligent life. If we were able somehow to transport the discussion backwards in time by a billion years, when nothing more advanced than single-celled organisms had evolved, the anthropic principle would seem considerably less interesting. Who knows whether it will still seem interesting in a billion years' time?

> **The universe may be very well adapted to the existence of carbon-based life, but unfortunately for the anthropic principle, it seems very *poorly* adapted to the existence of intelligence.**

There is a vast variety of species on the Earth, but only we are truly intelligent, and we have existed for less than one thousandth of the time during which life has been present here. Looking outside our own Solar System, there has been much discussion of the fact, first noted by Enrico Fermi in 1950, that in spite of systematic searches we have not been able to find any evidence of intelligent aliens. A few hundred planets outside the Solar System have been discovered in the last ten years, but as far as we know humans are the only truly intelligent species in the universe. If the new Allen Telescope Array and its successors find evidence of intelligent aliens over the next hundred years, then the claims of Christianity that we have a special status in the eyes of God will appear less convincing. Religions such as Buddhism and metaphysical statements that God is the 'ground of being' might not be affected by the existence of intelligent aliens, but the significance of the crucified Christ in the grand scheme of things would be greatly diminished. Perhaps this is the reason why the SETI institute in California receives no Federal funding for its search for intelligent aliens, in spite of the fact that the impact of a positive outcome would be so immense.

Some physicists, such as Paul Davies, have argued that the very existence of a universe in itself poses a metaphysical problem. Science seems to culminate in the description of the Big Bang, but even if there is something beyond that, science cannot explain why there is a universe, when there might literally be nothing – not even space and time. If one is religious one might say that the universe exists because God chose to create it. It is sometimes suggested that he might have done this because it is good to enter into loving relationships with other persons. The answers to such questions are highly speculative and dependent on the prior beliefs of the speculator. There is little point in pursuing them, even though they seem to be important.

5.4   The Existence of God

Swinburne's Existence Argument

Christian apologetics consists of attempts to provide rational arguments relating to the existence and nature of God. It is an immense subject and comes in many varieties, which are not all consistent with each other. The most famous is due to the thirteenth century theologian Thomas Aquinas.

He provided a series of arguments for the existence of God in his famous *Summa Theologica*. He called these proofs and discussed their merits and faults in a structured, logical manner. Aquinas scholars have not come to an agreement about the proper interpretation of his arguments, written in a theological and scientific culture very different from ours. The simplest course is not to worry about what Aquinas might have meant, but to discuss the issues in a modern context.

It should not be thought that the use of the word 'proof' in this context has the same meaning as it does in mathematics. It must be interpreted according to its primary meaning in the Oxford English Dictionary: facts, evidence, argument, etc. establishing *or helping to establish* a fact (my italics). It is often helpful to distinguish between deductive proofs, which are only applicable in a narrow range of logical and mathematical circumstances, and inductive proofs, in which the evidence does not render the conclusions certain.

Richard Swinburne is a philosopher of religion at Oxford University who is particularly noted for his commitment to natural theology, the attempt to prove the existence of God by arguments based on our experiences in the natural world. He does not believe that the existence of God can be proved deductively and has long argued in support of one particular inductive proof of the existence of God. In his book *The Existence of God* he tries to establish that the probability of God's existence is quite large, by arguments that use Bayes' theorem, a statistical result that provides a method of manipulating conditional probabilities.[23] His ideas are individually plausible, but one gradually realizes that his mathematical formulae have no real function: at no stage does he insert any numbers into the formulae or indicate the order of magnitude of the probabilities concerned. Occasionally he states, quite correctly, that one probability must be greater than some other, but his method does not allow one to quantify how much greater. The end result is that it is impossible to draw *any* quantitative conclusions from his book – as far as his arguments are concerned the probability of God's existence might be 1%, 99%, or any other value. His 'probabilities' are a literary device that have little relationship with probability as practised in science.

Take, for example, the conditional probability $P(h\,|\,c\ \&\ k)$ of the hypothesis h that God exists given the appearance of Christ, c and our prior knowledge, k of the development of civilization, physics, and the theory of evolution. Swinburne uses Bayes' theorem to write down[24]

$$P(h|c\ \&\ k) = \frac{P(c|h\ \&\ k)\,P(h|k)}{P(c|k)}.$$

One could easily make the case that $P(c|h \& k)$ is quite close to 1 on the grounds that if God exists he is very likely to reveal his love for, and empathy with, ourselves by offering up his only Son. This yields

$$P(h|c \& k) \leq \frac{P(h|k)}{P(c|k)},$$

so one is led to comparing the probabilities of the existence of God and of the appearance of a Christ-like figure in Palestine/Israel during the relevant period. If one did not already know that Christ did exist, one would judge that the probability of such a figure appearing at that time was small but not tiny on purely historical/political grounds. The real issue is whether the probability that God exists is so tiny as to remain insignificant after knowing of the existence of Christ, as many atheists believe, or big enough to be worth serious consideration in its own right, as theists believe. Somewhere or other such judgements must be made, and the outcome depends on those much more than it does on any mathematical formulae.

The situation changes substantially if c refers to a really astonishing miracle whose occurrence is impossible to deny. The prior probability of such a miracle occurring would then be so small as to increase the probability of God's existence a lot. But one does not need Bayes' theorem to tell one that – it is obvious without reference to any formulae. The problem, of course, is that people's willingness to believe in miracles, for example that of the resurrection of Christ, depends strongly on their prior belief in God.

The inadequacy of Swinburne's arguments may be also seen by applying them to a different type of God, one who shares all the transcendental attributes of Swinburne's God, but with his perfect goodness replaced by a completely amoral wish to create a world that will provide him with as much bizarre entertainment as possible. This would be achieved by creating people who consider that ethical behaviour is extremely important, while holding that it is justifiable to kill total strangers, people who manage to convince themselves that major natural disasters are the inevitable outcome of God's love, people who believe that their own religion is obviously superior to that of millions of others, people of great intelligence who manage to persuade themselves that quantum theory could be a true description of reality, and people who genuinely believe in alien abductions. It would be possible to construct a lengthy inductive argument for the existence of such a God by using similar arguments to those Swinburne employs. The issue is not whether anyone believes that God has such a character, but whether Swinburne's analysis only appears to succeed if the reader is already persuaded that only a narrow range of possibilities needs to be considered. Most approaches to natural theology fail for the same reason – they limit themselves to justifying an explanation of the world that only seems plausible in one particular community.

From the time of Augustine onwards, theologians have taken it for granted that God is perfectly good, or regard this as a part of the definition of God. Swinburne rejects the possibility of a totally amoral God by claiming that the concept is logically contradictory – in other words that God's goodness can be proved *deductively* from his omniscience and perfect freedom.[25] He argues that a free agent must choose to do one thing rather than another, because it seems to be a good thing; one does not deliberately make bad choices. This syllogistic argument confuses desiring something and considering its achievement to be *morally* good. Identifying the two is simply wrong-headed. Many of our actions are taken to increase our contentment or comfort; this may be good from our personal point of view but it is not morally good in any serious sense. Other actions are taken to improve our personal status in our career or our social community; this may well not promote the general good of society.

The Nature of God

The concept of God has long been associated with wisdom, love, goodness, being beyond space and time, not being material, and having infinite creative powers. It is said by some that all major religions are struggling towards the same ultimate truth, and even that the three Abrahamic religions all worship the same God. Unfortunately this has not prevented believers in those religions hating and even killing each other, sometimes with enthusiasm, for more than a thousand years.

The degree to which God has human characteristics has been a subject of much debate for centuries. The Scottish philosopher David Hume has a lengthy discussion of this is his *Dialogues Concerning Natural Religion*, published in 1779, shortly after his death. The book takes the form of a conversation between three people in which religious belief is not directly attacked; it adopts the more subtle strategy of accepting the existence of God, but arguing that every proposal about his nature is in the end either indefensible or incoherent. It is impossible to summarize the wide variety of arguments presented in a few lines, but the character Cleanthes warns throughout against holding too transcendent an image of God. Here is a brief extract from his argument that belief in a sufficiently incomprehensible deity is no different from atheism:

> *A mind, whose acts and sentiments and ideas are not distinct and succes-*
> *sive; one that is wholly simple, and totally immutable; is a mind, which has*
> *no thought, no reason, no will, no sentiment, no love, no hatred; or in a*
> *word, is no mind at all. It is an abuse of terms to give it that appellation.*

This type of description of God still persists. According to various speeches of Rowan Williams, the Archbishop of Canterbury, God is 'the explanation of why we look for explanations', he is 'the explanation of rationality itself', and he is not 'a member of any class of existent beings'. Williams' statements are consistent with the theologian Paul Tillich's description of God as 'the ground of being'. The problem with defining God this way is that those starting from this point regularly assume without argument that this very abstract God can be identified with the loving and personal God of the Christian religion. Even if God as the ground of being and God as a transcendent being are metaphors for something that we cannot comprehend, one has to comment these earnest theological abstractions have little to do with the religious beliefs of ordinary Christians.

In spite of its insistence on God's simplicity, Christianity has a layer of complexity that is absent in Judaism and Islam – the doctrine of the Trinity. This states that God the Father, Jesus Christ the Son, and the Holy Spirit are simultaneously three distinct beings, and all the same being, none subservient to another, all three with complete equality and a single will. Attempts to understand this may well lead the reader into one of the major heresies, with names such as docetism, monarchianism, Arianism, and Macedonianism. The declaration that the Father and Son are of the same substance and are co-eternal became official Church doctrine in the First General Council of Nicaea in 325, and is not stated explicitly in the Bible itself. It appears that reconciling the simplicity of God with the doctrine of the Trinity depends on faith rather than understanding.

Design Arguments

Aquinas presented five arguments for the existence of God, but only one is mentioned at all frequently today. This design (or teleological) argument was developed in considerable detail by William Paley, early in the nineteenth century. It states that one can infer the existence of a designer from the fact that living creatures are so perfectly adapted to their environments. One of the examples that he gave was that of the eye, which contains a number of very specialized parts – pupil, lens, iris, retina, etc. – that coordinate with each other almost miraculously. Paley felt that an object of such exquisite complexity cried out for the existence of a designer.

Unfortunately for Paley, Darwin was to show that this attractive argument had little substance. In his *Origin of Species*, published in 1859, he showed that it was entirely possible for such a structure to arise by a process of gradual adaptation driven by natural selection; since his time further evidence has amply supported his conjecture. Darwin, of course, believed that his theory of evolution provided a true account of the origins of species, but even if one does not agree with this judgement, as creationists do not, he established that Paley's argument was not logically decisive.

Hume had already shown how weak the design argument was in *Dialogues Concerning Natural Religion*, published posthumously in 1779. This criticized the argument from several points of view. It emphasized that the constant battle for survival among animals, and their inevitable suffering, did not support the idea that God was beneficent, even if he existed. Hume would also have been much more aware of human suffering than many people in the West are today, following the introduction of sewers, clean water, vaccination and many other life-transforming inventions.

The premise that the eye is almost perfectly adapted for its purpose is also flawed. 'The eye' is in any case an idealization – many people's vision is limited by short sight, long sight, astigmatism, and colour blindness, but seriously flawed vision is still far better than none. Even a normal eye also has two basic design faults. Everyone's accommodation (the ability to focus on objects at a variety of different distances) drops steadily with age until by the time they are sixty, it has often disappeared completely. Evolutionary theory explains this readily: until recently few reached this age, so there was no evolutionary pressure to improve the design. The second flaw is the existence of a blind spot to the side of the fovea, the point of our retina that provides the most detailed vision. This is a consequence of the way that the nerve fibres carry information from the light-sensitive cells in the retina to the brain. The eyes of squids and octopuses, which evolved independently, do not have this flaw. One could list a dozen design flaws in the human body with little effort, starting with the structure of our backbones, inherited from animals that did not stand upright. Many theologians today fully accept these criticisms of Paley's argument, and emphasize that religious belief cannot depend on factual matters. Unfortunately, in spite of its fatal flaws, further exposed in Dawkins' book *The Blind Watchmaker*, the design argument is still occasionally repeated by lay Christians of all denominations.

The latest incarnations of the design argument come from the creationist movement, and particularly Michael Behe, who has a large and receptive audience. The current focus of Behe's arguments involves the concept of irreducible complexity, but biologists have shown in one example after another that Behe is simply wrong. One of the recent cases concerns the bacterial flagellum, a minute rod that sticks out of the cell wall of a bacterium and rotates about its axis by using a biological analogue of an electric motor. The flagella of a bacterium may be much longer than its main body and the regular wave motions travelling down them propel it through its environment. A variety of different ideas about how such a peculiar and specific structure evolved are being pursued. The (Roman Catholic) cell biologist Ken Miller has noted that the 'irreducible complexity' argument has been decisively disproved, for flagella at least: a part of the molecular machinery in the flagellum also appears in another simpler structure that allows certain bacteria to inject toxins through the cell walls of their hosts. The co-option and modification of an existing structure to serve a new purpose is a familiar story in Darwinian theory. To disprove Behe's claims, one does not need to prove that the flagellum *actually* evolved this way; the irreducible complexity argument is that *no possible path* of evolution could have led to its appearance.

The Probabilistic Argument

In January 2009 the Atheist Bus Campaign put the following advertisement on the sides of hundreds of London buses:

> *There's probably no God. Now stop worrying and enjoy your life.*

The British Humanist Association supported this campaign, which was a response to an advertisement put out by evangelical Christians in June 2008. A few people claimed to have been offended by the atheists' advertisements but more regarded the lack of relationship between the first and second sentence as hilarious. The use of the word 'probably' also attracted comment.

Scientists believe that the appearance of the universe in which we live, the formation of the earth, and the evolution of human beings are all extremely improbable events. Even taking into account the existence of our species, the birth of each one of us depends on a further series of highly improbable events. However, the universe, the earth, the human species, and we individually do all exist. There is no point in trying to calculate the probabilities in any of these cases, because they would not alter the basic facts, which are settled by observation.

There are other situations in which the use of probabilistic ideas is simply not appropriate. If you are offered a bet on whether the hundredth digit in the decimal expansion of the number π is an 8, it would be better to think about the psychology of the person offering you the bet than to make your choice using probability theory.

The ideas just presented were used by Alister McGrath when criticizing a probabilistic argument against the existence of God by Richard Dawkins:

> *Perhaps we need to appreciate that there are many things that seem improbable – but improbability does not entail, and never has entailed, non-existence. We may be highly improbable – yet we are here. The issue, therefore is not whether God is probable, but whether God is actual.*[26]

McGrath's comment can be applied with equal force against his co-religionist Richard Swinburne when the latter tries to argue in favour of the existence of God on probabilistic grounds.

Swinburne errs even more seriously in trying to find support for his probabilistic approach to induction in the seventeenth century. He claims that 'Newton's theory of motion was judged to be highly probable on the evidence available at the end of the seventeenth century'.[27] In fact nobody in the seventeenth century would have argued that Newton's laws were true with high probability, because probability theory did not exist at that time, except in a rudimentary form in connection with games of chance. Indeed Bayes' theorem, Swinburne's main crutch, was not published until 1764. Newton did indeed argue that one should seek simple explanations, not on probabilistic grounds, but because he believed that Nature was simple. Swinburne is right to prefer simple explanations but not to give this preference a probabilistic gloss by references to Bayes' theorem that have no quantitative content.

Dawkins' Non-Existence Argument

In his book 'The God Delusion', written in 2006, Richard Dawkins presents several arguments against the existence of God. One of them has some novelty and he regards it as being of great significance. It claims that God must be at least as complex as his creation, the entire universe, and that one has not explained something if the explanation is as complex as the thing explained. In his book *The Dawkins Delusion*, discussed further below, Alister McGrath responds that the same argument should apply to the Theory of Everything. It is easy to agree: in their popular writings theoretical physicists and cosmologists often show strong signs of inventing metaphysical principles to order the world.

There is in fact no necessary connection between explanatory power and simplicity. A simple corkscrew may consist of a short wooden rod into which is fixed a piece of thick wire twisted into a spiral. The existence of corkscrews can only be explained by reference to vineyards, the properties of glass and cork, and the whole industry devoted to producing, storing, and transporting alcoholic drinks. So much for the idea that an explanation cannot be more complex than the thing explained. One can make a similar point about a paper-clip, as simple a manufactured item as one can imagine. A full explanation of its existence in terms of final causes would involve describing the properties of paper and the development of writing, while one in terms of efficient causes would require an account of the growth of the steel-making industry.

It might be thought that the above examples contradict the well-known principle that one should seek simple explanations rather than complicated ones. However, this is subject to the proviso that there may not exist a simple explanation, and if there is not, then one is bound to acknowledge that fact.

In other cases the cause is indeed much simpler than the result. A good example in the present context is the growth of civilization, traceable in some measure to the invention of writing. Once people learned how to keep records of their knowledge, civilization could start to grow beyond what any small group of individuals could remember. Knowledge became a cumulative process rather than a static one. The present universe could have developed from very simple beginnings, whether those consisted of natural laws or a creation act, provided those beginnings allowed the accumulation of complexity in an open-ended manner. Dawkins and others might prefer a natural explanation, but his simplistic argument is not valid.

All of the above assumes that the distinction between simplicity and complexity is always easy to recognize. Unfortunately this is not so. The Mandelbrot set, described on page 119, provides an example of a mathematical entity whose algebraic definition is fairly simple, but whose geometrical nature is so ramified as to be beyond apprehension. In the reverse direction a trefoil knot is simple to draw, but a description in words would be much more challenging. The importance of the perspective when assessing simplicity might justify the claim of theologians that God is in himself simple, even though from our point of view he must have a huge variety of capacities.

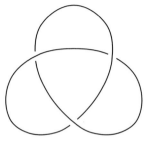

Fig. 5.1 A Trefoil Knot

Ward's Existence Argument

Keith Ward has given another argument for the existence of God in his book *God, Chance and Necessity*. He casts this as a refutation of claims made by Peter Atkins which I have no brief to defend; Atkins was arguing in favour of a world-view that Ward rejects and I find difficult to relate to; see pages 132 and 210. I agree with many of Ward's comments about Atkins' unconscious assumptions and preconceptions, but after this, part company with him. Ward's argument for the necessary existence of God involves the same kind of 'logical trickery' as he accuses Atkins of employing. The main difference is that he constructs his text around constant repetitions of the word 'possibility' rather than the word 'nothing'. The following short extract gives the flavour:

> *I am inclined to say that possibilities do exist. Even if no actual universe existed, its possibility would exist, together with the possibilities of every other possible universe, all comprising an infinite set of possibilities. We are back to the Platonic world of pure forms, pure possibilities. But how can mere possibilities exist? One must be logically ruthless, and say that either there are really no possibilities or that they exist in something actual. In that case, since possibilities will always, eternally, exist, there is never absolutely nothing.*[28]

This is not convincing. The use of the phrase 'logically ruthless' covers up the fact that the alternatives presented only exhaust the possibilities if one is a certain type of Platonist. Ward tries to avoid the fallacy of 'misplaced concreteness', a phrase introduced by Alfred North Whitehead early in the twentieth century, by claiming that 'the Platonic world' is just a metaphor for 'ideas in the mind of God'. (This metaphor is due to Augustine.) If this is the case, then he is not providing a proof of the existence of God, but assuming it.

Ward's reliance on Platonism is not an intrinsic part of Christianity. It might be contrasted with the rejection of Platonism by the mathematician Edward Nelson (see pages 123 and 125). Nelson is firmly committed to his Christian belief, but sees Platonism as a denial of the freedom of the human spirit.

Ward claims that possibilities must exist in something actual, namely the Platonic world of pure forms identified with ideas in the mind of God, in spite of the fact that God is generally agreed by theologians not to be a member of the class of existent beings. No doubt being actual while not existing makes sense to a theologian, but it involves using language in such a strange manner as to render it untranslatable into plain English. An obvious answer to this objection, that an infinite, transcendent God is indeed incomprehensible to our finite minds, abandons rational argument by assuming what is supposed to be the end point of the argument.

There is an alternative. Consider the possibility that there might have existed green swans. One is not obliged to believe that there must exist a world in which this possibility is actualized, or that the possibility must already have existed in God's mind in order for anyone to be able to entertain it. The obvious explanation is that the possibility of green swans is a figment of the author's imagination. The idea is pretty vague, like many other ideas that people have, in the sense that the author had not (actually could not have) thought through the ecological effects of the existence of green swans, or the genetic modifications that would make a swan green. There are green birds, so the idea is not self-evidently absurd, but it is simply a fantasy. Investing language about possibilities, ideas, or fantasies with theological significance is a device designed to lead to a desired goal, not a part of a rational argument.

After some other similar arguments, Ward comes to his theistic hypothesis, 'that there is a being which exists of necessity, but which creates this universe by a free act of will'. He then states the following:

> *Yet God's necessary nature can be expressed in many contingent ways, any one of which might properly manifest the love, creativity and wisdom that comprise the essential nature of God.*[29]

What immediately strikes one, at least if one is not already committed to Christianity, is the introduction of the word 'love', which has not been mentioned anywhere in the argument, and a few lines further down of the word 'goodness', again with no explanation. *In this context* these are entirely incongruous as necessary or essential properties of God, which Ward considers them to be. To do him justice, Ward later acknowledges that, in principle, the world might have been created by an utterly evil being who creates a world of intense and endless suffering, just for his own amusement.[30] He chooses between the two possibilities entirely on aesthetic grounds, that the 'best' explanation for the world is that it is one in which beauty, pleasure, and goodness prevail. It may seem so to him, but many millions of people living in desperate poverty and near starvation could well differ. The argument in this passage is fallacious for reasons pointed out by Hume two hundred years ago – the moral attributes of God do not follow from his necessary existence.[31] Ward's conclusion might be right, but, if so, his argument that love is a part of the nature of God is not based on necessity or reason.

Ward's chapters on the theory of evolution are even more disappointing. He starts by conceding that 'the theory of natural selection is a simple and extremely fruitful one', but gradually withdraws his support, arguing that 'it is too vague and flexible to provide a satisfyingly specific explanation of the evolutionary process'. He fails to distinguish between the low *predictive* power of evolutionary theory – that it cannot say how human beings evolved – and its very high *explanatory* power. As an example of the latter, consider the recent determination of the genetic code of the duck-billed platypus. Before its genetic code was determined it was possible that the platypus had no DNA in its cells, or that its DNA was unrelated to that of any other animal, or that there was no way of fitting it into the evolutionary tree. Neo-Darwinian theory predicted that none of these possibilities would arise, and also that the DNA was likely to be very interesting. It proved right on all counts. This was not a minor achievement: it involved correlating thousands of pieces of evidence about the DNA of the platypus with those of other species, all of which could have turned out differently. Ward seems not to be interested in such facts, focussing instead on the contingency of life as though it is a fatal weakness of the theory. In fact, the success of the theory *in spite of* the contingency of its subject matter has been an extraordinary achievement.

Ward finally declares that:

> It follows from all this that natural selection cannot be *the sole explana-
> tion of evolutionary change…In other words, natural selection is a nec-
> essary but not a sufficient condition for emergent evolution. In fact it
> would be entirely reasonable to think that on the principle of natural
> selection alone, very complex and delicately integrated structures would
> be less likely to replicate efficiently…(my emphasis)*[32]

Ward switches back and forth between what he considers reasonable and statements that evolution *must* have happened the way he prefers. His belief that it is possible to settle a scientific issue about the competitive advantages of multicellular organisms vis a vis single-celled organisms by armchair discussions shows that he has little concept of the nature of scientific enquiry. The emergence of multicellular organisms was of huge importance for us, and becomes more plausible if one keeps in mind the astonishing number of bacteria in the world at any one time: in 1998 Whitman, Coleman, and Wiebe estimated that the present number of prokaryotes in the world is around 10^{30}, in other words a million trillion trillion. One should also keep in mind the extremely short time that they take to reproduce by binary fission and the enormous length of time, about three billion years, that it took for the first multicellular organisms to appear. The number of new genes that must have appeared in that time is beyond imagination. Ward's 'explanation' is simply an expression of his personal preference. There is an obvious alternative: open-ended systems evolve and a viable mechanism for producing stable multicellular organisms only has to appear once. At the present time nobody can prove that either explanation is correct.

There is no point in attempting to list all of Ward's scientific blunders in these pages. Here is one of the most revealing. I will not dwell on what he might mean by the 'faith-postulates of science'. Science does not have beliefs and individual scientists have had many different beliefs over the centuries:

> One of the basic faith-postulates of science is that there is no ultimate chaos in nature.... Mutation does not occur in a vacuum, for no reason.... This leads one to suspect that mutation is only random in that we cannot detect or specify the causes leading to genetic change.[33]

He identifies radioactivity as one of those causes, but seems to have forgotten that earlier he had written

> This account entails that no reason can be given, for instance, for why a particular radium atom disintegrates at a particular time, rather than at some other time – that is one instance of what indeterminacy means.... There is a reason why things are as they are, but this precludes there being a reason for every specific event.[34]

The emphases in both quotations are mine. Quantum theory is a very hard subject to comprehend, and in the first quote above, Ward has apparently forgotten that it is important to distinguish between its laws and individual events, such as mutations, that happen at the molecular level. This is crucial because the effects of a single mutation may become more and more important as time passes.

Once again I emphasize that the purpose of scientific research in every field, including this one, is to discover how much can be explained by natural arguments supported by external evidence, not to prove that religious belief is wrong. The variety of forms of life is so great that Darwin's theory cannot be assessed without a serious engagement with the evidence. Philosophical discussions about the eventual triumph or limits of the neo-Darwinian programme have a certain interest, but evolutionary biologists do not need to assume, as an act of faith, that it will eventually provide a complete explanation of everything in biology in order to pursue their investigations. On the other hand it is already clear that it will be an ingredient of any future theory about the historical development of life forms on earth.

5.5   God's Nature and Acts

Most of this chapter is about Christianity, not because I consider Christianity to be the most important religion, but because it is the one I know most about. I will explain why a number of Christian beliefs cause non-Christians great difficulty. Many liberal Unitarians also reject the doctrines that are discussed below, while considering that the life and teachings of Jesus provide strong moral guidance for our society.

All Christians who have thought long enough about the questions that I raise below can probably answer them to their own satisfaction. Unfortunately, it does not take particularly wide reading to discover that they give a wide range of quite different answers. Some theologians claim that there is progress in their understanding of the problems, but that it is slow and many Christians do yet realize that their beliefs have been superseded. Others completely disagree and say that the so-called progress loses sight of fundamental truths that can only be revealed by reading the Bible itself.

People's willingness to believe some of the things described below is baffling to outsiders – although not as weird as the stories people tell about alien visits to Earth, and even about their personal encounters with aliens. It seems that such beliefs take hold of people very easily, and that they are very difficult to abandon. It is not easy to explain why this is so, but the fact itself is undeniable.

Let us start with miracles. If they occur, they are by definition outside the arena that scientists can deal with. Many religious people are committed to the existence of miracles, and eminent theologians defend their reality. It is often said that God's purpose depends on keeping his existence obscure, because faith in God would have no merits if his presence was obvious; as a result he ensures that his miracles are infrequent and carried out in circumstances that are hidden from general inspection. To a non-believer this already sounds suspicious, because Jesus is supposed to have carried out his own miracles quite openly.

The Virgin Birth

This is an example of a miracle that most Christians accept in spite of the fact that there is no good reason for doing so. For the sake of definiteness, we consider the arguments of Keith Ward in *God, Faith and the New Millennium*.

Ward accepts that many biblical scholars regard the virgin birth story as a legend, a symbolic insertion into the story of his life.[35] Such stories were commonplace at the time and were told about the Buddha, Krishna, and various Egyptian and Greek gods and rulers, including Perseus, the supposed founder of Mycenae. At that time assigning a virgin birth to someone gave them a special status, just as marking an event by a comet did; today the first claim would be received with amusement, while the second would be regarded as a mere coincidence. The story is only mentioned in two of the four gospels, those of Matthew and Luke. The relevant word in the Hebrew original of the 'virgin birth' prophecy in Isaiah can also be translated as 'young woman', but there are fierce disputes about which is the most appropriate translation.

It seems much better to think of the virgin birth as a legend or myth than as a historical fact, for the following reasons. It is extremely unlikely that women can ever bear children without the fertilization of an egg by a sperm, but if this happened on very rare occasions the resulting child would necessarily be female. If one relies on natural processes, virgin births of male children are simply not possible, so such an event must depend upon a miracle – a suspension of natural law for no good reason. The suspension is often said to indicate that Jesus was born without sin, or to mark God's liberation of humanity from its bondage to sin. Linking sexual intercourse to sin, whether this is taken literally or symbolically, is one of the most unattractive aspects of Christian belief, and it is sad that Ward cannot get away from it.[36]

In spite of admitting all these problems, Ward comes to the conclusion that Jesus was indeed 'born of the Virgin Mary'. The apparent reason is that he finds the symbolism so attractive that he would like the reality to match it. This is not a sensible way of deciding on an issue that he himself has cast serious doubt on, and which has no importance for the Messianic status of Jesus, unless one takes prophecies in the Old Testament literally. Surely one should only start thinking about a miraculous explanation when there is little doubt that the relevant event actually occurred, and it has an important spiritual significance; in this case *both* conditions are absent. Either Ward feels differently about miracles, or he is acquiescing in the tradition simply because it is well established.

Ward must also be aware that for the Anglican community to deny the doctrine of the virgin birth would provoke an irreparable rift with the Catholic Church. One only has to observe Easter processions in places such as Palermo or Seville to realize how embedded in Catholicism the cult of the Virgin Mary has become. Possibly Ward had to write what he did if he wanted to keep the ecumenical movement alive.

Rowan Williams also believes in the virgin birth, but explains it in a different way. In a television interview with Richard Dawkins in August 2008 he said that the birth of Jesus 'is not a suspension of the laws of nature, but Nature opening up to its own depths'. It is hard to understand what such poetic language really means, but that may well be his intention.

The Resurrection

Trying to find out what the doctrine of the Resurrection states is like drawing blood from a stone. The Apostles' creed and the thirty-nine Articles are quite explicit about the importance of the physical resurrection of Christ, and are not compatible with doubts about this. However, surveys indicate that a substantial proportion of clergy in the UK do not believe in a physical resurrection, and regard the story as having only metaphorical or mythical significance. Many others regard the literal truth of the resurrection as the centre point of their faith, and consider that the biblical accounts of it provide almost irrefutable evidence for its truth. The Catholic Church has no doubts about the resurrection, while Islam accepts Jesus as a prophet but denies that he was crucified.

In a response to twelve radical theses about Christian belief by the Episcopal Bishop Spong, Rowan Williams abandoned his usual obscurity to reveal a fundamental contradiction in his theology:

> *Thus God is never competing for space with agencies in the universe. When God acts, this does not mean that a hole is torn in the universe by an intervention from outside...For the record: I have never quite managed to see how we can make sense of the sacramental life of the Church without a theology of the risen body; and I have never managed to see how to put together such a theology without belief in the empty tomb. If a corpse clearly marked 'Jesus of Nazareth' turned up, I should save myself a lot of trouble and become a Quaker.*[37]

According to the last part of this quotation, Williams believes that when Jesus ascended into heaven, his physical body disappeared from the world; this is about as close to saying that his ascension left a 'hole in the universe' as one can get, without using the actual words. However, in his book *Resurrection: Interpreting the Easter Gospel* Williams says 'there is a sense in which the raising of Jesus...is not an event, with a before and after, occupying a determinate bit of time between Friday and Sunday'. By writing 'there is a sense' he equivocates – he can hardly be claiming that there is another sense in which the raising of Jesus from the dead was a physical event as we normally understand this term. Nor, given his comments about the empty tomb, can he be saying that there is no fact of the matter concerning his corpse. The problem with excessive subtlety is that it eventually turns into beautiful but empty poetic phrases. It is disturbing that such a prominent theologian cannot explain his position on so fundamental a doctrinal matter, in a form that others can understand. Understanding need not lead to belief, but it might help some to take the next step. I appreciate that this is an extremely sensitive matter in the Anglican Church, but we are left not knowing what he believes about the Resurrection as an event. Of course this may be deliberate. Anyone who is required by his position to lead conflicting groups without any real sanctions will know how difficult mediation can be if the various factions are determined to fight an issue to the bitter end.

Demonic Possession

It is easy to agree that there are morally good acts and morally bad acts, and that there are people who are so corrupted, either by their social environment or their own nature, that they enjoy committing acts that fill most people with horror. Good and evil are abstract nouns that might be useful when talking about such behaviour, but accepting them into the language is not the same as agreeing that evil is the responsibility of demons that possess people. This is, however, one of the beliefs of the Catholic Church.

> *According to Catholic belief demons or fallen angels retain their natural power, as intelligent beings, of acting on the material universe, and using material objects and directing material forces for their own wicked ends; and this power, which is in itself limited, and is subject, of course, to the control of Divine providence, is believed to have been allowed a wider scope for its activity in the consequence of the sin of mankind. Hence places and things as well as persons are naturally liable to diabolical infestation, within limits permitted by God, and exorcism in regard to them is nothing more than a prayer to God, in the name of His Church, to restrain this diabolical power supernaturally, and a profession of faith in His willingness to do so on behalf of His servants on earth.*[38]

Exorcism has been a part of Christianity throughout its history, but it is also a feature of other, earlier religions. It is highly regrettable that most major Christian sects still recognize it, and practise it to varying extents, and, with varying degrees of caution. The moderate Church of England does not like to talk about the subject, but every diocese has a 'Deliverance Ministry' responsible for exorcism, deliverance, and the paranormal. Exorcism might sometimes be a harmless ritual but in the charismatic context it can some-times degenerate into brutality; some horrific, recent exorcisms of children in England and America have led to major criminal convictions. To anyone who has any significant acquaintance with illnesses such as epilepsy and Tourette's syndrome, exorcism is a medieval superstition that the major world religions should by now have cast aside decisively. Perhaps its supporters feel bound to accept at face value the words and actions of Jesus as recorded in the Bible. This is not necessary: they could say that he was bound to use the language he did because he lived in a pre-scientific culture. Or perhaps the problem is that they feel that if they reject the personification of evil, the authority of the Church will be diminished – some believers might come to think that the obvious next step is to go on to reject the personification of good in Jesus.

Naturally Occurring Evil

Everyone except the most committed materialist recognizes the existence of good and evil. People without religious belief are just as convinced that one should try to reduce the amount of suffering in the world as those who are religious. When asked how a supremely good and all-powerful God tolerates the amount of human suffering, Christians usually concentrate on the evil caused by people, because this is the easier type to explain.

However, a creator God is also responsible for all natural disasters in a world that he himself has created. This is particularly the case if it is held that God is actively involved in the development of the world, and capable of intervening by occasional miracles if he so chooses. It has been argued that he cannot intervene in an obvious fashion because he must conceal his exist-ence; human faith is apparently only meritorious in the absence of objective evidence. Even if one accepts this proposition, it is hardly decisive. God could have prevented the Lisbon earthquake of 1755 without anyone being any the wiser. If he had done so, Voltaire would probably not have written his famous satire *Candide*, in 1759, ridiculing the idea that God could not have created a better world even if he had wished to do so. As I write, in May 2008, the Chinese are trying to cope with the destruction caused by a massive earthquake in Sichuan Province that has killed over seventy thousand people, while leaving up to five million homeless. No doubt poor building techniques contributed to this disaster, but the *primary cause* must be the earthquake itself, for which God cannot escape responsibility.

Arguments that the good on Earth substantially outweighs the natural evil have been particularly popular in England. Perhaps this is because England contains no volcanos, has no significant earthquakes, has a moderate climate throughout the year (by the standards of many other countries), is not subject to large-scale famine, and contains no large or particularly poisonous predators. In many other countries life is less pleasant, and the beneficence of nature less apparent. Nevertheless, even in England, Darwin had to come to terms with the loss of three of his children, one of whom was very close to him, and to realize that the constant struggle for survival applied to human beings just as much as to animals. This surely influenced his loss of faith.

It is often suggested that human suffering might be an inevitable consequence of allowing us genuine freedom; in other words it might flow inevitably from God's desire to create the possibility of the deepest kind of loving relationship. According to this argument, our mental capacities are so limited by comparison with those of God that we have no right to judge the considerations that motivate his actions. God's love and goodness are axiomatic, and the task is to explain the obvious problems associated with this belief. 'The problem of evil' has caused endless anguish to Christian theologians, but it is apparent from the amount that continues to be written about it, that they have failed to resolve the contradictions involved, even to their own satisfaction. Those who are not religious might be forgiven for concluding that the problem has not been solved because it is not soluble; the assumptions that give rise to the problem have no factual basis.

5.6   Life after Death

People have believed in the possibility of life after death since the construction of the Great Pyramid at Giza, and probably for a lot longer. Claims about the religious significance of prehistoric rituals should not always be taken seriously, but archeological evidence of the ritual burial of the dead makes it plausible that the belief is tens of thousands of years old. It has been incorporated in one form or an other into most major religions, but, once again, we restrict attention to the Christian tradition.

The nature of Heaven and Hell are not known and most believers agree that our images of them are wholly inadequate. The few descriptions of Heaven make it seem extremely boring, but those of Hell are much more graphic. At one extreme are the weekly sermons about hellfire and damnation that my father suffered as a child in his Baptist community in the Welsh coal-mining town of Tredegar. At the other, one should mention the avoidance of the notion of Hell by the liberal Anglican community, which seems to regard the word as signifying exclusion from Heaven, rather than as an entity in its own right. This liberal optimism does not have much in common with the views that Pope Benedict XVI presented in a sermon in Rome in March 2007. He stated that people who failed to admit blame risked 'eternal damnation – the inferno'. Hell 'really exists and is eternal, even if nobody talks about it much any more.'

Most Christians agree that sincere believers who have led blameless lives go to Heaven, and that those who have committed evil and refuse to repent, even after death, cannot. There is no such agreement about what happens to people who are neither wholly good nor wholly bad – in other words almost everyone. One solution to this problem is the Catholic notion of Purgatory. This allows people who have sinned to enter Heaven, after a period of punishment in which they compensate in some way for the evil that they have done. The notion of Purgatory is pagan in origin and was first given a definite form by Augustine in the fifth century. It only became an official article of faith in the Catholic Church in the fifteenth century.

There is no clear Biblical support for the notion of Purgatory, which is rejected by many Protestant sects. In particular the 22nd of the 39 Articles of the Anglican Church states that 'the Romish Doctrine concerning Purgatory, Pardons, Worshipping and Adoration, as well as Images of Relics, and also Invocation of Saints, is a fond thing, vainly invented, and grounded upon no warranty of Scripture, but rather repugnant to the Word of God.' Unsurprisingly, in view of his constant efforts to avoid doctrinal controversies, it is hard to find any reference to the issue by Rowan Williams.

The Anglo-Catholic theologian Keith Ward has presented a defence of the notion of Purgatory, in which he declares that, as a Christian, he thinks it is very odd to believe that a God of love would send people to Hell just for not having heard of Jesus, or for not having been baptised.[39] This is close to the orthodox Catholic position, but it is based on what he considers reasonable rather than any Biblical authority.

Imagine two people, A (for atheist) and B (for believer). Both are brought up in conventional but not particularly religious families, and both decide to devote their lives to working for Oxfam, helping people who live in a drought-ridden country in Africa. In the course of his work A is so appalled by the suffering of the population that he loses his belief in God. B, however, finds that his faith is the only thing that sustains him. After twenty years both die suddenly in an accident. Following his death, A learns that God does exist and immediately admits his error (sin?) in not retaining his faith. Since both are presumed for the sake of this discussion to have lived blameless lives, common sense suggests that God should allow both to enter Heaven more or less immediately. However, some evangelical Christians are sure that A does not go to Heaven. They follow the Lutheran doctrine that salvation is determined by faith alone; moreover faith comes to us as God's free gift through the work of the Holy Spirit and not through our own inward qualities, outward works, or satisfactions.

This disagreement about Purgatory is related to beliefs about whether prayers for the dead can have any effect. It is still very much alive within the Protestant community and cannot be resolved by reference to the Bible, which says many apparently contradictory things about conditions for entry to Heaven.

Some theologians and many lay Christians adopt a dualistic attitude towards the soul, considering it to be a separable entity that can survive the death of the body. In his book *Beyond Science*, Polkinghorne describes people's souls quite differently:

> I have already explained that I think we are psychosomatic unities and that the soul is the 'form' (the information bearing pattern) of the body. That pattern will be dissolved at death with the decay of my body. Yet it seems to me to be a perfectly coherent hope that the pattern that is me will be remembered by God and recreated in some new environment of his choosing in his ultimate act of resurrection...there is surely the possibility of there being a new 'matter' in which we can be re-embodied at our resurrection.[40]

This description of the soul is compatible with current scientific understanding of brain processes, but raises the issue of whether the gap between death and resurrection implies that the transformed entity is the original person or merely a copy. The philosopher Derek Parfit and others consider that psychological continuity is an essential aspect of individual identity, but Polkinghorne regards this as a 'peculiar conclusion'.[41] Indeed one might reasonably hold that there is the same degree of continuity if the patterns of people's personalities are held in God's mind after their death, as there is in them being held in their own brains when they are asleep.

A positive feature of this description of the soul is that it might allow him to restore a person after death to their state before their personality degenerated under the influence of dementia. God might also be able to remove various psychological traumas in the resurrected person. These comments presuppose that souls do survive the death of the body; if they do not, no explanation of the manner of their survival is needed. The contents of this section are equally irrelevant to the millions of Buddhists who believe in repeated reincarnation, but not in any God.

5.7 Keith Ward

In addition to his other positions, Keith Ward is the Joint President of the World Congress of Faiths. As one would expect from this, he constantly seeks common ground between the various religions and sometimes finds more than others might think is really there. The latest of his many books, *Is Religion Dangerous?*, is one of the better of the various responses to Dawkins' *The God Delusion*. It achieves this by ignoring Dawkins' text but by dealing in turn with each of the issues that Dawkins raised. I was convinced by many of the arguments that he put forward, but will focus on those which are less than adequate.

Ward grounds his belief in a world-view that includes the following propositions:[42]

- There is some explanation, whether scientific or not, for every event that happens (things do not happen for no reason).
- Human beings are basically good and well-meaning, but they are also subject to terrible corruptions of greed, hatred, and ignorance.
- People ought to consider the welfare of others, and ideally of all other sentient beings, at least to some extent.
- It is appropriate to feel awe and reverence at the beauty and complexity of nature, to feel gratitude for the fact of existence, and to sense the presence of some sort of transcendent power and value in moments of understanding truth, appreciating beauty, and enjoying friendship.

The first item was discussed on page 227, where Ward's lack of understanding of quantum theory became apparent. The second item is over-optimistic; controlling the basic human propensity for violence and even war involves first recognizing its full extent. The third item starts well, but most religious people would have little hesitation in voting for the elimination of head lice, tapeworms, and cockroaches, in spite of the fact that they are sentient beings. I have no idea how Ward would balance the welfare of tigers against that of their prey if he had to do so, and suspect that this aspect of his 'consideration' is vacuous. Ward's final proposition needs only one substantial change, the deletion of the reference to transcendent power, to make it acceptable to people who have no religious beliefs. The following humanistic version of Ward's four propositions demonstrates that there is a coherent alternative to materialism, idealism, and religious belief:

- Major events in our lives can happen for trivial reasons. For example, people die in road accidents as the result of momentary lapses of attention, often by others. People also die from cancer following tiny, random changes in a few cells of their bodies. We need not accept these facts passively, but should try to reduce their frequency.

- Human beings can be good and well-meaning, but they can also be subject to terrible corruptions of greed, hatred, and ignorance. We should aim to strengthen those social structures within which the better sides of our nature dominate.
- People ought to consider the welfare of others, and of animals that are sufficiently like ourselves, at least to some extent. We may seek to eliminate species that are actively harmful to us, provided we have considered the consequences carefully.
- It is appropriate to feel deeply moved by the beauty and complexity of nature, to appreciate the mere fact of existence, and to regard truth, beauty, and friendship as central values in one's life.

One aspect of Ward's book is particularly unsatisfactory. He claims that freedom of conscience has always been a fundamental principle of Christian thought, though it has often been counterbalanced by paternalistic considerations. This is an excessively optimistic reading, particularly of the behaviour of the Catholic Church over the ages. He is aware of its long-standing authoritarian character and condemnation of liberalism during most of its history, but places emphasis on the Second Vatican Council of the 1960s, which declared the importance of the freedom of conscience. This is now forty years ago, and all the evidence is that the Vatican regards it as having been an aberration. In 1979 Pope John Paul II revoked the teaching licence of the respected Catholic theologian Hans Küng – widely regarded as the architect of the Second Vatican Council – who had criticized him for misusing his papal authority to block debate about reforms. In July 2007 Pope Benedict XVI, criticized 'erroneous interpretations' of the Second Vatican Council and said that non-Catholic Christian communities were either defective or not true churches. In January 2009 he rehabilitated four ultra-conservative bishops who had rejected the Second Vatican Council, including Richard Williamson; the fact that he was a Holocaust denier was deemed to be irrelevant. The present day Catholic Church *prohibits* homoeroticism, extra-marital sex, contraception, abortion, and euthanasia. Individual Catholics may or may not agree with its values, but this is not the freedom of conscience that Küng has long advocated.

Ward's analysis of the long succession of wars that have characterized human society is very convincing. He rejects Dawkins' assertion that religious intolerance has played the central role as the cause of wars. He considers both religious and non-religious wars, and argues that the constant factor has been the desire for power and wealth. In many cases religion has been a convenient label for those who are being oppressed, but in other cases ethnicity or other 'justifications' are used.[43] One example illustrates this very well: the so-called 'troubles' in Northern Ireland between two indigenous, white communities, one Catholic and the other Protestant. The Catholic side wanted a united Ireland while the Protestants were intensely loyal to the British monarchy. The intensity of the feelings of both sides bewildered many English people. The two groups often lived in separate areas, particularly in Belfast, and their children went to different schools. Marriages between the two sides were rare, and in a few cases young people were murdered for trying to bridge the cultural barriers. The Catholic population were often subject to discrimination in employment. It is clear, in this case at least, that the conflicts were primarily cultural rather than religious, even though members of each group could be identified by their religions.

Ward points to the existence of millions of religious believers who function well in the ordinary affairs of life, whose faith seems to enable them to live well and be happy, and who can produce a reasonable and coherent defence of their beliefs.[44] This is of course true, but the same applies to people with many mutually contradictory religions, and to many atheists and humanists; their beliefs cannot all be right. In spite of his enthusiasm for 'religion' per se, the word is almost meaningless in its vagueness. Ward himself is unable to define it and admits that the concept embraces a wide range of mutually incompatible beliefs.[45]

In his book, Ward discusses the the more or less universal religious feelings that humans have had in all societies and over all ages. He considers that the natural conclusion to be drawn from these is also the correct one: we have religious feelings because there is something outside ourselves which makes such feelings appropriate. Ward calls this something, God. Edward Wilson, on the other hand, is confident that our strong religious instincts can be explained in adaptive biological terms without invoking any supernatural influence. Ward has anticipated this possibility and states that understanding the biological basis for a belief cannot demonstrate that the belief is false.[46] However, if one focusses on *a particular religious belief* (such as that about the resurrection) then one realizes there are hundreds of millions of religious people in the world whose views about it must be wrong. Even the existence of a God is denied by Buddhists, who must be numbered among those that one would regard as religious. Religiosity by itself has so little content that it cannot really be discussed intelligently.

5.8 Conclusions

It is time to draw together the various threads. Many scientists are struck by the grandeur of the universe, the simplicity of the laws that govern it, and even its very existence. Others are convinced that our existence as human beings must have some deep spiritual significance. Albert Einstein was astonished by our ability to comprehend it, and by the peculiar appropriateness of mathematics in this respect. I look into my soul and wonder why I have one, when all my scientific knowledge tells me that I do not. All of the above are religious responses to the world. Each appeals to some people but seems vacuous or plain wrong to others. Most are simply expressions of wonder, a component of religion to be sure, but only one. They lack any detail and are very difficult to develop any further. Nor do they make any contact with the ethical issues that Gould and others see as being at the core of the great religions. Famous scientists command a ready audience because of their important contributions to their own fields, but this does not mean that they have particularly deep views on other subjects.

One might expect religious leaders and theologians to have more coherent views about the great questions concerning our existence, but this chapter suggests that they do not. Some have well worked out beliefs but these can be quite different from those of others within the same sect, let alone those of people with different religions. If one asks whether a core Christian belief is to be taken as the literal truth or as a myth, different people give different answers, and some are quite unable to give a meaningful response. Theologians seem to accept this situation without drawing the obvious conclusions about the status of their beliefs.

When we look at political leaders, we find them equally lacking. With very few exceptions, such as Gandhi, Martin Luther King, and Nelson Mandela, they seem to devote as much energy to undermining their political opponents, as to increasing the feelings of cohesion between the various groups that they supposedly serve. Some, in all parts of the world, are quite obviously using their positions to pursue personal gain. In the West, politicians are heavily constrained by media that seek lurid headlines, and find it very hard to say anything original without being attacked while the ink is still wet. The British Prime Minister, Tony Blair, was a rare example of a charismatic political leader who might have unified large numbers of people behind his vision of the future, had it not been for his fatal error in backing the American President, George Bush, in the Iraq war. Why he did this is still unknown, but his strong religious beliefs might have been a contributing cause: politicians need to focus on what is achievable rather than on what they believe to be morally right in absolute terms. After stepping into the quagmire, every effort Blair made to justify his actions only made matters worse. President Barack Obama matches Tony Blair in terms of his eloquence, and one can only hope that this will be accompanied by real achievements in due course. His very premature Nobel Peace Prize will raise expectations and may make his task harder rather than easier.

One of my goals has been to persuade readers that the questions posed in this book do not have easy answers, and that those who claim otherwise are deceiving themselves. It is possible to live without knowing the answers to the great questions of life, and, in the end, it may be the most honest position to take, even though it does not provide the security that many people desire above everything else. I believe, as do Keith Ward and Rowan Williams, that we must learn to live with our differences and respect the sincerely held views of others. This is not the same as pretending to agree with them – we must be free to say what we ourselves believe even if we know that it may give offence to some. This is of enormous importance, because there are many parts of the world in which the freedom of expression is not accepted.

Religious belief is a key ingredient in human civilization, in the sense that one cannot understand the latter fully without reference to the former. It binds people together and also divides them, according to the circumstances, but the different religions have more in common than their mutual antagonisms would lead one to deduce. I, personally, am content to live in a secular country that formally adheres to a minimal Anglican tradition, and hope that it will not become less tolerant.

People's world-views are not founded on logic, and the most that one can expect is that they should be consistent with what science has taught us. In the long term, the conflicts between different religions may be more important than the current battles between fundamentalists and scientists. Science will survive because its products work: aircraft fly, binoculars improve our vision of distant objects, and electric power keeps our household devices working. The relative merits of the various competing sects and religions are not so easy to settle, because there is no agreed criterion for doing so. Some moderates describe the various religions as different routes to the same God, but there are just as many who consider it self-evident that their own is the only real truth. Since there is little likelihood of the various world religions disappearing, we must work towards tolerance of our differences.

One can puzzle indefinitely about the origin of our ethical standards, but our capacity for language and our appreciation of music are just as mysterious. All three are partly innate and partly acquired by exposure to whatever culture we are brought up in. In each case there are people with exceptional capacities and a few with almost none. Many people identify religion as the ultimate source of ethics, but others are completely secure in their ethical standards without believing that they were laid down by God. One does not need to be religious to be committed to the abolition of slavery and other human rights, such as those of women. They are evidence of our progress as an ethical species and must be valued if we are to preserve them.

I end with a poem of William Cecil Dampier, a noted historian of science in the first half of the twentieth century. This was copied and illuminated by my mother before I was born, and hung on a wall in my home. It made a great impression on me as a child, and the sentiments expressed have stayed with me throughout my life. Reading poetry has fallen out of fashion, but it demonstrates how far the human spirit has transcended the matter out of which we are all made.

> At first men try with magic charm
> To fertilize the earth,
> To keep their flocks and herds from harm
> And bring new young to birth.
>
> Then to capricious gods they turn
> To save from fire or flood,
> Their smoking sacrifices burn
> On altars red with blood.
>
> Next bold philosopher and sage
> A settled plan decree,
> And prove by thought or sacred page
> What Nature ought to be.
>
> But Nature smiles – a Sphinx-like smile –
> Watching their little day,
> She waits in patience for a while
> Their plans dissolve away.
>
> Then come those humbler men of heart
> With no completed scheme,
> Content to play a modest part,
> To test, observe and dream.
>
> Till out of chaos come in sight
> Clear fragments of a Whole;
> Man, learning Nature's way aright,
> Obeying, can control.

The great Design now glows afar;
But yet its changing Scenes
Reveal not what the Pieces are
Nor what the Puzzle means.

And Nature smiles – still unconfessed
The secret thought she thinks –
Inscrutable she guards unguessed
The Riddle of the Sphinx.

The riddle of our place in the universe may never be solved, and I am content that this should be so. The struggle to divine the meaning of life is a part of being human.

Notes and References

[1] Brooke, John Hedley (1991). *Science and Religion*, p.321. Camb. Univ. Press.

[2] See p.65 of http://www.pamd.uscourts.gov/kitzmiller/kitzmiller_342.pdf

[3] Ward, Keith (1998). *God, Faith and the New Millennium*, p.10. Oneworld Publ., Oxford.

[4] The historical origins of fundamentalism are traced in Armstrong, Karen (2004), *The Battle for God: Fundamentalism in Judaism, Christianity and Islam*, Harper Perennial, London.

[5] See his message delivered to the Pontifical Academy of Sciences on 22 October 1996.

[6] See *The Guardian* newspaper, 29 May and 1 June, 2007.

[7] Wilson, Edward O. (1975). *Sociobiology: The New Synthesis*, p.275. Harvard Univ. Press, Cambridge, Mass.

[8] Wilson (1975), p.284.

[9] See for example an article of Cardinal Murphy-O'Connor in *The Independent* newspaper on 8 December 2008. This is a preview of his contribution to Cooper Zaki and Lodge Guy, eds. (2008), *Faith in the Nation: Religion, identity and the public realm in Britain today*, Institute for Public Policy Research.

[10] New Statesman interview, 22 Dec. 2008, at http://www.archbishopof-canterbury.org/2065

[11] See http://www.acommonword.com/ for the many responses.

[12] Cantor, G. (1991). *Michael Faraday, Sandemanian and Scientist.* Macmillan Press Ltd., London.

[13] Gould, Stephen J. (2001). *Rocks of Ages*, p.129. Jonathan Cape, London.

[14] Gould (2001), p.72.

[15] Gould (2001), pp.130, 131.

[16] Polkinghorne, J. (1996). *Beyond Science*, p.98. Camb. Univ. Press.

[17] The Far-Future Universe: Eschatology From A Cosmic Perspective, Rome, Nov. 2000. Published by the John Templeton Foundation, 2002.

[18] McGrath, Alister (2007). *The Dawkins Delusion*, pp.12,23–6, 46. SPCK, London.

[19] Atkins, P. (1998). Awesome Versus Adipose, Who Really Works Hardest to Banish Ignorance? *Free Inquiry Magazine*, **18**, no.2.

[20] Carr, B. and Rees, M. (1979). The anthropic principle and the structure of the physical world. *Nature* **278**, 605–12.

[21] Weinberg, S. (2007). Living in the Multiverse. In B. Carr ed. *Universe or Multiverse?* Camb. Univ. Press.

[22] Adams, Fred C. (2008). Stars in other universes: stellar structure with different fundamental constants. *J. Cosmology and Astroparticle Phys.* **08**, 010.

[23] Swinburne, R. (2004). *The Existence of God*, 2nd edition. Clarendon Press, Oxford.

[24] Swinburne (2004), p.67.

[25] Swinburne (2004), pp.99–102.

[26] McGrath, Alister (2007). *The Dawkins Delusion*, p.10. SPCK, London.

[27] Swinburne (2004), p.69.

[28] Ward, Keith (1996). *God, Chance and Necessity*, p.36. Oneworld Publ., Oxford.

[29] Ward (1996), p.37.

[30] Ward (1996), pp.45–7.

[31] Hume, David (1779). *Dialogues concerning Natural Religions*, parts 5,10.

[32] See Ward (1996), pp.134–5 for full details.

[33] Ward (1996), p.120.

[34] Ward (1996), p.21.

[35] Ward, Keith (1998). *God Faith and the New Millennium*, p.176. Oneworld, Oxford.

[36] Ward (1998), p.176.

[37] *Church Times*, 17 July 1998.

[38] *Catholic Encyclopedia*, article on exorcism, http://www.newadvent. org/cathen/05709a.htm

[39] Ward (1998), pp.100–2.

[40] Polkinghorne, J. (1996). *Beyond Science*, p.100. Camb. Univ. Press.

[41] Polkinghorne (1996) pp.62, 63.

[42] Ward, K. (2006). *Is Religion Dangerous?*, p.86. Lion Hudson plc.

[43] Ward (2006), Chapter 3.

[44] Ward (2006), p.172.

[45] Ward (2006), p.8.

[46] Ward (2006), pp.176, 177.

Index